THE THEORY OF

DATABASE CONCURRENCY CONTROL

PRINCIPLES OF COMPUTER SCIENCE SERIES

ISSN 0888-2096

Series Editors
ALFRED V. AHO, *Bell Telephone Laboratories, Murray Hill, New Jersey*
JEFFREY D. ULLMAN, *Stanford University, Stanford, California*

Narain Gehani
C: An Advanced Introduction

David Maier
The Theory of Relational Databases

Leonard R. Marino
Principles of Computer Design

Christos H. Papadimitriou
The Theory of Concurrency Control

Theo Pavlidis
Algorithms for Graphics and Image Processing

Arto Salomaa
Jewels of Formal Language Theory

Stuart C. Shapiro
LISP: An Interactive Approach

Jeffrey D. Ullman
Computational Aspects of VLSI

ANOTHER BOOK OF INTEREST

Jeffrey D. Ullman
Principles of Database Systems, Second Edition

THE THEORY OF

DATABASE CONCURRENCY CONTROL

Christos Papadimitriou

Stanford University
National Technical Institute of Athens

COMPUTER SCIENCE PRESS

Computer Science Press, Inc.
1803 Research Boulevard
Rockville, Maryland 20850

1 2 3 4 5 6 Printing   Year 90 89 88 87 86

Library of Congress Cataloging-in-Publication Data

Papadimitriou, Christos H.
   The theory of concurrency control.

   Includes index.
   1. Data base management.   2. Parallel processing
(Electronic computers)   I. Title.
QA76.D3P344   1986   005.74   86-4221
ISBN 0-88175-027-1
PRINCIPLES OF COMPUTER SCIENCE SERIES
ISSN 0888-2096

Γιὰ τὴν μητέρα μου,

Τὴν γυναίκα μου

καὶ τὴν κόρη μου.

Contents

Preface

This book presents a rigorous approach to the problem of coping with concurrency in shared storage systems. This problem was clearly identified about ten years ago in the work of Jim Gray, and has since attracted the interest of a large community of researchers. Research in database concurrency control has advanced in a direction and style that clearly distinguishes it from areas that may appear related, most notably operating systems concurrency, concurrent programming languages, and verification of concurrent programs. A great variety of techniques and algorithms for maintaining consistency in multi-user databases have been developed, sometimes based on different assumptions and models; as a result the literature may appear a bit confusing in its wealth.

At the same time it also became clear that interesting mathematics can come out of research in concurrency control. Much of the work in this area deals with a particular syntactic abstraction of a program called a *schedule*, which turns out to be a surprisingly intricate combinatorial object. Besides, as in most areas of computer science, it is of interest to determine precisely the power and limitations of concurrency control techniques, and this gives rise to some beautiful problems.

My intention in this book is to present the main techniques and ideas in concurrency control within a simple, rigorous, and uniform model. The focus is on the few main ideas and principles underlying this area (serializability, locking, reliability, etc.), with an eye towards the development of a good mathematical understanding of these concepts. A surprising variety of mathematical tools are used, including graph theory, geometry, logic, and complexity (the latter is used to show certain basic negative results, which are useful as warnings about serious theoretical impediments in the applicability of certain techniques). All these tools are introduced in a reasonably self-contained manner, and used at a rather elementary level. Because of this wealth of formal techniques, and their instructive use in the pursuit of a fairly applied project, I hope that this material will also be of some value to computer scientists who are not otherwise interested in the particular motivating application.

I first organized the material in this book while teaching a graduate course on Database Concurrency Control at M.I.T. in the fall of 1981, and I have taught out of Chapters 1, 2, 4, and 6 twice at Stanford, during the last three weeks of a graduate course in Databases. I have also taught out of Chapters 1–6 a graduate seminar in the National Technical University of Athens, and a short course in the University of California at Santa Barbara in the spring of 1982. Chapters 1, 2, and 4 constitute a fairly self-contained introduction to database concurrency control, suitable to be part of the material covered in a graduate course in Databases.

I have used the problems in the end of each chapter less as an illustration of the material covered, and more as a way of disposing of uninteresting details that would threaten the continuity of the section, as well as for mentioning results that could not be covered in the chapter. I have used a crude notation for the difficulty of problems: One asterisk means that the I found the problem demanding, and two asterisks that I do not know how to solve it. Note that all problems whose answers can be found in published papers are not marked with respect to difficulty (naturally, references are provided).

Many results in this book first appeared in joint published work by myself and several coauthors, whom I want to thank for teaching me so many things; this applies to Phil Bernstein, Thanassis Hadzilacos, Paris Kanellakis, H. T. Kung, Jim Rothnie, Yannis Tsitsiklis, Mihalis Yannakakis, and Witek Lipski (a very talented researcher and friend who left us early). Above all I am indebted to Mihalis Yannakakis, who had a tremendous influence on my thinking in this area (on issues ranging from the definition of correctness to the notation for schedules), and has made many valuable suggestions and corrections on the manuscript. Albert Meyer encouraged me actively to write this book, and Jeff Ullman's suggestions substantially influenced the structure and philosophy of the book. Many other people have read parts of the book and given me their valuable opinion; these include Estie Arkin, Stélios Baltas, Ron Burback, Vassos Hadzilacos, Joe Mitchell, Peter Rathmann, and Ellen Silverberg. The National Science Foundation of the United States has generously supported my work on database concurrency control. Also, many thanks to all those who asked me over the years "How is the book coming along?"—without the embarassment they caused me I wouldn't have finished this book. Finally, it would have taken me even longer to write it, were it not for the constant encouragement and help of my wife, Xanthippi Markenscoff.

1

INTRODUCTION

1.1 DATABASES AND CONCURRENCY

A database is a collection of data stored in a computer system. But not all such collections can be called a database. First, all the data contained in a database are closely related, in that they are a description, at some level of detail, of a reasonably concrete and cohesive "part of the world." For example, a database might contain information concerning the personnel of an enterprise, the courses offered by a university, or the minerals found in a country. Another important requirement is that the data in a database must have a relatively long lifetime; they are essentially permanent except for updates and an occasional reorganization. This rules out data whose temporal scope coincides with the running of individual programs; it also suggests that databases are likely to be stored on longer term storage devices, such as disks and tapes. Perhaps the most important characteristic is that the structure of a database reflects a conscious effort to organize the data in a reasonably uniform manner. Although the data are ultimately stored in some precise way called the *physical data structure*, the user perceives a much less detailed and messy *conceptual data structure*, which can be operated on by clean, intuitive, and machine-independent high-level operations. A particular repertoire of data structures comprises a *data model*. For example, in the relational data model the allowed data structures are tables, and the allowed operations include projection, union, and Cartesian product. The language of the high-level operations of the data model is called the *query language*. Using this language, users can access and update the database directly. Also, one can write programs in an otherwise conventional programming language, except that input and output instructions can access and update the database instead of input and output devices.

The software that acts as the interface between the database and its users is called a *database management system*. Usually such a system is a commercially available product that can be adapted to manage any particular database application. The main function of the database management system is to maintain the mapping between the conceptual and the physical data structure, and, using this mapping, to translate queries and programs into operations on the physical data structure. However, besides this main task of supporting data abstraction, there are certain other important functions of the database management system. For example, one such function is *security*, that is, restricting access of data to authorized users. Another is *concurrency control*, the subject of this book. We examine next the reasons that make concurrency control a necessary part of any database management system.

The Problem of Concurrency

A database represents a part of the world, and this representation is done in terms of a complex data structure. This data structure consists of elementary parts called *entities* in this book (any subdivision of the data structure into entities is relevant). At any moment, the database is at a particular *state*, reflecting the current state of the part of the world represented. A state is an assignment of values to the entities.

Not all possible combinations of values of the entities represent a legal state of the world. For example, in a bank database no balance can be negative, and in an airline reservations database no flight should have more passengers than the capacity of the aircraft. Such real-world restrictions are called the *integrity constraints* of the database. A state of the database (i.e., a combination of values for the entities) that satisfies the integrity constraints is called a *consistent state*.

States, entities, and integrity constraints comprise the "static" aspect of a database. A database, however, represents a changing part of the world, and must, therefore, itself evolve. The dynamic elements of a database are the various *state transitions* ("jumps" from a state to another) reflecting changes in the world. Examples of state transitions are: the decrement of the balance of account number 1703 from $163 to $113; or the insertion of "JONES" in the list of passengers of flight 146.

In practice, many similar state transitions are grouped together and implemented by an *application program*. Examples are: the program which withdraws an amount from an account; or the program which reserves a seat in a flight. Such programs must be *correct*. That is, if a program is applied, all by itself, to a consistent database state, it must leave the database also in a consistent state. By this we do not mean that the state of the database remains consistent *throughout* the execution of the program. In fact, a program may drag the database through a sequence of inconsistent states, before it restores consistency in the end. In some sense this is unavoidable, because there may not be a way for the program to accomplish all changes it has to do in a single atomic step, without going through a sequence of smaller, individually inconsistent changes.

Individual programs run in isolation are correct. In database practice, however, we want many users to run their programs *concurrently*. This way the throughput and availability of the database system are enhanced. Unfortunately, if we allow the various steps of the different transactions to interleave indiscriminantly, serious errors may result as a result of unfortunate interactions between transactions.

Example 1.1:. Suppose that program A updates two entities, x and y, as shown in the following two steps:

$$A: \; x := x - 1; \; y := y + 1,$$

and program B updates the same entities as follows:

$$B: \; x := 2 * x; \; y := 2 * y.$$

Suppose further that the integrity constraints simply require that "$x + y = 0$". It is obvious that both programs are individually correct, because each maps consistent states to consistent states. It is also evident that certain interleaved executions of the two programs are *incorrect*. For example, the sequence

$$x := x - 1; \; x := 2 * x; \; y := 2 * y; \; y := y + 1$$

maps the consistent state $(x = -1, y = 1)$ to the inconsistent state $(x = -4, y = 3)$. $\square$

Evidently, the database system must monitor and control the concurrent execution of programs so that overall correctness is maintained, and erroneous executions, such as the one in the above example, are avoided. This task is called *concurrency control* and is the subject of this book.

The concurrency control problem for databases is quite reminiscent of similar problems in more classical concurrent systems, such as operating systems (see the notes and references at the end of the chapter). However, there are several important differences. In classical concurrent systems the interaction among different components of the system, as well as between the system and its users, is studied and designed carefully beforehand for the purpose of achieving maximum parallelism and utilization of resources. It is understood that many processes are to run concurrently; the problem is how to optimally design their interactions. In contrast, transactions in a database system are written as though each were to run *in isolation*. Their interaction is not understood, or even of interest. It is the responsibility of the database management system to make sure that this interaction is safe.

Another difference is that the more classical concurrent systems handle resources (printers, memory, processors) that possess a certain "robustness": At worst, you may run out of them. The resources handled by database systems are much more delicate: They are *data*, which may develop wrong values and, by propagation, soil the whole database.[1] For all these reasons the concurrency control problem for databases is very different, and quite a bit more complex, than the problems of concurrency motivated by operating systems.

1.2 THE MODEL

The database consists of a countable set of *entities*, $E = \{x_1, x_2, \ldots\}$. We shall usually denote entities not by a subscripted x, but by lower-case letters such as x, y, and z. Entities model parts of the database[2] that are indivisible, non-overlapping, and can be accessed and updated by a single atomic step. By "indivisible and non-overlapping" we mean that no part of an entity can coincide with another entity—or a part thereof. Thus updating an entity cannot have as a side-effect a change in the value of another entity. The only way to change the value of an entity is to update the entity explicitly. Any partition of the (physical or logical) data structure of the database into non-overlapping parts that can be updated atomically, can be the basis for our definition of the entities.

Each entity $x \in E$, has associated with it an enumerable set D_x called its *domain*. A *database state* is then an element of the Cartesian product of the domains; i.e., a mapping from each entity x to a value in D_x. The *integrity constraints* **C** are a *subset* of this Cartesian product. A state in **C** is called *consistent*.

Transactions

An application program is usually written in a high-level language such as PASCAL or COBOL, and may have a complex control structure, with loops and conditions. Much of the program involves "local" computation (i.e., computation involving not entities, but ordinary program variables local to the program). However, the program will occasionally communicate with the database via *database steps*. These steps are expressed in some database language which can be invoked from the programming language environment. A database step

---

[1] Operating systems do supervise access to data; however, they usually treat each such access by a process as an indivisible step, and isolate it from nontrivial interactions. There are, of course, exceptions, which in fact proved to be important precursors of database concurrency control.

[2] The fact that there are infinitely many entities is rather inconsequential; it will soon be clear from our model that at any instant only a finite number of entities can be relevant.

may *read* an entity (i.e., assign the current value of the entity to a program variable) or *write* an entity (i.e., change the current value of the entity to a value previously computed by the program).

From the point of view of concurrency control, the database steps are by far the most important element of a program. We capture this important part into an abstraction of a program execution called a *transaction*, a very central concept in this book. *A transaction is a sequence of database steps resulting from the execution of a program.* Thus, transactions are devoid of complex control structure: They are always straight-line programs. Furthermore, and more importantly, transactions ignore the precise nature of the computation happening between database steps, and are therefore to a large extent devoid of *semantics* as well.

This is the *top-down* way of thinking about transactions, as instantiations of more complex objects (i.e., programs). There is an equally informative *bottom-up* approach. What the database system sees of a program is a stream of database steps. This stream may drive the database through inconsistent states. This is not necessarily a disaster, the hope being that consistency will be restored in the end. Actually, passing through inconsistent states may be unavoidable. For example, in a bank database there is no way to transfer funds from an account to another in a single atomic step, without temporarily violating an integrity constraint stating that the sum of all balances equals the total liability of the bank. What is a transaction in this context? A transaction is a *unit of consistency*, a grouping together of several database steps, the combined execution of which is known to preserve the integrity constraints. A consequence is that there can be no "hidden restrictions" on inter-transaction behavior. For example, if correctness requires that steps from two "transactions" are executed in some predefined order, then these two "transactions" are in fact a *single transaction*.

The formal definition of transactions follows.

Definition 1.1: A *transaction* A is a finite sequence of steps $A = a_1 a_2 \cdots a_n$. The steps are assumed to be distinct symbols, and two different transactions cannot have steps in common. With each step a_j of A we associate an *action* ACTION$(a_j) \in \{W, R\}$, and an entity ENTITY$(a_j) \in E$. If for some step a_j we have ACTION$(a_j) = R$ and ENTITY$(a_j) = x$, then we say that step a_j *reads* entity x. This means that a particular program variable t_j in the underlying program is assigned the current value of x in the database: $t_j := x$. If ACTION$(a_j) = W$ and ENTITY$(a_j) = x$, then the step *writes* x. By this we mean that x is assigned a value computed by the program, which is potentially a function of *all previously read (by the same program) values of entities*: $x := f_j(t_{i_1}, t_{i_2}, \ldots, t_{i_k})$, where the i_p's are all indices smaller than j for which ACTION$(a_{i_p}) = R$.

A transaction, as defined above, is a purely *syntactic* object, subject to different *interpretations*. Intuitively, specifying an interpretation of a transaction means fixing a particular application program from which the transaction has originated, disregarding of course any control structure the program may have.

Definition 1.2: Let $A = a_1 \ldots a_n$ be a transaction. For each step a_j, $j \leq n$, let us define the set $B(a_j)$ of entities that are *read before* step a_j; that is,

$$B(a_j) = \{x \in E : \text{For some } i \leq j \text{ ACTION}(a_i) = R \text{ and ENTITY}(a_i) = x\}.$$

An *interpretation* of A is a pair $I = (\mathbf{D}, \mathbf{F})$, where $\mathbf{D} = \{D_x, D_y, \ldots\}$ is a set of *domains*, one for each entity in E; each domain is a set of values for the corresponding entity. $\mathbf{F} = \{f_a : a \text{ is a step of } A \text{ and ACTION}(a) = W\}$ is a set of *functions*, one for each write step of A. For each such step a, f_a is a mapping

$$f_a : \prod_{x \in B(a)} D_x \to D_{\text{ENTITY}(a)}.$$

Thus, an interpretation assigns a domain to each variable, and a particular function from values read to value written for each write step. In other words, it fills in the missing *semantics* of the transaction. □

It is quite natural—and, it turns out, simplifying—to make the following assumptions about the structure of the transactions.

(a) In a transaction, an entity is read at most once, and is written at most once.

(b) In a transaction, no entity is read after it is written.

Since a program is designed as though it would run in isolation, a violation of these assumptions would mean that the program contains redundant database steps, which can be easily eliminated.

We illustrate our transaction model by an example.

Example 1.2: In a bank database, we have written an application program for transferring an amount from one account to another.

```
program transfer (amt: integer);
entities x, y: integer;
variables temp1, temp2: integer;
begin
temp1 := x;
if temp1 ≥ amt then
  begin
  x := temp1 – amt;
  temp2 := y;
  y := temp2 + amt
  end
end.
```

Here x and y are names of entities representing the two balances, and amt is a program parameter, standing for the amount to be transferred from x to y. The variables $temp1$ and $temp2$ are local to the program. The database steps are those involving the entities x and y.

In a particular execution of this program, with $amt = 50$, the **then** path is taken. The resulting *transaction A* has four steps, $A = a_1 a_2 a_3 a_4$. In particular, the functions ACTION and ENTITY are as follows:

$$\text{ACTION}(a_1) = R, \text{ACTION}(a_2) = W, \text{ACTION}(a_3) = R, \text{ACTION}(a_4) = W$$

$$\text{ENTITY}(a_1) = x, \text{ENTITY}(a_2) = x, \text{ENTITY}(a_3) = y, \text{ENTITY}(a_4) = y$$

For clarity, we shall use in this book the following notation for transactions:

$$A = R(x)W(x)R(y)W(y)$$

It says that transaction A has four steps; the first reads entity x, the second writes x, the third reads y, and the last writes y. If we pretend for a moment that we do not know the precise program this transaction came from, then transaction A is a generic program of the form:

$$t_1 := x; \; x := f_2(t_1); \; t_3 := y; \; y :- f_4(t_1, t_3).$$

Transaction A can have many interpretations. The interpretation $I = (\mathbf{D}, \mathbf{F})$ corresponding to the particular execution of the original program is the following: The two domains are $D_x = D_y = \mathbf{integer}$, and the two functions are $f_2(t_1) = t_1 - 50$ and $f_4(t_1, t_3) = t_3 + 50$.

Naturally, this is not the only possible interpretation. Another interpretation would have the domain of x be records containing passenger names, and the domain of y be files (ordered sequences) of such records. The interpretations of the two functions are: $f_2(x) = x$ (the identity function), while $f_4(x, y)$ is the result of inserting x to y, if y contains no more than N records, N a constant. This interpretation could come from a program that reads an entity x (for example, a buffer holding a passenger's name), and, given that there is space in a particular flight, it appends the passenger's name to the list y of passengers for this flight. $\square$

In the course of this book we shall see that, in the theory of concurrency control, much depends on the *information* one has concerning the transactions. Situations such as this of Example 1.2, in which we have complete information about the application programs and the values of their parameters, are rare in concurrency control. Our working hypothesis will be that the interpretations of our transactions are not known (see the next chapter for a detailed discussion of this point). Thus, a transaction for us is just a sequence of read and write steps. We call this the *read-write model* of transactions. In this model, we would not distinguish between the two very different interpretations of the previous example. Occasionally (e.g. in Section 6.1) we shall not even know—or care—whether each step is a read or a write, and on which entity. In this *fully uninterpreted model* we shall denote transactions as sequences of symbols, e.g., $A : a_1a_2a_3a_4$.

Schedules

Transactions are submitted and run concurrently, with their steps interleaved. An interleaved execution of several transactions is termed a *schedule* (sometimes called *history* or *log* in the literature). Formally, a schedule of the transactions $A_1, A_2, \ldots, A_k$ is a sequence of steps in the *shuffle* $A_1 * A_2 * \cdots * A_k$ of the transactions (recall that the shuffle of two or more sequences consisting of distinct elements is the set of all sequences that have the given sequences as subsequences, and contain no other elements.)

For example, if $A = a_1a_2a_3a_4$ and $B = b_1b_2b_3$ are transactions, then $s = a_1b_1b_2a_2a_3a_4b_3$ and $s' = b_1b_2a_1b_3a_2a_3a_4$ are schedules. If we are working in the read-write model of transactions (as we shall in most of this book), we can use a more transparent notation. For example, if $A = R(x)W(x)R(y)W(y)$ and $B = R(z)W(x)W(z)$, then we represent s above as

$$s = \begin{array}{ll} A: & R(x) \qquad\qquad\quad W(x)R(y)W(y) \\ B: & \qquad R(z)W(x) \qquad\qquad\qquad W(z) \end{array}$$

That is, time increases from left to right, and each transaction occupies a separate line.

We now extend our notion of interpretation, so far defined for single transactions, to schedules. If s is a schedule involving the transactions $A_1, \ldots, A_k$, then an *interpretation* I of s is a k-tuple of interpretations $I_j = (\mathbf{D}, \mathbf{F}_j)$, all with the same choice $\mathbf{D}$ of domains for the entities.

Definition 1.3: A schedule, together with its interpretation, is tantamount to a real computation that acts on the database. The way to formalize this is the following: Suppose that s is a schedule, I an interpretation, and X an initial state, that is, a value for each entity. We say that every database step a of s *computes* a value $a_s(I, X)$. In particular, if a is $R(x)$, then $a_s(I, X)$ is defined to be equal to $w_s(I, X)$, where w is the latest $W(x)$ step before a in the schedule; if no such write step exists, then $a_s(I, X)$ is the value of entity x in the state X. If a is a $W(x)$ step, then let $r^1, \ldots, r^k$ be the read steps in the same transaction that preceed a. Then, $a_s(I, X)$ is defined as $f_a(r^1_s(I, X), \ldots, r^k_s(I, X))$. The *final state resulting from the execution of s*, denoted $s(I, X)$, is the state that has as value for each entity x the value computed by the last $W(x)$ step of s; if no such step exists, then naturally entity x has in $s(I, X)$ the same value as in X. $\square$

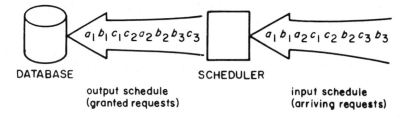

DATABASE   SCHEDULER

output schedule   input schedule
(granted requests)   (arriving requests)

Figure 1.1. The Scheduler.

A *serial schedule* is a schedule consisting of a succession of transactions, without any interleaving. For example, $a_1a_2a_3a_4b_1b_2b_3$ is a serial schedule, and so is

$$A: \qquad\qquad R(x)R(y)W(x)W(y)$$
$$B: \quad R(z)W(x)W(z)$$

Serial schedules play an important role in concurrency control, for the following reason. Recall that each transaction is correct, that is, if run in isolation it is guaranteed to map consistent database states to consistent database states. Call a schedule *correct* if it has the same property (after all, a transaction is a special case of a schedule!). Since transactions are correct, it is easy to show, by induction on the number of transactions involved, that *all serial* schedules are correct. Thus, serial schedules provide us with a firm foundation for our search for the appropriate notion of correct schedules that takes place in the next chapter.

Schedulers

The *scheduler* is the part of the database system which is responsible for concurrency control. The scheduler receives as input a stream of user requests for the execution of database steps, originating from different transactions (Figure 1.1). The scheduler grants or delays the arriving requests. The output of the scheduler is another schedule of the same transactions; it is executed by the rest of the database system. In Figure 1.1, for example, the scheduler delays steps a_2 and c_3 until the execution of steps c_2 and b_3, respectively. All other steps in the example are granted on arrival. We shall give a far more detailed view of our model of schedulers in Chapter 4.

The goal of the scheduler is to safeguard the consistency of the database by outputting only correct schedules. This problem, however, has an annoyingly trivial solution: Since all serial schedules are correct, the scheduler could fulfill its mission by delaying the steps of all but one transaction at a time, thus avoiding all interleavings and outputting a serial schedule. So, what is the rest of this book all about?

The trivial scheduler described above has one serious drawback: It introduces many unnecessary delays. It effectively forbids concurrency and multi-programming, and therefore would degrade such important aspects of the performance of our database system as *response time* and *transaction throughput*. It is not an acceptable solution. *The goal of the scheduler is to preserve consistency while maintaining a high level of parallelism or performance.* We shall try to capture mathematically these concepts in Chapter 5, where we examine in detail the subject of schedulers.

APPENDIX

In this Appendix we review some basic concepts and facts from Graph Theory and Complexity Theory that will be handy in later chapters.

Graph Theory

A *graph* is a pair $G = (V, E)$, where V is a finite set of *nodes* or *vertices*, and E is a set of subsets of V of cardinality two, called *edges*. Two nodes are *adjacent* if they define an edge, and a node is *incident* upon an edge if it belongs to the edge. We denote an edge $\{u, v\}$ as $[u, v]$, using brackets instead of the set notation. Graphs are represented pictorially as in Figure 1.2, where vertices are represented as points, and each edge $[u, v]$ is a line joining u with v. The *degree* of a node in a graph is the number of edges that are incident upon the node. For example, the degree of node v_4 in Figure 1.2 is four.

A *walk* in a graph $G = (V, E)$ is a sequence $[v_1, \ldots, v_n]$ of vertices in V, such that for $i = 1, \ldots, n - 1$, $[v_i, v_{i+1}] \in E$. A walk in which there is no repetition of nodes is a *path*; if only the first and last nodes coincide, we have a *cycle*. For example, in Figure 1.2, $[v_1, v_4, v_3, v_1, v_2, v_4]$ is a walk, $[v_1, v_4, v_3, v_6, v_5]$ is a path, and $[v_1, v_4, v_3, v_1]$ is a cycle.

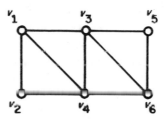

Figure 1.2. An Undirected Graph.

A *directed graph* is a pair $D = (V, A)$, where V is a finite set of *nodes* or *vertices*, and A is a set of *arcs*. Each arc is an ordered pair of distinct nodes, called its *tail* and its *head*, respectively. An arc is pictured as an arrow from the tail to the head. The number of arcs with node v as their tail is called the *out-degree* of v; the *in-degree* is the number of arcs with v as their head. In Figure 1.3(a), for example, we see a directed graph with four nodes and five arcs; the in-degree of v_2 is two. A *walk* in a directed graph $D = (V, A)$ is a sequence of nodes $(v_1, \ldots, v_n)$ such that $(v_i, v_{i+1}) \in A$ for $i = 1, \ldots, n - 1$. A walk with no nodes repeated is called a *path*; it is a *cycle* when only the first and last node coincide. In Figure 1.3(a), for example, (v_1, v_2, v_3) is a path, and (v_2, v_3, v_4, v_2) is a cycle. When it is clear by context that a walk is indeed

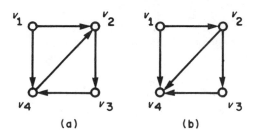

Figure 1.3. Two Directed Graphs.

a cycle, we may omit the second occurrence of the first node; thus, the cycle
above is (v_2, v_3, v_4).

A directed graph with no cycles is called a *directed acyclic graph*. For
example, the directed graph in Figure 1.3(b) is acyclic. The following is a
useful property of directed acyclic graphs:

Proposition 1.1: A directed graph is acyclic if and only if its vertices can be
ordered so that for all arcs the tail comes before the head.

Proof: We shall first establish that a directed acyclic graph has a node with
zero in-degree; such nodes are called *sources*. Start with any vertex v_1. If it is a
source, then we are done. Otherwise, there are arcs coming into v_1; we choose
the tail of such an arc, call it v_2. If v_2 is a source we stop, otherwise we pick one
of its predecessors, call it v_3, and so on. Since there are finitely many nodes,
either this process terminates (in which case we have identified a source), or a
node is repeated, say $v_m = v_n$, $m < n$. In the latter case, however, we have
discovered the cycle $(v_m, v_{m+1}, \ldots, v_n)$, contradicting our assumption that the
directed graph is acyclic.

Thus, any directed acyclic graph has a source. To show the Proposition,
we use induction on the number of nodes in the graph; it holds trivially for
directed acyclic graphs with one node. For the induction step, given a directed
acyclic graph $D = (V, A)$ we identify a source $s \in V$, and place it first in the
ordering. If we remove s and all arcs having it as tail from D, we obtain a new
directed graph $D' = (V - \{s\}, A - \{(s, v) \in A\})$. This directed graph is also
acyclic, since any cycle of D' would also be a cycle of D. Hence, by induction,
the nodes of D' can be ordered so that tails come before heads. Arranging them
in this order after s completes the proof. $\square$

An order on the nodes of a directed acyclic graph in which the tail of each
arc is numbered lower than the head, such as the one constructed in the proof
of Proposition 1.1, is said to be *compatible* with the directed acyclic graph.
For example, the vertices of the directed acyclic graph in Figure 1.3(b) are

numbered according to an order compatible with the graph. A directed acyclic graph (V, A) is sometimes called a *partial order*[3] on V; this means that an order is imposed on the nodes, but this order is not completely specified (as evidenced by the fact that in the proof of Proposition 1.1 we can choose any source as the next node, and there may be more than one of them). If there is only one order compatible with a directed acyclic graph, the graph is called a *total order*. The directed acyclic graph in Figure 1.3(b), for example, is a total order.

Algorithms and Complexity

An algorithm is a systematic and mechanical way of solving a computational problem. A computational problem is defined in terms of an infinite set of *instances*, of which we ask a particular *question*. For example, testing directed graphs for acyclicity is a particular computational problem. The possible instances are all directed graphs; the question asked of each is: "Is this directed graph acyclic?" Instances are represented as strings over some alphabet. For example, using typewriter symbols we can represent directed graphs in a number of ways. One particularly useful way is via *adjacency lists*. In this representation, we list the nodes of the graph one by one, each immediately followed by a listing of the heads of the arcs, of which the node is the tail. For example, the directed graph in Figure 1.3(a) would be represented as follows: $v_1(v_2, v_4); v_2(v_3); v_3(v_4); v_4(v_2)$.

We measure the performance of an algorithm in terms of the number of steps it takes to reach the answer. Since we expect an algorithm to spend more time on large instances than on small ones, we consider this performance as a function of the size of the input, that is, the number of symbols in the string which encodes the instance. Of all inputs with the same size, it is the one that has the largest time requirements that determines the performance of the algorithm for this size. The function which maps each integer n to the largest number of steps taken by the algorithm on any input of size n is called the *complexity* of the algorithm. To make our measure independent of the specific computer, available instruction set, etc., we express the complexity of an algorithm using the "big O" notation. A function $f(n)$ is said to be $O(g(n))$ if there is a constant c such that for all n we have $f(n) \leq c \cdot g(n)$.

For example, the proof of Proposition 1.1 above suggests an algorithm for determining whether a directed graph (V, A), presented in terms of its adjacency lists, is acyclic. The algorithm works in $|V|$ stages. At the ith stage, the algorithm scans the adjacency lists of the graph, to discover a source (i.e., a

---

[3] Strictly speaking, a partial order is an acyclic directed graph which is *transitive*, that is, if (u, v) and (v, w) are arcs, then so is (u, w). From any acyclic directed graph we can obtain a unique partial order by adding all possible edges implied by transitivity.

node not mentioned in any adjacency list). If none is found, then the algorithm concludes that the graph has a cycle. Otherwise, the source found is proclaimed the ith node of the graph, and its adjacency list is deleted from the input (thus deleting the source and its arcs from the graph).

What is the complexity of this algorithm, as a function of n, the length of the input? There are $|V| \le n$ stages. Each stage involves scanning the adjacency lists to discover one that contains no outgoing arcs, and deleting this list from the input. Both of these operations can be carried out in $O(n)$ steps. As a result, this algorithm has complexity $O(n^2)$. In fact, by a more careful implementation of these ideas an algorithm with complexity $O(n)$ is possible (see Problem 1.4).

NP-Completeness

There are many other ways of testing whether a directed graph is acyclic. We could examine one by one all sequences $(v_1, \ldots, v_n)$ of distinct vertices to see whether any of them forms a cycle. Another way would be to use Proposition 1.1, and test each permutation of the vertices whether for all arcs the tail is arranged before the head. The problem with these two algorithms is that they are too *inefficient*; both require a number of steps that is an *exponential* function of the length of the input. Fortunately, we know that for the acyclicity problem there is an algorithm whose time requirements grow as n^2—a *polynomial* in the length of the input. This distinction between polynomial and exponential time requirements is considered to mark the boundary between efficient and inefficient algorithms. The class of all problems, such as testing a graph for acyclicity, for which polynomial-time algorithms exist, is denoted P.

For some problems no efficient algorithms are known. Consider, for example, the following problem, superficially similar to the previous one. We are given a directed graph (V, A), and we are to determine whether there is a permutation $v_1, v_2, \ldots, v_n$ of the nodes of the graph such that, for $i = 1, \ldots, n-1$, $(v_i, v_{i+1}) \in A$. This problem, called the *Hamilton path problem*, can certainly be solved by trying all permutations. But unlike the problem of acyclicity, *no significantly better algorithm is known* for the Hamilton path problem. After many decades of efforts at devising a polynomial algorithm for this problem, mathematicians are conjecturing that no such algorithm exists, in other words, that the Hamilton path problem is not in P. Unfortunately, no proof of this impossibility conjecture is currently available.

Whether or not the Hamilton path problem belongs in P, it does belong in a wider class of problems called NP. This class can be defined rigorously using material that would be a long diversion now. Informally, NP can be defined as follows: Recall that a computational problem is an infinite set of instances, each with a question asked. NP is the class of all computational problems, in which the question is whether there exists an object having a particular relationship with the instance; moreover, once the desired object is found, its appropriateness can be verified in time polynomial in the length of the input. For example, the Hamilton path problem asks whether a permutation in which all successive nodes are connected by an arc exists. Although we do not know how to determine whether such a permutation exists, it is clear that, once such a permutation is found, the desired property can be easily established. The object sought in relation to an instance of a problem in NP is sometimes called the *certificate* for this instance.

It can be argued that P is a subset of NP. Because we can reformulate any problem in P so that we are asked whether a particular object exists: The certificate sought is simply the record of the computation of the appropriate program that solves the problem in polynomial time. Such a record can obviously be checked for validity in polynomial time. But is P a *proper* subset of NP, or are the two classes equal? The answer is not known.

In another important problem in NP, called the *satisfiability problem*, we are given a *Boolean formula in conjunctive normal form*. A Boolean formula is a formula involving Boolean variables (that is, variables taking only the values **true** and **false**), connected by the Boolean operations **or** (denoted $\vee$), **and** (denoted $\wedge$), and **not** (denoted by a bar above the variable) more or less in the same way that ordinary variables are connected by addition, multiplication, and square root to form ordinary formulas. For example, $x \vee (\bar{y} \wedge \bar{x})$ is a Boolean formula. A Boolean formula is in conjunctive normal form if it consists of the conjunction (that is, joining together by *and*s) of several terms, called *clauses*, each of which is the disjunction (joining by *or*s) of some *literals*. A literal is either a Boolean variable or the negation of one. For example,

$$(\bar{x} \vee y \vee z) \wedge (x \vee \bar{z}) \wedge (x \vee y \vee \bar{z})$$

is a Boolean formula in conjunctive normal form, with three variables and three clauses. A *truth assignment* is a function mapping each variable to {**true**, **false**}. A truth assignment is said to satisfy a Boolean formula in conjunctive normal form if each clause contains a literal that is **true** under the assignment. Finally, SATISFIABILITY is the following computational problem: Given a Boolean formula in conjunctive normal form, is there a satisfying truth assignment? Evidently, this problem is also in NP, as it can be easily tested whether a given truth assignment satisfies the formula. Naturally, we can solve SATISFIABILITY by trying all possible truth assignments, but this is again an exponential algorithm. No polynomial algorithm for SATISFIABILITY is known, and it is widely suspected that none exists. But again, we have no proof that SATISFIABILITY (or any other problem in NP) is not in P.

Even in the absence of a concrete proof that SATISFIABILITY is not in P, we have very substantial evidence that it is not. What we *can* prove is that SATISFIABILITY is in a certain precise sense *the least likely among all problems in NP to be in P*. This is shown using the concept of a *reduction*. A reduction from problem A to problem B is a polynomial-time algorithm which transforms any given instance of A to some instance of B such that the answer to the produced instance of B is the same as that to the original instance of A. Many reductions are possible among problems in NP. For example, the Hamilton path problem can be reduced to SATISFIABILITY (see Problem 1.5 for details). Also, SATISFIABILITY can be reduced to the special case of the same problem in which all clauses have at most three literals (see Problem 1.6). Clearly, if problem A can be reduced to B, and B is in P, then also A is in P.

A problem B is called *NP-complete* if all other problems in NP can be reduced to B. By the last remark, if an NP-complete problem is in P, then so are all problems in NP, and P=NP. Given that this possibility is considered extremely unlikely, we are led to believe that no NP-complete problem is in P, and NP-completeness is a serious evidence of intractability. An important result shown by S. A. Cook in 1971 is that *SATISFIABILITY is NP-complete*. In fact, even the special case in which all clauses have at most three literals is NP-complete (see Problem 1.6).

How does one go about proving that a problem in NP is NP-complete? Once Cook's Theorem has been proved and problems known to be NP-complete are available, we can show a new problem to be NP-complete by exhibiting a reduction from SATISFIABILITY (or any other known NP-complete problem) to the problem in hand. We shall illustrate the use of this methodology several times in later chapters.

PROBLEMS

1.1 In the personnel database of an enterprise, which of the following is *not* an integrity constraint, as defined in the text. (i) Each department has at most one manager. (ii) No employee earns more than the manager of his/her department. (iii) No salary can ever be decreased.

1.2 In databases, transactions may cause the dynamic *creation* of new entities, or *destruction* of entities. Discuss how our model of entities can simulate the behavior of such operations by equipping each of the infinitely many entities with an "exists" bit.

1.3 Suppose that no step of a transaction can arrive while the previous step of the same transation is being delayed by the scheduler. This is a reasonable assumption in the case of read steps, since presumably the computation of the transaction cannot continue without the value to be read. It turns out that, under this assumption, not all pairs of schedules of the same transactions could be the input and output of a scheduler. For example, if the scheduler receives the same input as in Figure 1.1, the output cannot be $a_1 a_2 c_1 c_2 c_3 b_1 b_2 a_3 b_3$: Since step c_3 arrives after b_2, it cannot arrive and be output while b_1 is waiting. Define carefully the relationship that must hold between the input and the output of any on-line scheduler under this assumption.

1.4 Describe an $O(n)$ algorithm for determining whether a directed graph is acyclic. (*Hint:* Maintain a data structure which allows the determination of a source in constant time, and the deletion of arcs in time proportional to the number of arcs deleted.)

1.5 Give a reduction from the Hamilton path problem to SATISFIABILITY. (*Hint:* Given a directed graph, we have to construct a Boolean formula which is satisfiable if and only if there is a numbering of the nodes of the graph such that any two consecutive nodes define an arc. The formula may involve variables such as x_{ij}, which is **true** if node v_i is jth in the numbering.) Can you find a reduction in the opposite direction?

1.6 Show that SATISFIABILITY can be reduced to the special case of the same problem in which all clauses have three of fewer literals. (*Hint:* Replace a clause with more than three literals by an equivalent set of three-literal clauses.)

NOTES AND REFERENCES

Two good textbooks on the subject of databases are [Date 1981] and [Ullman 1982]. Each of them has a chapter on concurrency control. Treatments of concurrency control, which are less rigorous and more pragmatic than ours, can be found in [Gray 1978] and [Bernstein et al. 1986]. See also [Casanova 1981]. For an introduction to graph theory see [Even 1979], and for more on algorithms, complexity, and NP-completeness see [Aho et al. 1974], [Garey and Johnson 1979], [Papadimitriou and Steiglitz 1982]; you can find more about problems 1.14, 1.15 and 1.16 in any one of these books. SATISFIABILITY was shown NP-complete in [Cook 1971].

2

CORRECTNESS

2.1 INTRODUCTION

The input of the scheduler is the sequence of steps submitted by the users for execution by the database system; its output must be a correct schedule. In this chapter we examine in detail what "correct schedule" means. In doing so, we shall maintain a rather "static" view of the scheduler, namely as a mapping from schedules to schedules. We shall discuss in great detail the issue of its implementation by an algorithm (in fact, an efficient, on-line one) in the next chapters.

It is clear that, for an output of the scheduler to be correct, it must meet two basic criteria: First, it should preserve the integrity constraints of the database, as discussed in the previous chapter. Second, the transactions appearing in the output should be *the same* as those in the input. The latter requirement rules out such absurdities as a scheduler which maintains integrity constraints by refusing to grant *any* step; or a scheduler which invents a transaction in order to salvage consistency—for example, when in doubt it reinitializes the database.

The question facing the scheduler at any moment is whether the proposed schedule s appearing in the input maintains the integrity constraints $\mathbf{C}$. [1] There is an established and active field of computer science, called *Program Verification*, dealing with precisely this type of problem (see the notes at the end of the chapter). In the notation used in this field, the scheduler must prove the

---

[1] Actually, the question a scheduler must answer is whether the prefix of the schedule which has arrived so far can be extended to one that maintains the integrity constraints. More about this point in Chapter 5.

following assertion:

$$\text{``C } \{s\} \text{ C''}$$

The meaning of this assertion is: "If the execution of program s C holds, then after the execution of s C is guaranteed to hold again."

The problem of verifying such assertions mechanically is by no means solved. However, it is certainly well-studied, and it would be very exciting if that body of knowledge could be put in use for database concurrency control. Unfortunately, this approach is inappropriate, because of a number of reasons.

First, we have the problem of *performance*. Proving reasonably complicated assertions of this form, when it can be carried out mechanically at all, is an awesome computational task (see Problem 2.1 for one of the reasons why). It can be feasible in a case in which s is an important program that must be proven correct once and for all, and a substantial amount of time can be invested in this effort. In our case, however, s is an ever-changing interleaving of steps, and the scheduler must make decisions about it in a speed comparable with the rate of arrival of requests.

But efficiency is not the only problem. If we were to take the mechanical proof approach, we would have to understand precisely what the application programs are doing—their *semantics*—and not just the database steps. However, application programs are long and complex pieces of code that are best left ununderstood.[2] How much is it reasonable to assume that we know about the application programs? It is safe to assume that the database management system knows about *the interaction of the programs with the database*, either by acquiring the relevant information as the interaction progresses, or by "soliciting" such information off-line. This is precisely the kind of "syntactic" information that the read-write model captures.

A further difficulty with the semantic approach is that the scheduler is usually designed *before* the application programs, and by a different group of people. Typically, the same commercially available database management system, including the concurrency control subsystem, is adapted to different applications. Necessarily, the concurrency control must be *application-independent*, which clearly means that it cannot take into account the precise semantics of the application programs.

However, the ultimate argument against the semantic approach is that, in practice, *we do not even know the integrity constraints*. The writers of application programs are guided by their insight into the application domain to write correct programs, but usually nobody cares to spell out all integrity

---

[2] In this book we have introduced transactions as executions of tangible programs. However, sometimes a transaction is just a *session* of a user interacting with the database through a terminal, and thus its semantics may not even be well-defined.

constraints of the system. *Usually what we know about the integrity constraints is that application programs preserve them!*

This last observation points the way towards the appropriate definition of correctness. All we know about correctness is that transactions are correct. What can we say about schedules? Certainly that any *serial* schedule is correct—by an induction on the number of transactions involved. And likewise for any schedule that can be shown *equivalent* to a serial schedule. If a schedule behaves differently from any serial schedule, for all we know it violates the integrity constraints.[3] Thus we are lead to the following principle: *A schedule is correct if it is equivalent to a serial schedule.*

We have not quite defined correctness, though. We have simply *reduced* defining correctness to defining equivalence. As a result, the various notions of correctness that we shall examine in this chapter are in fact different notions of equivalence. Predictably, they are all of a syntactic nature.

2.2 FINAL-STATE SERIALIZABILITY

Definition 2.1: Let s and s' be schedules.[4] We say that s and s' are *final-state equivalent* if

(a) They involve the same transactions, and

(b) For each interpretation $I = \{(\mathbf{D}, \mathbf{F}_i)\}$ of s (which is at the same time an interpretation of s' by (a) above) and all choices $X \in \prod_{x \in E} D_x$ of initial values for each entity in E we have $s(I, X) = s'(I, X)$.

That is, two schedules are final-state equivalent if they are identical as mappings from states to states, under all possible interpretations. $\square$

This is a very intuitive definition, but it has a serious drawback: It is stated in terms of an extremely general condition. How are we to test whether two schedules differ under some among the unimaginably many possible interpretations? Fortunately, there is a convenient graph-theoretic characterization of final-state equivalence, which we describe next.

Given a schedule s, let us first define an object called the *augmented schedule of s*, denoted $\hat{s}$. This schedule contains two new transactions A_0 and A_∞, besides those in s. A_0 consists solely of *write* steps, one for each entity read or written in s, and A_∞ of read steps, again one for each entity read or written in s. Schedule $\hat{s}$ starts with A_0 followed by s, and ends with A_∞.

The intuitive justification of this definition is the following. Our notion of final-state equivalence involves the concepts of initial and final state, which a schedule fails to capture. The augmented schedule is designed to correct this.

---

[3] This quite intuitive statement can be made rigorous; see Chapter 5.

[4] We shall henceforth use the read-write model of transactions, unless it is stated explicitly otherwise.

The "pseudotransaction" A_0 defines the initial values X of the entities, while A_∞ "senses" the final results $s(I, X)$ of the execution of s.

Example 2.1: Consider the schedule

$$
\begin{array}{ll}
A_1 : R(x)R(y) \quad\ W(z)W(x) & \\
s = A_2 : \qquad\quad R(y) & \qquad\qquad W(y)W(x) \\
A_3 : \qquad\qquad\qquad\qquad\quad R(z)W(z)R(x)W(y) &
\end{array}
$$

Its augmented schedule, $\hat{s}$, is the following:

$$
\begin{array}{ll}
A_0 : W(x)W(y)W(z) & \\
A_1 : \quad\ R(x) \qquad R(y) \qquad W(z)W(x) & \\
A_2 : \qquad\qquad\qquad R(y) & \qquad W(y)W(x) \\
A_3 : \qquad\qquad\qquad\quad R(z) \quad W(z)R(x) \quad W(y) & \\
A_\infty : & \qquad\qquad R(x)R(y)R(z)
\end{array}
$$

Starting from the augmented schedule $\hat{s}$, we next construct a directed graph $D(s) = (V, A)$. The set of nodes V is the set of all steps of transactions in $\hat{s}$. The set A contains two kinds of arcs:

(a) If a_i and a_j are steps in the same transaction with $i < j$, ACTION$(a_i) = R$, and ACTION$(a_j) = W$, then we add the arc (a_i, a_j) to A. These arcs denote dependencies within the same transaction.

(b) If a_i and b_j are steps in different transactions, with ACTION$(a_i) = W$, ACTION$(b_j) = R$, ENTITY$(a_i) = $ ENTITY(b_j), and a_i is the *last* step in $\hat{s}$ before b_j which writes ENTITY(a_i), then we add the arc (a_i, b_j) to A. These arcs denote dependencies across transactions.

Example 2.1 (continued): For the schedule s in the previous example, $D(s)$ is the directed graph shown in Figure 2.1 below. In the figure we use the notation, for example, "$A_i : R(x)$" to distinguish among different steps reading x. Intuitively, the graph $D(s)$ captures the "flow of information" among the steps of s and the initial and final values of the entities. $\square$

Finally, from $D(s)$ we construct the directed graph $D_1(s)$ by deleting all nodes of $D(s)$ from which *no step* of A_∞ can be reached. We also delete all arcs incident upon such nodes. For example, in Figure 2.1 $D_1(s)$ is $D(s)$ with the part included in the broken line deleted. It is in terms of $D_1(s)$ that the promised graph-theoretic characterization of finite-state equivalence is stated.

Theorem 2.1: *Two schedules s and s' are final-state equivalent if and only if they involve the same transactions, and $D_1(s) = D_1(s')$.* [5]

We first need some terminology. If D is a directed graph we say that node u is a *predecessor* of node v if there is a path from u to v. If there is an *arc* directly from u to v, u is termed an *immediate predecessor* of v. The *preceding*

---

[5] Two directed graphs are equal if they have the same sets of nodes and arcs. This is equality of *labeled* graphs, not graph isomorphism.

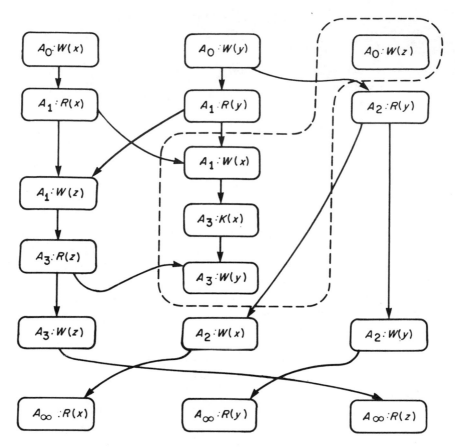

Figure 2.1. An Illustration of the Construction of $D(s)$ and $D_1(s)$.

directed graph of v, denoted $\text{pre}_D(v)$, is D restricted to v and its predecessors, with all other nodes deleted. Also, recall the notation $v_s(I, X)$ for the value computed by step v of schedule s under interpretation I, assuming that the initial state was X.

Proof of Theorem 2.1:   For the *if* direction we shall show the following stronger inductive assertion:

"Suppose that, for some step v of s and s', we have that $\text{pre}_{D_1(s)}(v) = \text{pre}_{D_1(s')}(v)$. Then under any interpretation I of s and s' and any initial state X, we have $v_s(I, X) = v_{s'}(I, X)$."

We shall prove the assertion by induction on the number of nodes in $\text{pre}_{D_1(s)}(v)$. For the basis, if this graph contains just v, then v must be a write step, and in fact one that is not preceded by any read step in its transaction. Because, if v were a read step, then there would be an immediate predecessor of v, namely the write step with the same entity which is last before v in s'—such a step always exists, since our schedule s' starts with steps writing all entities. Also, if v is a write step preceded by a read step in the same transaction, then this read step is by our definition of $D(s)$ an immediate predecessor of v. Therefore, the function for step v in the interpretation I has 0 arguments: it is a *constant* depending on I—or X, if v is a step of A_0—and thus the assertion holds.

Let now $\text{pre}_{D_1(s)}(v)$ contain more than one node. Suppose first that v is a read step, and consider the immediate predecessor of v in $D_1(s)$ (read steps have only one). Since we know that $\text{pre}_{D_1(s)}(v) = \text{pre}_{D_1(s')}(v)$, it follows that this immediate predecessor is the same step w in both graphs, and furthermore, that the preceding graph of w will be the same in the two graphs. Node w has a smaller preceding graph than v does (for example, the preceding graph of w does not contain v, by acyclicity), and therefore by induction we know that $w_s(I, X) = w_{s'}(I, X)$. However, w is the last write step before v in s to write the same entity that v reads. Therefore, $v_s(I, X) = w_s(I, X)$; similarly, $v_{s'}(I, X) = w_{s'}(I, X)$, and we have the desired equality.

The case in which v is a write step is similar. First we note that for all read steps r^i, $i = 1, \ldots, k$ that precede v in its transaction (and are therefore the only immediate predecessors of v in both graphs) we have $\text{pre}_{D_1(s)}(r^i) = \text{pre}_{D_1(s')}(r^i)$, for $i = 1, \ldots, k$. Thus, by the induction hypothesis we have $r_s^i(I, X) = r_{s'}^i(I, X)$. Consequently, for any interpretation f of the function associated with v, and any initial state X, we have

$$v_s(I, X) = f(r_s^1(I, X), \ldots, r_s^k(I, X)) = f(r_{s'}^1(I, X), \ldots, r_{s'}^k(I, X)) = v_{s'}(I, X)$$

The assertion has been proven.

It is now easy to complete the proof of the *if* part. Since $D_1(s) = D_1(s')$, it follows that, for each entity x, the step $R(x)$ of A_∞ has the same preceding graph in both graphs. By our assertion, the values read by this step in both schedules are the same. This, however, is the final value for entity x in the schedules s and s'. It follows that they indeed are final-state equivalent.

Only If: Suppose now that s and s' are final-state equivalent. This means that, for all domains for the entities, all initial values, and all interpretations of the write steps, both schedules arrive at the same final state.

Since we can choose any domain of values for the entities, let us consider a rather unusual one: *The set of all directed graphs with nodes that are steps of $\hat{s}$, and which have a single sink* (node with no outgoing arcs). As our initial value for an entity x, we choose the *single node* labeled $A_0 : W(x)$. Finally, let us define the interpretations of the functions. Suppose that $A_j : W(x)$ is preceded

in the same transaction by the read steps $R(y_1), \ldots, R(y_k)$. We must define a
function f mapping any k-tuple of directed graphs $G_i = (V_i, E_i)$, $i = 1, \ldots, k$,
each with a single sink v_i, to a new directed graph $G = f(G_1, \ldots, G_k)$. The
graph G is defined as follows:

(a) The nodes of G are all nodes in $\bigcup_{i=1}^{k} V_i$, together with the nodes with
   labels $A_j : R(y_i)$, $i = 1, \ldots, k$, and one node labeled $A_j : W(x)$. The latter
   is the sink.

(b) The arcs of G are also those in $\bigcup_{i=1}^{k} E_i$, together with the arcs $(v_i, A_j :$
   $R(y_i))$ and $(A_j : R(y_i), A_j : W(x))$, $i = 1, \ldots, k$.

This completes the definition of the interpretation. For example, if $k = 2$,
$j = 3$, $y_1 = y$, $y_2 = z$ and G_1, G_2 are as shown in Figure 2.2 (a) and (b), then
$f(G_1, G_2)$ is shown in Figure 2.2 (c).

It should be obvious that this interpretation and initial state "reconstructs"
the graph $D_1(s)$, in the sense that, for each write step v, $v_s(I, X) = \mathrm{pre}_{D(s)}(v)$.
Applying this to the last step, call it v, which writes x in each augmented schedule, we obtain:

$$\mathrm{pre}_{D(s)}(v) = v_s(I, X) = v_{s'}(I, X) = \mathrm{pre}_{D(s')}(v),$$

where the first and last equalities follow from the above observation. The second
equality holds because the value read by step $A_\infty : R(x)$ in a schedule is, by
definition, the final value for x in that schedule, and by our hypothesis s and
s' are final-state equivalent.

Thus, for each step v of A_∞ we have $\mathrm{pre}_{D(s)}(v) = \mathrm{pre}_{D(s')}(v)$. However,
this is identical to the statement that $D_1(s) = D_1(s')$, since $D_1(s)$ was defined
as the union of all the preceding graphs of steps in A_∞. $\square$

Corollary : *Given two schedules s and s', we can test whether they are final-
state equivalent in $O(n)$ time, where n is the length of the schedules.*

Proof: The graphs $D(s)$, $D_1(s)$, as well as the corresponding graphs for s',
have a number of arcs at most proportional to the square of the length of the
input, and can be constructed in time proportional to their size. This estimate,
however, is wasteful, since the important arcs of these graphs are those that
go from write steps to read steps (not vice-versa), and there are linearly many
such arcs (one for each read step). Testing whether these arcs are the same in
both graphs can be done in linear time; equality of the remaining parts of the
graphs can be done by simply making sure that the transactions involved are
identical. $\square$

An important notion of correctness is based on final-state equivalence:

Definition 2.2:   Let us call a schedule s *final-state serializable* if it is final-
state equivalent to some serial schedule. $\square$

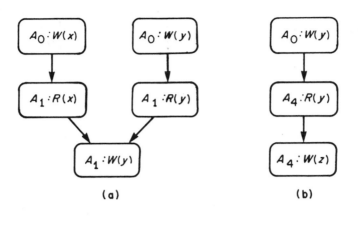

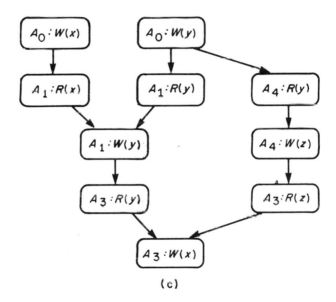

Figure 2.2. The Interpretation of f.

Example 2.2: Consider the following schedule

$$s' = \begin{array}{llll} A_1 : R(x) & W(y) & & W(x) \\ A_2 : & R(y) & & R(x)W(z) \\ A_3 : & & R(z)W(z) \end{array}$$

This schedule is final-state serializable, since it is equivalent to the following serial schedule:

$$\begin{aligned}
&\quad\; A_1: &&\qquad\qquad\qquad R(x)W(y)W(x) \\
s'' = &\quad\; A_2: &&\quad R(y)R(x)W(z) \\
&\quad\; A_3: &R(z)W(z)
\end{aligned}$$

This fact can be easily checked by applying the construction in Theorem 2.1. In contrast, the schedule s in Example 2.1 *is not final-state serializable*. One way to show this would be to repeat the construction of Theorem 2.1 for the $3! = 6$ serial schedules involving the three transactions of s. (As we shall see later in this chapter, it is unlikely that a much better algorithm exists!) An *ad hoc* argument for showing the non-serializability of s is the following: Consider the transactions A_2 and A_3. Which one comes first in the alleged equivalent serial schedule? If it is A_2, then the final value of y is written by A_3 and not by A_2, and final-state equivalence does not hold. If A_3 comes first, then A_2 reads the value of y written by A_3 instead of the initial value, as it does in s. $\square$

2.3 THE CRITIQUE OF FINAL-STATE SERIALIZABILITY

Final-state serializability has been quite controversial as a criterion of correctness. There are two lines of criticism: One says that final-state serializability is *too restrictive* (it rules out schedules that it shouldn't), the other says it is *too permissive* (it allows schedules that it shouldn't).

Using Semantics

Final-state serializability is certainly "syntactic," in that it ignores the semantics of the transactions and the integrity constraints of the database. In the beginning of this chapter we defended this approach by arguing that the semantics are complex and hard to obtain. There are, however, certain kinds of semantic information that are quite "simple" to argue about, and, moreover, they could conceivably be solicited from the writers of the application programs. We discuss some of these below.

Commutativity. It is often the case that the functions computed by programs *commute*. For example, if we knew that the functions corresponding to the write steps are increments of a counter (i.e., $f(x) = x + 1$), then the part of the schedule shown below

$$\begin{aligned}
A_1: &\quad \dots \; R(x)W(x) &&\qquad\qquad\quad \dots \\
A_2: &\quad \dots &&\quad R(x)W(x) \; \dots
\end{aligned}$$

is equivalent to

$$\begin{aligned}
A_1: &\quad \dots &&\qquad\quad R(x)W(x) \; \dots \\
A_2: &\quad \dots \; R(x)W(x) &&\qquad\qquad\quad \dots
\end{aligned}$$

even though the two schedules are *not* final-state equivalent.

Copiers. It is often the case that the function computed by a write step is in fact the *identity* function in one of its arguments: $f(\ldots, x, \ldots) = x$. This can be valuable information, as far as concurrency control is concerned. For example the schedule

$$
\begin{array}{llll}
A_1 : R(x) & & & W(z) \\
A_2 : & & W(x) & \\
s = A_3 : & R(x)W(y) & & \\
A_4 : & & R(y)W(x) & \\
A_5 : & & & R(x)W(z)
\end{array}
$$

is not final-state serializable, but becomes equivalent to the serial schedule $A_5 A_1 A_3 A_2 A_4$ if we know that the transactions A_3 and A_4 compute the identity function. One can define a more relaxed version of final-state serializability, which takes into account this information (see Problem 2.2).

Integrity Constraints. The integrity constraints are usually the most obscure part of the database. Nevertheless, some information concerning the integrity constraints may be quite easy to obtain and use. For instance, we may know that a specific variable x does not appear in the integrity constraints. Also, integrity constraints are usually the conjunction (i.e., the logical *and* of several partial constraints called *clauses*). We might have some information concerning the structure of these clauses—e.g., the entities appearing in each. Such information can be used to arrive at more liberal notions of correctness than ordinary final-state serializability (see Problem 2.3.)

Dead Transactions

Our basic definition of correctness (end of Section 2.1) requires that the equivalent serial schedule contain the same set of transactions as the schedule in hand. It can be argued that this is unnecessarily restrictive. After all, what we need is the maintenance of the integrity constraints, and this can be accomplished by *any* serial schedule, whether or not it contains the same set of transactions as the input of the scheduler.

In particular, it is sometimes the case that a schedule is equivalent to a serial schedule involving a *subset* of the transactions. Consider for example the following:

$$
s = \begin{array}{lll}
A_1 : R(x) & W(y) & \\
A_2 : & R(y) & W(y)
\end{array}
$$

Schedule s is not final-state serializable, as it can be easily checked. It is, however, final-state equivalent to the serial schedule consisting of the transaction A_2 alone! Obviously, s does preserve the integrity constraints. Why is it then that it must be excluded from the schedules that we regard correct?

The issue here is that of *dead steps and transactions*. A step is *live* in a schedule s if, intuitively, it affects the final state. In terms of the directed graph $D(s)$, a step v is live if a step of A_∞ can be reached from it. To phrase it inductively:

(a) A write step is live in s if either it is the last write step on this entity, or it is the last write step for that entity *before a live read step for the entity*.

(b) A read step is live in s if there is a subsequent live write step in the same transaction.

A step of s is *dead* in s if it is not live in s. Evidently, dead steps do not influence the computation; their effects are "overwritten" by subsequent steps, before anybody had a chance to see them —except possibly for other dead steps. They are the steps that we delete in our construction of $D_1(s)$ out of $D(s)$.

We say a transaction is *dead* in s if all of its steps are dead in s. Notice that transaction A_1 in s above is dead in s. This is why equivalence is preserved when A_1 is omitted.

We claim that it is reasonable to consider s incorrect, as we did. Here is the argument: Two users submitted transactions. They were both left to believe that their transactions –say, seat reservations– were executed. Yet, A_1 in effect *did not* execute, because it was scheduled in a way that made it dead in the resulting schedule. Even though the integrity constraints were preserved, the overall schedule cannot be considered correct. Hence our insistence that the equivalent correct schedule contain all transactions.

This is not to say that if a schedule contains a dead transaction it is necessarily incorrect. Consider, for example, the following augmented version of s:

$$s' = \begin{array}{ll} A_1: & R(x) \quad W(y) \\ A_2: & \quad\quad\quad R(y) \quad\quad W(y) \\ A_3: R(z)W(y) \end{array}$$

A_1 is also dead in s'. Yet s' is final-state serializable, and therefore correct from our point of view, since it is equivalent to the serial schedule $A_1 A_3 A_2$—this can be checked by applying Theorem 2.1. The informal justification for considering s' correct, but not s, is the following: In the case of schedule s', the database system includes a transaction, namely A_3, which can render A_1 dead in serial execution.[6] The user who submitted A_1 is presumably aware of the fact that the effects of her/his transaction can be legitimately annulled by A_3. For example, most likely this is not a seat reservation system.

---

[6] Of course, it could be the case that such a transaction was also present in the system in which s was submitted and rejected for execution. The point is that A_3 appears in s', and therefore this information is now available to the scheduler.

Infinite Schedules

Databases operate continuously (or let's assume they do). Transactions are submitted, interleaved, and executed in a never-ending fashion. This can result in the following paradox: It is possible that during the lifetime of the database *the integrity constraints never hold*, and yet the operation of the database is intuitively "correct." Suppose, for example, that the integrity constraints are "$x = y$," and consider the following infinite schedule:

$$
\begin{array}{llll}
A_1 : x := x + 1 & y := y + 1 & & \\
A_2 : & x := x + 1 & y := y + 1 & \\
A_3 : & & x := x + 1 & y := y + 1 \\
A_4 : & & & x := x + 1 \quad y := y + 1
\end{array} \quad \cdots
$$

Here we have replaced pairs of steps of the form $R(x)W(x)$ and $R(y)W(y)$ with their interpretations $x := x + 1$ and $y := y + 1$, respectively. Suppose that we start from the consistent state $(x = 0, y = 0)$. The database undergoes a never-ending sequence of *inconsistent* states $(x = 1, y = 0), (x = 2, y = 0), (x = 2, y = 1), (x = 3, y = 1), (x = 3, y = 2), \ldots$. Still, this infinite schedule is intuitively "correct," although it is correct in a sense which final-state serializability fails to capture.

Strict Serializability

We next examine arguments that final-state serializability is too liberal a notion of correctness. Consider the following schedule:

$$
\begin{array}{llll}
A_1 : R(x) & & W(y) \\
s - A_2 : & R(x)W(x) & \\
A_3 : & & R(y)W(y)
\end{array}
$$

Schedule s is final-state serializable. An equivalent serial schedule—in fact, the only one— is $s' = A_3 A_1 A_2$. There appears to be a problem, though. In s, transaction A_3 starts after A_2 has terminated, whereas in s' A_3 comes before A_2. If a schedule is equivalent to a serial one, in which no such "inversion" occurs, then it is termed *strictly serializable*. It has been proposed that schedules, such as s, which are final-state serializable but not strictly serializable, are of questionable correctness. The rationale for this is that, in our example, perhaps the two transactions A_2 and A_3 were to be executed in this order, and therefore their switching is a dangerous change.

This is not a serious problem. The serial schedule s' should be regarded merely as a *proof* of the correctness of s, and as a proof it is certainly a valid one. The scheduler will still schedule the steps of s in their right order in s, and not in their order in s'. In particular, A_2 will be executed before A_3.

Incorrect Views

Let us consider this schedule:

$$s = \begin{array}{ll} A_1 : R(x)W(x) & W(y) \\ A_2 : & R(x)R(y)W(y) \end{array}$$

It is final-state serializable, because it is equivalent to $A_2 A_1$. Still, it has a serious problem. Transaction A_1 updates both x and y. For all we know, it may increment them both by 1, preserving some integrity constraint of the form "$x < y$". Now A_2 reads x after it is updated, and yet reads an unupdated version of y: It saw an "inconsistent view," in which possibly the integrity constraint is violated. Since transactions are guaranteed to work correctly only when they are run at a consistent state, it is possible that A_2 wrote a grossly incorrect value for y. Luckily, A_1 came back to *overwrite* this value, and so s came out final-state serializable.

Inconsistent views can cause concurrency errors, even though the overall schedule is final-state serializable. Recall that the transactions are runs of programs. Suppose that transactions A_1 and A_2, are runs of the following programs, respectively:

```
program P1;
entities x, y: integer;
variable t1: integer;
begin
t1:=x;
x:=t1+1;
y:=t1+2;
end

program P2;
entities x, y, z: integer;
variables t1, t2: integer;
begin
t1:=x;
t2:=y;
if t1 < t2 then z:=1
    else y:=t2+1
end
```

So, A_2 is an execution which took the **else** branch of $P2$. If we execute $P1$ and $P2$, in this order, starting from the state $(x = 0, y = 1, z = 0)$, then we get to the state $(x = 1, y = 2, z = 1)$. The same state results if we execute the programs in the order $P2$, $P1$. If however we execute the *schedule* s from the same state, we obtain $(x = 1, y = 2, z = 0)$. Therefore, s is not equivalent to any serial execution of the *programs*. Consequently, s must be regarded as incorrect, despite the fact that it is final-state serializable.

2.4 VIEW SERIALIZABILITY

The infinite schedule in the previous section must be considered "correct" essentially because the pair of x and y values read by each transaction is consistent —$(0,0)$ for A_1, $(1,1)$ for A_2, etc. We say that each transaction "sees a consistent view." In contrast, the final-state serializable schedule s of the last subsection was incorrect, because transaction A_1 sees an inconsistent view. Evidently, views must be taken into account in our improved definition of correctness.

Definition 2.3:   Suppose that a transaction A has k read steps, $r^1, r^2, \ldots, r^k$. The *view* of A in a schedule s under interpretation I and initial state X is the k-tuple $(r_s^1(I, X), \ldots, r_s^k(I, X))$ of the values of the variables read by the read steps of A in s. Two schedules s and s' are called *view equivalent* if
(a) They are final-state equivalent, and
(b) Under any interpretation and initial state, the views of each transaction in both schedules are the same. $\square$

Note that, since the final state can be considered as the view of the pseudo-transaction A_∞, view equivalence can be rephrased as equality of views for all transactions in $\hat{s}$ and $\hat{s}'$. We can now state a graph-theoretic characterization of view equivalence completely analogous —both in statement and proof— to Theorem 2.1.

Theorem 2.2: *Two schedules s and s' are view equivalent if and only if they involve the same set of transactions and $D(s) = D(s')$.*

Proof: Problem 2.6. $\square$

Corollary: *Given two schedules s and s', we can test in $O(n)$ time whether they are view equivalent.* $\square$

Definition 2.4:   A schedule is called *view serializable* if it is view equivalent to a serial schedule. For example, the schedule s in the "Incorrect Views" subsection of the previous section is not view serializable, although it is final-state serializable. $\square$

Notice that, since the requirements in the definition of view equivalence are stronger than those of final-state equivalence, we have immediately the following result:

Proposition 2.1: *All view serializable schedules are final-state serializable.* $\square$

We can rephrase Theorem 2.2 in simple terms as follows: Two schedules are view equivalent if and only if each read step reads its entity from the same write step in the two schedules. Compare with final-state equivalence: The condition of Theorem 2.1 states that each *live* read step reads its entity from the same step in both schedules. Notice that this has the following interesting implication:

Corollary: *Two schedules with no dead steps are final-state equivalent if and only if they are view equivalent. Consequently, a schedule without dead steps is final-state serializable if and only if it is view serializable.* $\square$

It is a bit non-trivial to understand the difference between final-state serializability and view serializability. Very roughly, view serializability is a stronger, more restrictive notion, and therefore a safer one. Their set-theoretic difference is not very extensive, since it consists only of schedules with dead steps, as was pointed out above. Which criterion should concurrency control systems adopt? If our application programs are straight-line programs, then it is easy to argue that final-state serializability is an adequate notion of correctness. As was illustrated in the previous section, however, it is the presence of non-trivial control structure (e.g., the **if - then - else** in program $P2$) that made us adopt view serializability. In the rest of this section we shall formalize this connection between control and view serializability, by extending our notion of interpretation to include program control. We show that, with this generalized notion of interpretation, view serializability coincides with final-state serializability (Theorem 2.3 below).

Definition 2.5: A *free schema* is a finite tree with two kinds of nodes: *predicates*, which have outdegree two, and *steps*, with outdegree one or zero. Steps with zero outdegree are called *leaves*. The intention of this definition is that free schemas are the control skeletons of loop-free programs (or of programs with loops, after these loops have been "unwound"). Steps are ordinary database steps, whereas predicates stand for "**if-then-else**" conditions. We distinguish among the left ("**true**") and right branch of a predicate. $\square$

For example, in Figure 2.3 we show a free schema. A *path* in a free schema is a sequence of nodes from the root to a leaf, with all predicate nodes deleted. For example, in the schema of Figure 2.3, $R(x)W(y)W(z)$ and $R(x)W(y)R(z)W(x)$ are paths. Notice that paths in a free schema are transactions. We extend to free schemas our assumptions on transactions, namely that no read step is preceded by a read or write step on the same entity, and likewise no write step is preceded by a write step on the same entity.

Definition 2.6: Let A be a transaction. A *full interpretation I of A* consists of

(a) A free schema S_A such that A is a path in S_A;

(b) For each entity $x \in E$, a domain D_x;

(c) For each write step $W(x)$ appearing in S_A, we have in I a function f : $\prod_i D_{y_i} \rightarrow D_x$, where the y_i's are the entities read by the read steps pre-

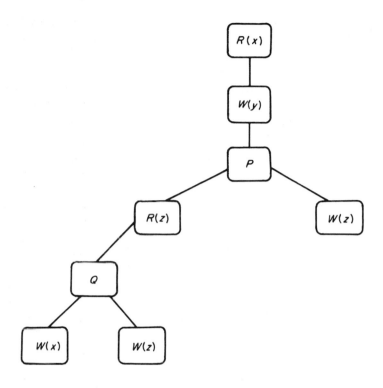

Figure 2.3. A Free Schema.

ceding $W(x)$ in S_A; and

(d) For each predicate P of S_A, I contains a subset p of $\prod_i D_{y_i}$, where the y_i are the entities in the read steps preceding P in S_A (this subset contains the combinations of values that make P true). $\square$

For example, consider the transaction $A = R(x)W(y)R(z)W(z)$. A full interpretation of A could be the free schema in Figure 2.3, with domains of all variables the reals, say. The two functions could be $f_2(x) = x - 1$, and $f_4(x, z) = \frac{1}{z+x}$. As for the predicates, $P(x)$ might be all x such that $x \geq 1$, whereas $P(x, z)$ could be all pairs (x, z) such that $x + z \neq 0$.

Let s be a schedule, and let I be a full interpretation for s, that is, a full interpretation S_A for each transaction A appearing in s, all with the same domains. Let X be an initial state, that is, a value in D_x for each entity x. We say that s is *legal* for I and X if for each transaction A of s and each predicate P in S_A the following holds: Transaction A corresponds to a path of S_A which, for each predicate P of S_A, takes the left branch at P if $(v_s^1(I, X), \ldots, v_s^k(I, X)) \in p$, and the right branch otherwise, where the v^i's are the read steps which precede

P in A, and p is the interpretation of P.

Let $\pi : \{A_1, A_2, \ldots, A_n\} \to \{A_1, A_2, \ldots, A_n\}$ be a permutation of the transactions in s, and let I and X be an interpretation and initial state, respectively. A *π-serial execution* of the free schemas in I starting from X is a *legal* schedule $s = s_1 s_2 \ldots s_n$, where s_i is a path in $S_{\pi(A_i)}$ for $i = 1, \ldots, n$. It is not hard to see that there is only one π-serial execution for each I, π and X.

Theorem 2.3: *Let s be a schedule. Then s is view serializable if and only if there is a permutation π of the transactions in s such that, for all full interpretations I of s and for all initial states X for which s is legal, the π-serial execution s' of the free schemas in I satisfies $s(I, X) = s'(I, X)$.*

Proof: Suppose that s is view serializable. Then there is a serial schedule s' which is view equivalent to s. Since view equivalence is stronger than final-state equivalence, we know that s' has the same transactions as s, and furthermore for all interpretations I and states X, the two schedules satisfy $s(I, X) = s'(I, X)$. If we show that s' is legal for all full interpretations and initial states for which s is legal, then the *only if* direction of the theorem would follow, with π the permutation of the transactions as they appear in s'. But this is very easy to see. The definition of legal schedules is based solely on values read by the read steps, and these values are identical in s and s', by view serializability.

For the other direction, suppose that s is not view serializable. Let π be a permutation of its transactions; we have to exhibit a full interpretation and initial state for which the π-serial execution of the schemas behaves differently from s. If the serial schedule s' in which the transactions are ordered according to π is not final-state equivalent to s, we are done: Just take the (ordinary) interpretation and initial state which differentiates s from s' (an ordinary interpretation is a special case of full interpretation). Otherwise, since s was assumed not to be view serializable, there must be a read step $v = R(x)$ in s which reads values $v_s(I, X) \neq v_{s'}(I, X)$ for some interpretation I of the write steps, and some initial state X.

Let y be an entity not written by any step in s. We now extend I to a full interpretation as follows: We let the interpretations of all transactions except A be the same as before, and we insert to transaction A a predicate P right after the step v. The left (true) branch of this predicate is the continuation of the transaction A, whereas the right branch is a single step $W(y)$. The interpretation of this write step is a constant function, different from the value of y in X (since y is not written in s, it is not a loss of generality to assume that the domain for y in I has at least two elements). If $v^1, \ldots, v^k = v$ are all read steps of A preceding (and including) v, the interpretation p of the new predicate is $p = \{(v_s^1(I, X), \ldots, v_s^k(I, S))\}$. That is, p is the predicate which is true only when the view seen by A coincides with that seen by A under I and X. This ensures that s is a legal schedule under this full interpretation and X.

We claim that the π-serial execution of the schemas in this full interpretation, call it s'', does not yield the same final values as s when started on X. To see this, notice that s'' consists of the serial schedule s', except that the remainder of transaction A after the step v is replaced by the step $W(y)$. This follows from the fact that the view seen by A in s'' is different from this seen by A in s, and thus the right branch of P must be taken, if the schedule s'' is to be legal. Now, schedule s'' yields different final value for entity y than does s, and therefore the theorem is proven. $\square$

2.5 THE COMPLEXITY OF VIEW SERIALIZABILITY

Given a schedule s, how can we tell whether it is view serializable—or final-state serializable? There is an obvious exhaustive algorithm: Using the test of Theorem 2.2 (Theorem 2.1 for final-state serializability), check whether each of the serial schedules of the transactions in s is equivalent to s. If s has m transactions, this algorithm takes time proportional to $m!n^2$, which is an exponential function in the size of s. This approach becomes impractical when a reasonably large number of transactions are involved—say, ten. In this Section we show a result which suggests that this is an inherent limitation. In particular, we prove that view serializability is NP-complete—see the Appendix to Chapter 1 for definitions. The same is true of final-state serializability.

In the coming chapters we shall see that such a result rules out the possibility of designing an efficient scheduler that *realizes* view serializability, that is, allows all view serializable schedules and just these. However, an NP-completeness result has certain important implications that go beyond the efficiency of algorithms. In the field of *combinatorial optimization* (see the notes and references), for example, problems that are NP-complete do not just lack efficient algorithms; they are equally short in powerful theorems and interesting characterizations. The fact that a problem is NP-complete is usually taken as evidence that the underlying concept (view serializability in our case) is combinatorially nasty and intricate, likely to resist all attempts at deepening our understanding of it.

For our study of the combinatorics of view serializability we shall need a generalization of the directed graph called a *polygraph*. A polygraph is a triple $P = (V, A, C)$, where

   V is a finite set of vertices,

   $A \subset V \times V$ is a set of *arcs*, and

   $C \subset V \times V \times V$ is a set of *choices*. If $(u, v, w) \in C$, then the three vertices are necessarily distinct, and in fact $(w, u) \in A$.

Example 2.3: In Figure 2.4(a) we see a typical polygraph P. A choice (u, v, w) is shown as two broken arrows (u, v), (v, w), joined by a circular arc centered at v. $\square$

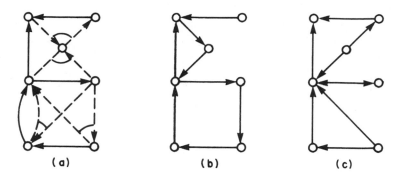

Figure 2.4. A Polygraph and Two Directed Graphs.

Suppose that $P = (V, A, C)$ is a polygraph, and let $D = (V, B)$ be a directed graph with the same set of nodes. We say that D is *compatible* with P if $A \subset B$, and for each choice $(u, v, w) \in C$ either $(u, v) \in A$ or $(v, w) \in A$. Polygraph P is called *acyclic* if there is an acyclic directed graph D that is compatible with P.

Example 2.3 (continued): The directed graphs shown in Figure 2.4(b) and (c) are both compatible with the polygraph of Figure 2.4(a). In particular, this polygraph is acyclic, since it is compatible with the acyclic directed graph in Figure 2.4(c). $\square$

There is an interesting connection between polygraphs and view serializability of schedules. Let s be a schedule, and let $\hat{s}$ be its augmented version. The *polygraph associated with* s, $P(s)$, is defined as follows: The set of vertices of $P(s)$ is the set of transactions in $\hat{s}$, including A_0 and A_∞. The arcs and choices of $P(s)$ depend on the relative order of the various steps of $\hat{s}$. To start, we have all arcs of the form (A_0, A) and (A, A_∞) for all transactions A of s. Notice that this means that, in all digraphs compatible with $P(s)$, A_0 must precede all other transactions, and all transactions must precede A_∞. Suppose that A_1, A_2 are transactions of $\hat{s}$, such that there is a step $R(x)$ in A_2 such that the last $W(x)$ step in $\hat{s}$ before the $R(x)$ step of A_2 is a step of A_1. Then we add an arc (A_1, A_2) to $P(s)$. If furthermore there is a $W(x)$ step of transaction A_3 somewhere else in s, then we add a choice (A_2, A_3, A_1) to C. The polygraph that results if we repeat this for every read step of s is denoted $P(s)$, and called the polygraph associated with s.

Example 2.4: Consider the following schedule:

$$
\begin{array}{llll}
A_1 : R(x) & & W(y) & \\
s = A_2 : & W(y) & & W(x) \\
A_3 : & & R(y) &
\end{array}
$$

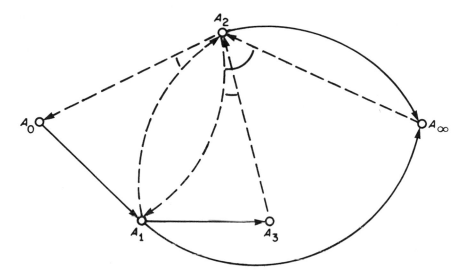

Figure 2.5. The Polygraph $P(s)$.

The polygraph associated with s, $P(s)$, is the polygraph shown in Figure 2.5, where we have omitted for clarity the trivial arcs out of A_0 and those into A_∞. The arcs and choices of $P(s)$ capture the "reads from" relation between whole transactions of s—and not individual steps as was the case with $D(s)$. Dealing with transactions is now appropriate, because we are interested in finding equivalent serial schedules, and in such schedules steps appear clustered in transactions. Intuitively, the meaning of the arcs and choices of $P(s)$ is that if a transaction, say A_3 in our example, reads a variable, say y, from another transaction A_1, then A_3 must come after A_1 in any equivalent schedule. Moreover, a third transaction, say A_2, which writes y, must come either *after* transaction A_3, or *before* transaction A_1, if equivalence is going to be preserved. Obviously, if A_2 were to come between A_1 and A_3, then this would change the "reads-from" relation of the schedule. Naturally, A_0 must be the first transaction in the augmented serial schedule, and A_∞ must come last. $\square$

The previous comments suggest that there is a connection between the polygraph $P(s)$ and the directed graph $D(s)$ of Theorem 2.1. The polygraph $P(s)$ can be thought of as resulting from $D(s)$ by

(a) shrinking all nodes of $D(s)$ corresponding to a transaction A into a single node (so that the arcs stand for "reads-from" relationships between transactions), and then

(b) adding a choice for each arc of $D(s)$, and each other transaction writing the same variable.

These operations are completely defined once we have $D(s)$. Therefore, by Theorem 2.2, we have the following interesting fact:

Lemma 2.1: *If two schedules s and s' are view equivalent, then $P(s) = P(s')$.* $\square$

What if a schedule is serial? What special structure does its polygraph have?

Lemma 2.2: *If schedule s is serial, then $P(s)$ is acyclic.*

Proof: Suppose that s is serial. Let us define the following directed graph G with nodes the transactions of $\hat{s}$: There is an arc connecting any two transactions A and B in $\hat{s}$. The direction of this arc is from the transaction among A and B that comes earlier in $\hat{s}$ to the one that comes later.

The directed graph G is a total order, and therefore acyclic. We claim now that G is compatible with $P(s)$. To see this, consider any arc of $P(s)$; it is certainly an arc of G, since it connects a transaction that writes an entity to a subsequent transaction with a read step on this entity. Suppose now that we have a choice (A, B, C) in $P(s)$. Evidently, there is a step in B which writes a variable that A reads from C. This step, and therefore all of B, must be either before the write step in C on that variable, and thus before all of C, or after the write step in A, and therefore after all of A. It follows that in either case G contains an arc which makes G compatible with $P(s)$. $\square$

Our next theorem establishes a combinatorial criterion for view serializability:

Theorem 2.4: *A schedule s is view serializable if and only if $P(s)$ is acyclic.*

Proof: For the *only if* direction, suppose that s is view serializable. Then there is a serial schedule s' which is view equivalent to s. By Lemma 2.1, the polygraphs associated with s and s' are identical. However, Lemma 2.2 says that the polygraph associated with s' is acyclic.

For the other direction, suppose that $P(s)$ is acyclic. In fact, let G be a directed graph which is acyclic and compatible with $P(s)$. Since in $P(s)$ we have arcs from A_0 to all transactions, and from all transactions to A_∞, G has no arcs entering A_0 and leaving A_∞. Therefore we can complete G into a total order in which A_0 comes first and A_∞ last, and let s' be the serial schedule in which the transactions are executed in this order. We claim that s and s' are view equivalent.

To show this we must show, by Theorem 2.2, that the directed graphs $D(s)$ and $D(s')$ are identical. How could these directed graphs differ? The only way is, by having some read step $R(x)$ in some transaction A read its value from the $W(x)$ step of some transaction B in $\hat{s}$, and from some other transaction C in $\hat{s}'$. The polygraph $P(s)$ contains the choice (A, C, B), and, by compatibility, the directed graph G contains arc (B, A). So, in $\hat{s}'$ transaction B comes before A. Since in $\hat{s}'$ transaction A reads x from C and not from B, it follows that

C is after B and before A in $\hat{s}'$. So, in G there is no arc from A to C, neither from C to B, and yet in $P(s)$ we have the choice (B, C, A). This, however, contradicts the fact that G is compatible with $P(s)$. We must conclude that s and s' are view equivalent, and thus s is view serializable. $\square$

Final-state serializability can be treated in a very similar manner. In constructing the version of the polygraph associated with a schedule for final-state serializability, we add choices to C not for every read step of the schedule, but for every *live* read step. With this subtle difference, the same results hold for final-state serializability as well (see Problem 2.8).

Theorem 2.4 appears to be a hopeful sign in our search for algorithms for view serializability and serializability. According to this theorem, all we have to do is test a polygraph for acyclicity. How hard can this be?

Theorem 2.5: *Telling whether a polygraph is acyclic is NP-complete.*

Proof: The problem of recognizing acyclic polygraphs is clearly in NP. An acyclic polygraph always has a succinct certificate of its acyclicity, namely, an acyclic directed graph compatible with it. Our proof of NP-completeness is based on a polynomial transformation from the problem SATISFIABILITY (see the Appendix to Chapter 1 for an introduction to complexity, NP-completeness, and the methodology used in this proof).

In fact, we shall need a somewhat restricted version of SATISFIABILITY. A variable appearing on a clause unnegated is called a *positive* literal. Occurrences of negations of variables are *negative* literals. A clause is *mixed* if it contains both positive and negative literals. Call a formula *simple* if it has no mixed clauses.

Lemma 2.3: *SATISFIABILITY remains NP-complete even if it is restricted to simple formulae with two or three literals per clause.*

Proof of the Lemma: Suppose that F is a Boolean formula with three literals per clause, and let x be any variable appearing in it m_1 times unnegated, and m_2 negated. Let $m = \max\{m_1, m_2\}$, and let $x_1, x_2, \ldots, x_{2m}$ be new variables. We replace in F the first positive occurrence of x by x_1, the second positive occurrence by x_3, the third by x_5, and so on. As for its negative occurrences, we replace the first with x_2, the second by x_4, and so on, with the even variables. Finally, we add to F the clauses

$$(x_1 \vee x_2) \wedge (\bar{x}_1 \vee \bar{x}_2) \wedge (x_2 \vee x_3) \wedge (\bar{x}_2 \vee \bar{x}_3) \wedge \ldots \wedge (x_{2m} \vee x_1) \wedge (\bar{x}_{2m} \vee \bar{x}_1)$$

which is the conjunctive normal form of $x_1 \equiv \bar{x}_2 \equiv \ldots \equiv \bar{x}_{2m}$. If we repeat this for all variables of F, the resulting formula has no mixed clauses, since the initial clauses have only positive literals, and the introduced clauses are not mixed. Also, the original clauses have three literals each, and the new ones two. More importantly, it is easy to see that the resulting formula is equivalent

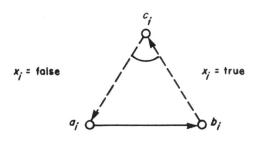

Figure 2.6. A Variable.

to F. Furthermore, the construction requires a polynomial amount of time. It follows that the SATISFIABILITY problem for simple formulae with two or three literals per clause is NP-complete. $\square$

Suppose that we are given a Boolean formula F with variables $x_1, \ldots, x_m$ and clauses $C_1, \ldots, C_n$, which is as described in the previous lemma. We shall show how to construct for every such formula a polygraph $P(F)$ such that $P(F)$ is acyclic if and only if F is satisfiable. $P(F)$ will consist of several parts, reflecting the structure of F.

Variable. For each Boolean variable x_i appearing in F, in $P(F)$ there is a separate part as shown in Figure 2.6. If the directed graph D includes the arc (b_i, c_i), we take this to mean that x_i is **true**; otherwise (if, that is, (c_i, a_i) is in D), x_i is taken to be **false**.

Fan-out. We can use the part of $P(F)$ in Figure 2.7 to create any number of "copies" of the literal x_i. If x_i is **true** —that is, (b_i, c_i) is in D— and this part of D is to be acyclic, then arc (b_i', c_i') must also be in D. A similar construction can be carried out for "copying" $\bar{x}_i$.

Clause. In each clause not all literals can be false. This is achieved by the hexagonal structure in Figure 2.8, where the broken arcs are supposed to be copies of the *negations* of the literals in the clause C_j. For example, for the clause $(\bar{x} \vee \bar{y} \vee \bar{z})$ we would use the copies indicated in Figure 2.8. If all literals in the clause are false, then all three broken arcs are in the graph D, and thus D contains a cycle, contrary to specifications.

If the clause contains just two literals, the hexagon contains, instead of a third broken arc, a regular arc.

The construction of the polygraph $P(F)$, starting from F, is now easy to describe. For each variable x_i of F we add to $P(F)$ a "variable" subgraph

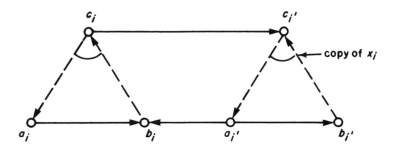

Figure 2.7. The Fan-out.

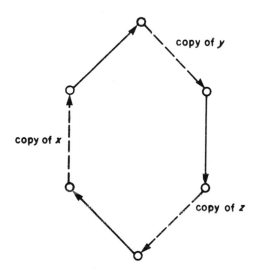

Figure 2.8. A Clause.

as shown in Figure 2.6. For each clause, we add a "clause" subgraph (Figure 2.8). We then connect via "fan-outs" each of the three broken arcs of each clause subgraph with the part of the negation of a literal in the clause. The construction is illustrated in Figure 2.9 for the case of the formula $(\bar{x}_1 \vee \bar{x}_2 \vee \bar{x}_3) \wedge (x_1 \vee x_2)$. The acyclic directed graph indicated in this figure by checkmarks on the choices corresponds to the satisfying truth assignment $x_1 = x_3 = \textbf{true}, x_2 = \textbf{false}$.

We now have to show that $P(F)$ is acyclic if and only if F is satisfiable.

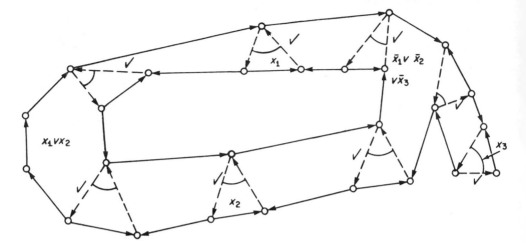

Figure 2.9. Illustration of the Construction in the Proof of Theorem 2.5.

Suppose first that $P(F)$ is acyclic, that is, there is an acyclic directed graph D compatible with $P(F)$. For each variable x_i, D must contain either the arc (b_i, c_i), or the arc (c_i, a_i). This implies a truth assignment, call it T, for F. Also, for each clause of C, the corresponding hexagon must be missing at least one broken arc in D. However, it also follows that for each fan-out subgraph D contains either both arcs (b_i, c_i) and (b_i', c_i'), or both (c_i, a_i) and (c_i', a_i'). From the last two observations, it follows that T satisfies F.

Suppose now that there is a truth assignment T satisfying F. Let us construct a directed acyclic graph D compatible with $P(F)$. D contains all arcs of $P(F)$, and, for each choice (b_i, c_i, a_i) or (b_i', c_i', a_i') of $P(F)$, it contains the first arc if x_i is **true**, in T, and the second otherwise.

Directed graph D is clearly compatible with $P(F)$. It remains to be shown that it is acyclic. It clearly avoids the "local" cycles in the clause and the fan-out graphs. How about larger cycles, however, involving many variables, fan-outs, and clauses?

Here is where we use the fact that F is simple. Think of cycles in D as "visiting" variables and clauses of F, via the correspondence implicit in the construction. It is not hard to see that the only possible cycle is one that visits a clause, then a variable appearing positively on the clause, then a clause on which the same variable appears negatively, then another variable which appears positively on the latter clause, and so on until the cycle is closed. However, it is evident that all clauses on this cycle are mixed, and this contradicts the fact that F is simple. It follows that D is acyclic, and the theorem is proved. $\square$

We are not done proving that view serializability is NP-complete. What we must show is that view serializability is no easier than testing a polygraph for acyclicity. This is accomplished as follows:

Lemma 2.4: *Given any polygraph P, we can construct in polynomial time a schedule s such that s is view serializable if and only if P is acyclic.*

Proof: Schedule s consists of several *segments*, corresponding to the various parts of P. It has a transaction for each vertex of P, and another transaction, called A_ω. For each arc $a = (A_1, A_2)$ of P, s contains the segment

$$A_1 : \;...W(a) \qquad ...$$
$$A_2 : \;... \qquad R(a) \;...$$

where a is an entity particular to this arc, not appearing in any other part of s. Also, for each choice $c = (A_1, A_2, A_3)$ in P, s contains the segment

$$A_1 : \;... \qquad R(c) \qquad ...$$
$$A_2 : \;... \qquad\qquad W(c) \;...$$
$$A_3 : \;... \; W(c) \qquad\qquad ...$$
$$\vdots$$
$$A_\omega : \;... \qquad\qquad\qquad ... \; W(c)$$

Here c is again an entity that does not appear anywhere else in s. The precise order of the various segments in s is not important, as long as the groups of consecutive steps above are indeed consecutive in s, and A_ω comes last.

It is easy to check that the polygraph associated with s, $P(s)$, is P itself, with three additional vertices: A_0, preceding by arcs all other nodes; A_∞, preceded by arcs from all other nodes; and A_ω, preceded by all nodes except A_∞. It follows that $P(s)$ is acyclic if and only if P is. From this and Theorem 2.4 we have the Lemma. $\square$

We have finally arrived at the main result of this Section:

Theorem 2.6: *The problem of deciding whether a given schedule is view serializable is NP-complete.* $\square$

2.6 CONFLICT SERIALIZABILITY

Showing a problem NP-complete has sometimes a salutary effect: It helps redirect the research effort towards more well-behaved *alternatives* or *approximations* to the original problem. The material of this section can be viewed as a reaction to the NP-completeness of view serializability[7]. In particular, in this section we study yet another notion of correctness. This notion "approximates"

---

[7] However, this material appeared in the literature before the other notions of correctness; see the references.

view serializability, in that it is stronger (so that no incorrect schedules are allowed) and yet "not too strong" (so that it can be the basis of concurrency control algorithms with acceptable performance). Furthermore, and perhaps more importantly, this notion is free from negative complexity results such as those in the previous section. Quite to the contrary, we shall prove that there is a very efficient algorithm for testing whether a schedule is correct in this new sense.

This new correctness criterion is based on the notion of a *conflict*. We say that two steps, originating from different transactions, *conflict* if the following is true: Both steps read or write the same entity, and not both are read steps. Each instance of a pair of conflicting steps is called a *conflict* between the corresponding transactions.

This definition is in line with our intuitive notion of "conflict" or "interaction" between concurrent processes. If two programs have no common variables, then they do not interact at all. If they do have common variables, but both use them in a read-only manner—say, as value parameters—then again their interaction is nil. If, however, they share variables, and at least one of them writes on these common variables, then there is a non-trivial interaction between the two programs.

In studying the properties of schedules, it is intuitively clear that only the order in which conflicting steps are executed is important. We say two schedules are *conflict equivalent* if they contain the same transactions, and any pair of conflicting steps is ordered the same way in both. Once again, there is a graph-theoretic characterization of this version of equivalence, although now it follows so directly from the definition that it is almost tautological. For a schedule s let us define $D_2(s)$ to be the directed graph with vertices the steps of s, and arcs all those pairs (u, v) such that u and v are conflicting steps from different transactions in s, and v comes after u in s. Notice that in this case we do not need to add the pseudotransactions A_0 and A_∞.

Theorem 2.7: *Two schedules s and s' are conflict equivalent if and only if* $D_2(s) = D_2(s')$. $\square$

As with any notion of equivalence, conflict equivalence suggests a correctness criterion: A schedule is called *conflict serializable* if it is conflict equivalent to a serial schedule. It can be argued that this is an even more restrictive notion of correctness than view serializability—which is, by its definition, a restriction on final-state serializability. To see this, just notice that the directed graph $D(s)$ used to test for view equivalence *is uniquely determined* once $D_2(s)$ is given. This is because $D(s)$ records for each read step the last write step on the same entity that preceded the read step. This information is uniquely determined, once we know the order of all conflicting pairs of steps. Therefore, we have:

Proposition 2.1: *If a schedule is conflict serializable, then it is view serializable.* □

Example 2.5: Notice that the converse does not hold. Consider, for example, the schedule

$$
s = \begin{array}{llll}
A_1 : R(y) & & W(y)W(x) & \\
A_2 : & R(y) & & W(x)W(z) \\
A_3 : & R(w) & & & W(x)
\end{array}
$$

This schedule is view equivalent to the serial schedule $A_2 A_1 A_3$, as can be easily checked. In fact, this is the only serial schedule view equivalent to s. However, $A_2 A_1 A_3$ is *not* conflict equivalent to s. To see this, notice that the two (dead) $W(x)$ steps of A_1 and A_2 are in opposite orders in the two schedules, even though they certainly conflict. Therefore, there are view serializable schedules that are not conflict serializable, and thus conflict serializability is indeed a more restrictive notion of correctness than those studied so far.

Can we test efficiently a schedule for conflict serializability, or is the curse of NP-completeness still with us? Let us define, for each schedule s, a directed graph $G(s)$ called the *conflict graph* of s (this is the analog of the *polygraph* associated with s, $P(s)$ for conflict serializability). This graph has the transactions of s as its nodes, and it contains an arc (A, B), where A and B are distinct transactions of s, whenever there is a step of A which conflicts with a subsequent (in s) step of B.

Theorem 2.8: *A schedule s is conflict serializable if and only if the conflict graph $G(s)$ is acyclic.*

Proof: Suppose that s is conflict serializable. Then there is a serial schedule s' that is conflict equivalent to s. Thus, $D_2(s) = D_2(s')$. However, it also follows that $G(s) = G(s')$; this is so because the conflict graph $G(s)$ can be thought of as resulting from $D_2(s)$ by shrinking all steps belonging to one transaction into a single node. Furthermore, the conflict graph $G(s')$ of the serial schedule s' is necessarily acyclic, since it must be a subgraph of the total order under which the transactions are executed in s'. We conclude that $G(s)$ is acyclic.

Suppose now that $G(s)$ is acyclic. Let us find a total order of the transactions which is compatible with the arcs of $G(s)$—that is, let us *topologically sort* the conflict graph. The resulting total order suggests a serial schedule s'. We claim that s is conflict equivalent to s'. This follows from the fact that, for any two transactions A, B of s, either all steps of A precede the conflicting steps of B, or vice-versa, depending on whether A precedes B in $G(s)$, or the other way around—otherwise we would have a cycle of length two involving A and B in $G(s)$. Furthermore, the same is true in s', since the order of transactions in s' is compatible with the arcs of $G(s)$. It follows that s and s' are conflict equivalent. □

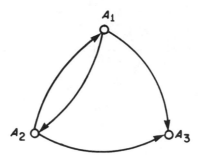

Figure 2.10. The Graph $G(s)$.

Corollary: *We can test in $O(n^2)$ time whether a schedule is conflict serializable.*

Proof: We can determine whether the conflict graph has cycles in time linear in the number of edges of the graph. $\square$

Example 2.5 (continued): The conflict graph $G(s)$ for the schedule s in Example 2.5 is shown in Figure 2.10. It does have a cycle. $\square$

Conflicts and Commutativity

There is an appealing alternative definition of conflict equivalence. Let us write $s \sim s'$ for two schedules if one can be obtained from the other by changing the order of two consecutive non-conflicting steps, from different transactions. For example, if

$$s = \begin{matrix} A_1 : R(x) & & W(x) \\ A_2 : & R(x)W(y) & \end{matrix}$$

and

$$s' = \begin{matrix} A_1 : R(x) & & W(x) \\ A_2 : & R(x) & & W(y) \end{matrix}$$

then $s \sim s'$, because the two write steps of the two transactions do not conflict.

Let $\overset{*}{\sim}$ be the *reflexive-transitive closure* of the relation $\sim$. In other words, $s\overset{*}{\sim}s'$ if s can be transformed to s' via zero or more switchings of non-conflicting steps. It turns out that this is another formulation of conflict equivalence:

Theorem 2.9: *Two schedules s and s' are conflict equivalent if and only if $s\overset{*}{\sim}s'$.*

Proof: Each switching of non-conflicting steps clearly preserves conflict equivalence. It follows by induction that any finite number of such switchings also preserves conflict equivalence, and thus any two schedules related by $\overset{*}{\sim}$ are conflict equivalent.

Suppose now that two schedules s and s' are conflict equivalent. Let k be the number of pairs of steps of the two schedules which occur in different order in s than in s'. We shall show, by induction on k, that $s \overset{*}{\sim} s'$. Our claim is clearly valid for $k = 0$, in the case, that is, in which the two schedules are identical. Suppose now that $k > 0$. This means that there are two steps out of order in s'. Among the pairs of steps which are out of order in s', choose a pair of steps which are consecutive in s'. We claim that this is always possible. Because, if the two steps have another step separating them in s', then the third step is also out of order with respect to at least one of the two, and thus we can repeat the argument until there is no other step in between.

Since the two schedules are assumed conflict equivalent, the two steps cannot be conflicting ones. Therefore, we can switch them, and obtain a schedule s'' such that $s' \sim s''$. However, s'' differs from s in at most $k - 1$ pairs of steps, and thus, by induction, $s \overset{*}{\sim} s''$. We can conclude that $s \overset{*}{\sim} s'$. $\square$

What this definition of conflict equivalence says is that, in order to define conflict serializability, we do not need even the rudimentary information on whether a step is a read or write one, and on which entity. All we need is to be told *which steps conflict*. It turns out that this approach can go surprisingly far: We can start our discussion of correctness on the *fully uninterpreted model* of transactions (recall Section 1.3), in which steps are plain symbols and there is no information concerning whether a step reads, writes, and which entity. All we know about the steps is that *some pairs conflict*, and therefore cannot be switched when they are consecutive steps of a schedule, if equivalence is going to be preserved. All other pairs of consecutive steps can be switched freely. Obviously, this defines a notion of equivalence between schedules, which we may as well call *conflict equivalence*—there is no danger of confusion, since this notion generalizes its namesake. The corresponding notion of correctness is, of course, *conflict serializability*. It should be obvious that we already know how to test whether a schedule is conflict serializable in this generalized sense: Our original definition of conflict serializability is in fact a special case, in which the conflicts are given implicitly by the read-write information on the various steps. The test of Theorem 2.8 is valid for generalized conflict serializability as well, since it is based on the notion of conflict only.

Example 2.6: We are given the schedule $s = a_1 b_1 a_2 c_1 a_3 b_2 c_2 c_3 a_4 c_4 b_3$ of the transactions $A = a_1 a_2 a_3 a_4$, $B = b_1 b_2 b_3$ and $C = c_1 c_2 c_3 c_4$, and we are told that the following steps conflict: $\{a_2, b_1\}, \{a_2, c_1\}, \{b_1, c_1\}, \{b_3, c_4\}$. This schedule is not conflict serializable, and we can check this by applying the test of Theorem 2.8. The conflict graph $G(s)$ has an arc from one transaction to another if a step of the first conflicts with a subsequent (in s) step of the second—exactly as before. The conflict graph $G(s)$ is shown in Figure 2.11. It does have a cycle.

As we shall see in our discussion of multiple versions in the next chapter,

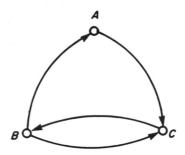

Figure 2.11. The Graph $G(s)$.

the definition of correctness based on commutativity leads to some interesting generalizations of the notion.

Conflicts and Projections

Important concepts usually come in a number of alternative formulations, and conflict serializability is a good example. We shall show in this subsection still another interesting characterization of conflict serializability. The new characterization is phrased in terms of a "monotonicity" property, quite interesting by itself. We first need to define the *projection* of a schedule:

Definition 2.7: Let s be a schedule, let τ be the set of transactions appearing in s, and let $\tau' \subset \tau$. The *projection* of s to τ', denoted $s_{\tau'}$, is the schedule obtained from s if we delete all steps of transactions not in τ'. $\Box$

Let us call a property of schedules "monotonic" if it is closed under projection, that is, if s has the property, so does $s_{\tau'}$ for any τ'. Interestingly, view serializability is *not* a monotonic property. For example, the schedule

$$s = \begin{array}{llll} A_1 :W(x) & & R(y)W(y) \\ A_2 : & W(x) & \\ A_3 : & & R(x)W(y) \\ A_4 : & & & W(x) \end{array}$$

is view serializable (view equivalent to $A_2 A_3 A_1 A_4$), whereas $s_{\{A_1,A_3,A_4\}}$ is not. In contrast, it is easy to see that conflict serializability is monotonic. In proof, suppose that a schedule s is conflict serializable. By Theorem 2.8, this means that $G(s)$ has no cycles. However, notice that for every subset τ' of the transactions in s, $G(s_{\tau'})$ is just $G(s)$ with all nodes not in τ' deleted. Therefore, if $G(s)$ has no cycles, then neither does $G(s_{\tau'})$ for any τ'. Therefore, any projection of s is conflict serializable as well.

Our result in this subsection says something much stronger: Not only is conflict serializability a monotonic property and view serializability is not, but the set of conflict serializable schedules is the *largest monotonic subset* of view serializability.

Theorem 2.10: *A schedule s is conflict serializable if and only if, for all subsets τ' of the transactions in s, $s_{\tau'}$ is view serializable.*

Proof: One direction of the theorem is implied by the fact that conflict serializability is monotonic, shown in the discussion above. For the *only if* direction, suppose that s is not conflict serializable. We shall exhibit a projection of s which is not view serializable. In this proof we shall use several times the following simple fact about view equivalence:

Lemma 2.5: *Let s be a schedule. Suppose that two transactions A and B of s conflict on entity x, and no transaction of s other than A and B writes x. Then in any serial schedule s' view equivalent to s, the two transactions must be in the same order as the two conflicting steps are in s.*

Proof of the Lemma: If both steps write x, then their relative order determines the final value of x (since no other step writes x), and thus this order cannot differ in two view equivalent (or even just final-state equivalent) schedules. If A writes x and B reads it, then the relative order of the two conflicting steps determines the view seen by B, and therefore it must again be the same in any two view equivalent schedules. $\square$

To continue the proof of the theorem, suppose that s is not conflict serializable. Consider then the shortest cycle $(A_1, A_2, \ldots, A_k, A_1)$, $k \geq 2$, in the conflict graph $G(s)$ (which exists by Theorem 2.8), and consider $s_{\{A_1,\ldots,A_k\}}$, that is, s projected to the transactions of the cycle. We claim that $s_{\{A_1,\ldots,A_k\}}$ is not view serializable. There are three cases:

Case 1: $k = 2$. There are two pairs of conflicting steps of the two transactions in $s_{\{A_1,A_2\}}$, one in which the step of A_1 precedes the step of A_2, and one vice-versa. Naturally, there is no third transaction in $s_{\{A_1,A_2\}}$ to write these entities, and so the Lemma applies. It follows that in any serial schedule view equivalent to $s_{\{A_1,A_2\}}$ A_1 must come before A_2, and also A_2 must come before A_1; no such schedule exists.

Case 2: $k = 3$. There is a pair of conflicting steps of A_1 and A_2 such that the step of A_1 comes first in $s_{\{A_1,A_2,A_3\}}$. Does A_3 write the same variable? If so, that step of A_3 would conflict with both conflicting steps of A_1 and A_2. If the write step of A_3 came before the step of A_1, then there is an arc (A_3, A_2) in G(s), forming a cycle of length two and contradicting our assumption that the shortest cycle in $G(s)$ is of length three. Similarly if the write step of A_3 is between the two conflicting steps, or after them. So, we conclude that A_3 does not write the entity on which A_1 and A_2 conflict. So, the Lemma applies, and we can conclude that in any serial schedule view equivalent to $s_{\{A_1,A_2,A_3\}}$ transaction A_1 comes before A_2. However, we can similarly argue that A_2 must come before A_3, and A_3 before A_1; so $s_{\{A_1,A_2,A_3\}}$ is not view serializable.

Case 3: $k > 3$. Consider two consecutive transactions on the cycle, A_i and A_{i+1} (addition modulo k), conflicting on x. We claim that no other transaction in the cycle writes x. Because if A_j did, then there would be an arc between A_j and A_i, as well as between A_j and A_{i+1} (in either direction). At least one of these arcs would create a cycle of length less than k, contrary to our assumption that $(A_1, A_2, \ldots, A_k, A_1)$ is the shortest cycle. So, Lemma 2.5 is applicable. We conclude that in any serial schedule view equivalent to $s_{\{A_1,A_2,\ldots,A_k\}}$ transaction A_1 must come before A_2, A_2 before A_3, and so on, up to A_k before A_1, a contradiction. $\square$

A similar result, relating final-state serializability with a variant of conflict serializability, can be shown, albeit by arguments that are quite a bit more involved (Problem 2.12).

2.7 SPECIAL CASES

One reaction to complexity is to seek "approximations" of the original goal; we took this path in the previous section. Another interesting approach is to consider whether the original problem, becomes any easier when restricted *to important special cases*. In this section we shall examine certain plausible and practically relevant restrictions on the transactions, under which testing for view serializability (and final-state serializability) becomes easy.

No Blind Writes

Suppose that our transactions are such that every write step must be preceded in the transaction—not necesarily immediately—by a read step on the same entity. That is, no transaction is allowed to write an entity, unless it has previously read it. We call this the *restricted model* of transactions. If we assume that all transactions are in the restricted model, the theory of correctness is simplified considerably. The reason is essentially the following:

Lemma 2.6: *Let s be a serial schedule in the restricted model of transactions, and let x be an entity. Then the $W(x)$ steps are totally ordered in $D(s)$ (recall the definition in Section 2.2). That is, there is a path in $D(s)$ between any two $W(x)$ steps, in one of the two directions.*

Notice that, in particular, the lemma implies that there can be no dead write steps in a serial schedule of restricted transactions.

Proof: We shall prove the lemma for pairs of $W(x)$ steps without a third $W(x)$ step in between them in s. The general statement will then follow by an easy induction. Let $A : W(x)$ and $B : W(x)$ be two such steps, occurring in this order in the serial schedule s. The latter one must be preceded by a $B : R(x)$ step, since B is in the restricted model of transactions. Recall that s is a serial schedule. Now, the latest $W(x)$ step before this $R(x)$ step is, by our hypothesis, $A : W(x)$. Thus, B reads x from A, and thus there is an arc from $A : W(x)$ to $B : R(x)$ in $D(s)$. Furthermore, in B the $R(x)$ step comes before the $W(x)$ one, and therefore there is an arc from $B : R(x)$ to $B : W(x)$. The proof is complete. $\square$

Theorem 2.11: *For transactions in the restricted model, a schedule is view serializable if and only if it is conflict serializable.*

Proof: By Proposition 2.1 conflict serializability implies view serializability. Therefore, it suffices to show that view serializability implies conflict serializability. Suppose that schedule s is view equivalent to some serial schedule s', that is, $D(s) = D(s')$. We claim that s and s' are also conflict equivalent. To see this, take any two conflicting steps u and v of s; we shall show that they are in the same order in s as in s'. By Lemma 2.6, all write steps on each entity are totally ordered in $D(s)$, and thus in $D(s')$. Thus, if both u and v are write steps there is nothing to prove. So, let us assume that u is a $R(x)$ step and v is a $W(x)$ step. Since the two schedules are view equivalent, u reads x from the same $W(x)$ step, say w, in s as in s'. If $w = v$, then clearly u comes after v in both schedules, and we are done. Otherwise, does w come before or after v in the linear order? If it comes after v, then u comes even later, and thus after v in both schedules. If w comes before v, then u must also come before v in both schedules, since otherwise u would have read x from v, contrary to the property of the restricted model. We conclude that s is indeed conflict equivalent to s', and thus conflict serializable. $\square$

Does final-state serializability also coincide with the other two correctness criteria? The answer is no, but for a trivial reason: Serial schedules can still have *dead read steps*, which can be used to differentiate between final-state serializability and view serializability (see Problem 2.11).

The Action Model

Suppose that each step of a transaction consists of *both* reading the entity and immediately writing a new value computed in terms of all values of previously read entities (including the entity just read). In terms of our model, we can rephrase this as follows: In each transaction, the read and write steps come in pairs of the form $R(x)W(x)$ (and thus the transactions are in an even more special form than those in the restricted model discussed in the previous subsection). Furthermore, these pairs, called *actions*, always appear together in a schedule. We call this the *action model* of transactions. In this model, we usually replace a pair $R(x)W(x)$ of steps denoting an atomic action on x by the symbol $A(x)$.

Example 2.7: Two typical transactions in the action model would be $A_1 = A(x)A(y)A(z)$ and $A_2 = A(y)A(x)$. A possible schedule of these transactions is the following:

$$s = \begin{matrix} A_1 : A(x)A(y) & A(z) \\ A_2 : & A(y) & A(x) \end{matrix}$$

Is this schedule view serializable? We do not need to define view serializability—or final-state serializability, or conflict serializability—from scratch for the action model. We just think of s as the following schedule in the read-write model:

$$\begin{matrix} A_1 : R(x)W(x)R(y)W(y) & R(z)W(z) \\ A_2 : & R(y)W(y) & R(x)W(x) \end{matrix}$$

By using the test of Theorem 2.2, we conclude that s is view serializable. It is also final-state serializable, and of course conflict serializable. And this is no coincidence. □

Theorem 2.12: *In the action model, final-state serializability, view serializability, and conflict serializability all coincide.*

Proof: Since the set of schedules in the action model is a subset of those in the restricted model, that view- and conflict serializability coincide follows from Theorem 2.11. For final-state serializability, recall that, by Theorems 2.1 and 2.2, serializability and view serializablity differ only in that the former ignores the "reads-from" information of dead read steps. However, it is quite easy to see that, in the action model, no step is dead. □

In the next chapters, we shall use the action model quite frequently. The reason is that, as evidenced by Theorem 2.12, the simplicity of the action model irons out the complexities of serializability, and makes correctness a simple, stable concept. This will be quite important when we study schedules in contexts—such as *distributed databases* and *locking policies*—that are quite complex by themselves.

A Review

We have studied several notions of correctness, each defined in terms of some version of equivalence to serial schedules. We started with final-state serializability, which corresponds to final-state equivalence. Issues of correctness forced us to retreat to a less general notion, view equivalence, and the corresponding correctness criterion, view serializability. We then observed that both of these versions of correctness are NP-complete to check, and as a consequence too complex to study seriously (or, as we shall see, to implement). This led us to a new, even more restricted, notion of correctness, conflict serializability, which turned out to be of considerable interest. The situation is depicted in Figure 2.12, in which we represent the space of all schedules (H), final-state serializable

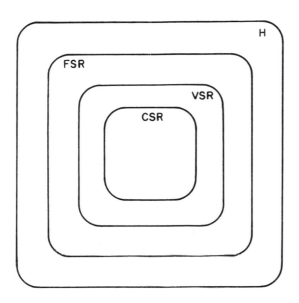

Figure 2.12. The Various Notions of Correctness.

schedules (FSR), view serializable (VSR) and conflict serializable (CSR) ones. Classes of schedules are represented as regions on the plane. (In Chapter 5 we shall argue see that the "area" of such a region is a reasonable measure of the "parallelism" supported by the corresponding notion of correctness.) Finally, we noticed that restricted models for transactions can cause many of these distinctions to disappear.

PROBLEMS

*2.1 Suppose that s is a sequence of assignments of the form $x := y \otimes z$, where x, y, and z are integer-valued entities, and $\otimes$ is an operation among $\{+, -, *, /\}$. Let **C** be an assertion concerning the entities (that is, a set of $|F|$-tuples of integers).

    (a) Show that it is undecidable to determine, for a given sequence s and constraints **C**, whether "**C** $\{s\}$ **C**," that is, whether the assertion **C** is preserved by the schedule s. (*Hint:* A simple proof involves Hilbert's Tenth Problem.)

    (b) Suppose now that s is a schedule, that is, it results from the shuffling together of various transactions, each of which is itself a sequence of assignments. Show that it is undecidable to tell whether there is a serial execution of the transactions such that, for all initial values of the variables, the serial execution produces the same final values as s.

2.2 Suppose that in a schedule s, $R(x)$ is the only read step before $W(y)$ in transaction A, and we know that the interpretation of the step $A : W(y)$ is the identity function on x—that is, A copies into y the value of x. Define what final-state

equivalence means when this information is available for several steps of the
schedule. Formulate and prove a version of theorem 2.1 for this case.

2.3 In a database system, the integrity constraints are the conjunction of simpler
assertions. Each subassertion does not involve all entities, but a particular subset
of the entities called a *clause*. For example, if the integrity constraints are "$x+y \leq$
$z \wedge z = w + 1$", then the clauses are $\{\{x, y, z\}, \{z, w\}\}$. If the clauses of the
integrity constraints are known, then final-state serializability can become more
liberal. Give a schedule which is not final-state serializable, but is intuitively
correct if the clauses are known to be as above. Define formally the appropriate
notion of correctness, when the structure of the clauses is known, and prove a
Theorem analogous to Theorem 2.1 concerning a test for correctness.

2.4 A schedule is called *live serializable* if it is equivalent to a serial schedule involving a subset of its transactions (where equivalence is meant as part (b) of the
definition of final-state equivalence). Give an example of a schedule that is live
serializable, but not final-state serializable.

2.5 Call a schedule *serializable in the broad sense* if it is equivalent to a serial schedule
involving *zero or more copies of each transaction* of the original schedule. Prove
or disprove: A schedule is serializable in the broad sense if and only if it is live
serializable.

2.6 Prove Theorem 2.2.

*2.7 A schedule is *weakly view serializable* if for all interpretations of the transactions
and all initial values of the entities the following is true: For each transaction
there is a serial schedule such that the transaction sees the same view in the
serial schedule and the original one.
  (a) Show that if a schedule is view serializable then it is weakly view serializable.
      Give an example of a weakly view serializable schedule which is not view
      serializable. Is weak serializability an attractive notion of correctness?
  (b) What is the complexity of telling whether a schedule is weakly serializable?

2.8 Let s be a schedule. Define a polygraph $P'(s)$ exactly as we have defined $P(s)$,
except that the addition of arcs and choices does not take place for each read
step, but for each *live* read step.
  (a) Show that $P'(s)$ is acyclic if and only if s is final-state serializable.
  (b) Show that determining whether a given schedule is final-state serializable is
      an NP-complete problem.

2.9 A schedule s is *strictly serializable* if it is final-state equivalent to a serial schedule
in which transactions that do not overlap in s are in the same order as in s.
  (a) Show that strict serializability is incomparable to view serializability (i.e.,
      neither a superset nor a subset thereof).
  (b) Show that it is NP-complete to tell whether a schedule is strictly serializable.

*2.10 Suppose that we are given a schedule s in fully uninterpreted form (that is, the
steps are just distinct symbols from some alphabet), and a set of equations of the

form $\sigma = \rho$, where σ and ρ are arbitrary subschedules, possibly involving new steps, not in s.

  (a) Show that it is an undecidable problem to tell whether a schedule can be transformed into a serial schedule of the same transactions by repeatedly replacing subschedules appearing on one side of an equation by the other side.

  (b) Suppose now that we restrict the equations so that the right side is a permutation of the steps appearing on the other side. Show that the problem of telling whether a schedule can be transformed into a serial schedule of the same transactions becomes *PSPACE-complete* (see Section 3.2 for a definition). Prove that the problem remains PSPACE-complete even if the two sides of all equations have length bounded by a small constant, such as five.

2.11 Construct a schedule in the restricted model that is final-state serializable, but not view serializable.

2.12 We can define a variant of conflict serializability as follows: Call a conflict in a schedule *live* if neither of the steps is a dead read step, and call two schedules *live conflict equivalent* if all pairs of live-conflicting steps are in the same order. A schedule is *live conflict serializable* if it is live conflict equivalent to a serial schedule. Finally, if s is a schedule, define $l(s)$ to be the same schedule with all dead read steps deleted.

  (a) Show that a schedule is live conflict serializable if and only if $G(l(s))$ is acyclic.

  (b) Show by a counterexample that it is *not* true that a schedule is final-state serializable if and only if all of its projections are live conflict serializable.

  (c) Show that all projections of a schedule are final-state serializable if and only if they are all live conflict serializable.

2.13 Show that the results of Theorems 2.12 and 3.5 (in the next Chapter) for the action model of transactions also hold in the less restricted model in which transactions are such that each read step is followed by a write step on the same entity, and each write step is preceded by a read step on the same entity.

2.14 Give an example of a schedule without dead steps which is view serializable but not conflict serializable.

2.15 Show the following stronger version of Theorem 2.3: Schedule s is view serializable if and only if for each full interpretation I and initial states X for which s is legal, there is a π such that the π-serial execution s' satisfies $s(I, X) = s'(I, X)$. That is, there may be different π's for different interpretations.

NOTES AND REFERENCES

Two early papers that address the issue of correctness of concurrent transactions are [Eswaran et al. 1976] and [Stearns et al. 1976]. The former paper assumes the action model of transactions, and the latter the restricted model (Section 2.7) and therefore in both papers correctness coincides with what we call here conflict serializability. Another early work on the subject is [Schlageter 1978]. Final-state serializability was formally defined in [Papadimitriou et al. 1977], and further explored in [Papadimitriou 1979]; the material in Section 2.5 is from these papers. The concept of view serializability was implicit in the work of [Stearns et al. 1976], proposed in [Rosenkrantz et al. 1982]. Theorem 2.10 and Problem 2.12 is from [Yannakakis 1984]. [Yannakakis 1980] is an excellent exposition on the many possible variants of correctness, some of which are defined in the problems, and the intricate relations between them; unfortunately, this paper is not widely available. A good source for information about program verification is [Manna 1984]. For information on undecidable problems (Problem 2.1) see [Hopcroft and Ullman 1979]. Problem 2.9 is from [Sethi 1981], Problem 2.7 is due to J. A. Brzozowski, and Problem 2.15 is due to Mihalis Yannakakis. A book in combinatorial optimization is [Papadimitriou and Steiglitz 1982].

3

MORE ON CORRECTNESS

In the previous chapter we examined in detail what it means for a schedule to be correct. Among other notions, we have studied view serializability, a natural but computationally complex criterion, and conflict serializability, an elegant compromise between generality and simplicity. In this chapter we shall examine two subtler concepts related to correctness. They are both motivated by important implementation issues in concurrency control: Multiple versions of entities, and reliability in the face of transaction failures.

3.1 MULTIPLE VERSIONS

Surprisingly, we can define an important new notion of correctness for schedules, which is more liberal than view serializability. We must first revise one of our most basic assumptions: That an entity at any time has only one value, namely the value supplied by the last transaction which wrote this entity (or the initial value, if there is no previous write step on this entity in the schedule). The scenario is this: The scheduler receives a write step on x, which is essentially a request by a transaction to replace the present value of entity x by a new one. What happens to the old value? So far, we had been assuming that it is forgotten forever, overwritten by the new version. There is, however, an intriguing possibility to consider. Suppose that *we keep both values around.* Next, if a transaction requests to read the value of x, we have the option to supply it with either version. Which one do we supply? The answer is, whichever serves best our ultimate goals, which are *correctness* and *performance*.

Example 3.1: Let us consider the following schedule:

$$s = \begin{array}{l} A_1 : R(x)W(x) \qquad\qquad R(y)W(z) \\ A_2 : \qquad\qquad R(x)W(y) \end{array}$$

Schedule s is not view serializable—or final-state serializable for that matter. We can argue this informally as follows: Transactions A_1 and A_2 see in s inconsistent views. In particular, transaction A_1 sees that A_2 runs before A_1, while A_2 sees the opposite. The problem is worth "animating." Imagine that we are scanning the schedule from left to right, as a scheduler would do, implementing the read and write requests. We first supply A_1 with the initial value of x, and replace the value of x with the one written by A_1. We supply this value to transaction A_2, and it gives us in return a new y value to write. Next, we receive the $R(y)$ step of A_1, and we immediately realize the impasse. We cannot supply A_1 with the new value of y, because this would lead to an inconsistency. The only y value that is consistent with A_1's view so far would be the *old* one, by now lost forever, overwritten by A_2. If only we had kept that old value of y! We could supply it to A_1, thus pretending our schedule was

$$s' = \begin{matrix} A_1 : R(x)W(x)R(y) & & W(z) \\ A_2 : & R(x)W(y) & \end{matrix}$$

which is a perfectly correct one. $\square$

There are concurrency control algorithms that do exactly this: They keep old versions of the entities in case they will be needed in the future to supply to some read step, and thus salvage the correctness of the schedule. This approach is called *multiversion concurrency control*. It is the basis of a new, more relaxed, correctness criterion for schedules: We consider those schedules correct which, even though they may not be view serializable, they can be made to *behave* like view serializable ones by appropriately manipulating versions. We must first define this formally.

Version Functions

Definition 3.1: Let s be a schedule. A *version function* for s is a function V mapping each read step of $\hat{s}$, the augmented schedule containing transactions A_0 and A_∞, to a previous write step of $\hat{s}$ on the same entity, and each write step of $\hat{s}$ to a previous write step *or* one of the symbols ν and λ, such that (1) if a is a read or write step of s then $V(V(a)) \neq \lambda$ and (2) if a is a read or write step of s and w a previous write step on the same entity, then $V(a) \neq V(w)$. $\square$

The intuitive meaning of this definition is that the version function supplies to each read step a version of its entity: The read step r reads the value written by $V(r)$. Also, the version function assigns to each write step w a version to overwrite, namely the version written by $V(w)$. $V(w) = \nu$ means that a new version is created; $V(w) = \lambda$ that the write step is *ignored*, and no record of the value written is kept. (This is not as self-defeating as it may seem; see the next subsection.) Evidently, the steps of A_0 are necessarily mapped to ν or λ, since they are not preceded by a write step on the same entity. The two conditions in the definition simply say that we cannot read or overwrite a version that was never kept, and that we cannot read or overwrite a version after it has been overwritten.

If V maps each read and write step in $\hat{s}$ (except A_0) to the write step on the same entity that *immediately* precedes it in $\hat{s}$, then V is called *the standard version function*. The unique standard version function of a schedule s is denoted by V_s.

Example 3.1 (continued): A possible version function for schedule s above may map step $A_1 : R(x)$ to the step $A_0 : W(x)$ of the initial pseudotransaction; step $A_2 : R(x)$ to $A_1 : W(x)$; and step $A_1 : R(y)$ to $A_0 : W(y)$. Each read step of A_∞ is mapped to the last write step of s on the same entity. All write steps are mapped on the last write step on the same entity, except of course that steps of A_0 are mapped to λ. This version function is a formalization of the method suggested in Example 3.1 in order make s "serializable." This is not the standard version function for s, since, for example, step $A_1 : R(y)$ is mapped to $A_0 : W(y)$, and not the latest $W(y)$ step that precedes it in s, namely $A_2 : W(y)$. $\square$

A schedule together with a version function, (s, V), is called a *full schedule*. A full schedule determines a particular interaction of the transactions with the entities of the database. Notice that, up to now, only a plain schedule was needed to determine such an interaction; this is because the standard version function was implicitly assumed. Given a full schedule (s, V), an interpretation I of its transactions, and an initial state X of the database, we can formalize the effect of the full schedule on X under interpretation I as follows: Recall the notation $a_s(I, X)$ of Section 2.2 for the value read or written by step a of schedule s under interpretation I and from initial state X (with the standard version function). We now add the superscript V for the version function: $a_s^V(I, X)$. In particular, if a is a write step with the read steps b and c, say, preceding it in its transaction, then $a_s^V(I, X) = f_a(b_s^V(I, X), c_s^V(I, X))$, where f_a is the function assigned to step a by I. If a is the step $W(x)$ of A_0, then a_s^V is of course the value of x in X. Finally, if a is a read step, then $a_s^V(I, X) = b_s^V(I, X)$, where $b = V(a)$ is the write step to which the version function V maps a. The resulting state is denoted $s^V(I, X)$.

Notice that ordinary schedules are in fact a *special case* of full schedules: They are the ones whose version functions are standard. We may wish to extend to full schedules any notion that we have defined for schedules. For example, now that we have a notion of the effect of a full schedule on the database, we can define what it means for two full schedules to be view equivalent. As with plain schedules, we say that (s, V) and (s', V') are view equivalent if, for all interpretations I and initial states X, the values read by each transaction (including the final pseudotransaction) in both schedules are identical.

We wish to state a condition for view equivalence of full schedules analogous to Theorem 2.2. This theorem relates view equivalence of two schedules s and s' with the equality of two directed graphs $D(s)$ and $D(s')$. These directed graphs essentially capture the same "reads from" information contained in the version functions. It turns out that the following simple generalization of Theorem 2.2 holds for full schedules.

Theorem 3.1: *Two full schedules (s, V) and (s', V') are view equivalent if and only if s and s' have the same transactions, and V and V' agree on all read steps.*

Proof: The proof of this theorem is almost identical to the proof of Theorem 2.1 (as was slightly amended in Section 2.4 to account for view equivalence). For the "if" part, the same inductive hypothesis works; in the only place where equality of the directed graphs was needed, namely the inductive step for write steps, all that is really needed is agreement of the version functions on their read steps. For the "only if" direction, that same argument works. If the two resulting directed graphs are equal, then it easily follows that the two version functions agree on all read steps. $\square$

We have not yet defined what it means for a full schedule to be correct. Evidently, it must be equivalent to a serial full schedule, that is, a full schedule (s, V) such that s is serial. But with which version function V? To answer, we must recall our motivation in adopting serial schedules as our archetypical correct schedules: Serial schedules have the important property that they can be inductively shown correct, starting only from the assumption that transactions are correct. This, however, is the property of serial schedules *with the standard version function*. Serial full schedules with non-standard version functions are in this respect as unpredictable as nonserial ones. Thus, our notion of correctness for full schedules is the following: *A full schedule is view serializable if it is view equivalent to a serial schedule (with the standard version function).* As it is shown in Problem 3.3, there is a test of view serializability for full schedules, based on polygraphs, which is completely analogous with the one for schedules with the standard interpretation. Naturally, testing a full schedule for view serializability is NP-complete (remember, this is a generalization of the same question for ordinary schedules, so it is at least as hard).

Example 3.2: The schedule s defined in Example 3.1, together with the version function described there, comprise a view serializable full schedule. It is view equivalent to the serial schedule $A_1 A_2$. $\square$

Let us recall now the schedule s of Example 3.1. It is certainly not view serializable. However, it does have an interesting property that partially compensates for this: There is a version function V, also given in Example 3.1, such that the *full* schedule (s, V) is view serializable. In other words, schedule s is not completely hopeless: Under the proper management of versions, there is hope that it can be made to behave like a correct schedule. An interesting question arises now. Do all schedules that are not view serializable have the same property, that is, they are at least view serializable under some nonstandard version function?

Example 3.3: Consider the following schedule.

$$t = \begin{array}{ll} A_1 : R(x) & W(x) \\ A_2 : & R(x)W(x) \end{array}$$

This schedule is certainly not view serializable. But is there some version function V such that (t, V) is view serializable? The answer is "no"!

To see this, let us attempt to construct such a V. It has to map both $R(x)$ steps in t to $A_0 : W(x)$, because no other $W(x)$ step comes before either of them in $\hat{t}$. We are already doomed to failure: The standard version function of both possible serial schedules maps only one of the $R(x)$ steps to $A_0 : W(x)$, and this can be easily checked. As a result, there is no version function that will make t view serializable. $\square$

This leads us to a new definition of correctness for *schedules* (not full schedules). We call a schedule s *multiversion serializable* if there is a version function V such that (s, V) is view serializable. Evidently, any view serializable schedule is also multiversion serializable, since its standard interpretation renders it view serializable. As demonstrated by Examples 3.2 and 3.3, multiversion serializable schedules is a proper subset of all schedules, and a proper superset of the view serializable schedules. It is an interesting notion of correctness, clearly a relaxation on view serializability. Multiversion serializable schedules are not necessarily view serializable: It is just possible to "make them" view serializable, by interpreting their read steps in terms of some version function.

Storage Costs

The incorrect schedules that are "salvaged" by the multiversion approach, and the additional performance and parallelism implied by this, do not come for free. One aspect of the cost is, of course, the additional complexity of maintaining and making available several versions of the same entity. Another is the additional *storage* required for keeping all needed versions available. Our formalism of multiple versions allows us to discuss this cost, and observe its rather interesting behavior.

Definition 3.2: Let s be a schedule, and V a version function for s. The *storage cost* of V, denoted $c(V)$, is the total number of write steps of s (not $\hat{s}$) that are mapped by V to ν. The *storage cost* of s, denoted $c(s)$, is the minimum $c(V)$ over all version functions V such that the full schedule (s, V) is view serializable. This is a measure of the cost incurred in "salvaging" s. If s

is view serializable, this cost is zero (but see the next section for the failure of the converse). $\square$

Example 3.4: The cost of schedule s in Example 3.1 is at most one, as only one step of s (namely, $A_2 : W(y)$) is mapped to ν by the version function V described there. It is at least one, since, we argued, the only version functions V that make (s, V) view serializable must map the step $A_1 : R(y)$ to $A_0 : W(y)$, and thus incur cost of at least one. Therefore, $c(s) = 1$.

Consider now the following schedule s_2

$A_1 :R(x)W(x)W(y)$
$A_2 :$ $R(x)W(x)$ $R(y)$
$A_3 :$ $R(x)W(x)W(y)$
$A_4 :$ $R(x)W(x)$ $R(y)$
$A_5 :$ $R(x)W(x)W(y)$

This schedule is multiversion serializable; just map the $A_2 : R(y)$ and $A_4 : R(y)$ steps to $A_1 : W(y)$ and $A_3 : W(y)$, respectively, and all the remaining ones to the latest previous write step on the same entity. The cost of this version function is two.

We claim that this is the minimum possible cost of any version function such that (s_2, V) is view serializable, and thus $c(s_2) = 2$. The idea in the argument is that the only serial schedule to which any full schedule (s, V') can be view equivalent is $A_1 A_2 A_3 A_4 A_5$. The reason for this is that all five transaction start by reading and writing x. Any serial schedule would thus have each transaction read x from the immediately preceding one, and thus the only choice for a version function would be to map $A_i : R(x)$ to $A_{i-1} : W(x)$.

Since $A_1 A_2 A_3 A_4 A_5$ is the only possible view equivalent serial schedule, it follows that A_3 must write a *new* version of y, so that the one written by A_1 can survive and be read by A_2 later on; similarly for A_5 and A_3. Thus, at least two new versions of y are needed in order to make s_2 view equivalent to some serial schedule, and $c(s_2) = 2$. $\square$

The argument in Example 3.4 can be generalized to a schedule s_k with $2k + 1$ transactions, of which the odd-numbered ones are identical to the odd-numbered transactions of s_2, and the even-numbered to the even-numbered ones. The $R(y)$ steps of the even-numbered transactions are always at the end. Schedule s_k, as defined above, can be shown to have $c(s) = k$; so we have:

Proposition 3.1: *There are multiversion serializable schedules with arbitrarily large storage cost.* $\square$

Thomas' Write Rule

There is a class of schedules which have zero storage cost, and yet are not view serializable. A simple example is the following:

$$s = \frac{A_1 :R(x) \qquad W(x)}{A_2 : \qquad W(x)}$$

It is clear that s is not view serializable. It is, however, multiversion serializable. The appropriate version function V differs from the standard one only in that it maps $A_\infty : R(x)$ to $A_2 : W(x)$ instead of $A_1 : W(x)$ (and therefore $A_1 : W(x)$ to λ). (s, V) is view equivalent to $A_1 A_2$ with the standard version function. Still, notice that the cost of V is zero. Intuitively, the effect of V is that the write step of A_1 is simply *ignored*. No extra versions are kept.

This interesting phenomenon, namely that a schedule can be rendered correct by simply ignoring a write step that arrived "too late", is known as *Thomas' write rule*. Historically, it was one of the first manifestations of the multiversion approach to concurrency.

The Complexity of Multiversion Serializability

How hard is it to tell whether a schedule is multiversion serializable? The next Theorem says, very hard.

Theorem 3.2: *Testing whether a schedule is multiversion serializable is NP-complete.*

Proof: Multiversion serializability is in NP. In proof, given a schedule s, we can guess a version function V and a serial schedule s' such that (s, V) is equivalent to s' under the standard interpretation.

To show completeness, we shall reduce polygraph acyclicity to multiversion serializability. Our proof is quite similar in spirit to the proof of Lemma 2.4. Given any polygraph $P = (V, A, C)$ we shall construct in polynomial time a schedule s, such that s is multiversion serializable if and only if P is acyclic. For simplicity, we shall assume that for each arc $(u, v) \in A$ there is at least one choice $(v, w, u) \in C$. It is easy to see that the polygraphs produced in the NP-completeness proof in Chapter 2 have this property (which can be forced very easily anyway by adding a new vertex w and choice (v, w, u) where needed).

First, we have a transaction for each vertex in V. Also, for each choice $c \in C$, we have entities c and c'. Now for describing the schedule s itself, we shall construct it in several segments, the precise order of which is unimportant. For each choice $c = (A_1, A_2, A_3)$ in C, our schedule s contains the segment

$$
\begin{array}{lll}
A_1 : \ldots & R(c)W(c') & \ldots \\
A_2 : \ldots & W(c) & \ldots \\
A_3 : \ldots W(c)R(c') & & \ldots
\end{array}
$$

Intuitively, the read and write steps on c' force transaction A_3 to come before A_1 in any serial schedule which is view equivalent to (s, V), for any V. This is because the only transaction in s that writes entity c', A_1, does so after A_3 reads c', and so any version function must map the step $A_3 : R(c')$ to the initial step $A_0 : W(c')$. It follows that A_3 comes before A_1, and therefore any version function must map the step $A_1 : R(c)$ to $A_3 : W(c)$. How about A_2? It cannot come in between A_3 and A_1, because then the serial schedule would not be view equivalent to this version function of s.

It follows from the above arguments that s is multiversion serializable if and only if there is an order of the nodes of P such that, for each choice (A_1, A_2, A_3), A_3 comes before A_1, and A_2 does not come in between. However, such an order exists if and only if an acyclic digraph compatible with P exists. $\square$

Conflict Multiversion Serializability

Our previous theorem suggests that multiversion serializability, a novel correctness criterion of which we shall see many applications, shares with view serializability the drawbacks implied by NP-completeness. We shall describe next an interesting subset of multiversion serializability, which is easy to test, and still retains much of the generality enjoyed by multiversion serializability. This is analogous to the manoeuvre that led us to conflict serializability, in Section 2.6, and our reasoning will not be unlike the arguments of that section.

Theorem 2.9 defines conflict serializable schedules as those schedules which can be transformed to serial ones by some sequence of allowable "switchings" of adjacent steps. We first identified the types of pairs of steps from different transactions (we called them "conflicts") for which *order matters*. These were of three types:

1. A $W(x)$ step followed by another $W(x)$ step.
2. A $W(x)$ step followed by a $R(x)$ step.
3. A $R(x)$ step followed by a $W(x)$ step.

Which are the disallowed switchings for multiversion serializability? Pairs of type (1) now can be inverted. When multiple versions are supported, it does not matter which transaction wrote the entity last; both versions can survive. It is a bit more subtle to argue that switchings of type (2) are also allowed. Reversing the order of such a pair means *giving up* a legal version mapping for the read step, and should be allowed. It is the opposite change that should be illegal. Bringing a write step in front of a read step of the same entity produces a schedule that cannot be "simulated" by the original one via multiple versions. Thus, in multiversion serializability, pairs of type (3) are our only "conflicts."

We define a schedule to be *conflict multiversion serializable* if it can be made into a serial schedule by a sequence of zero or more transformations, in which any pair of adjacent steps (from different transactions) can be interchanged, unless they are a read step followed by a write step on the same entity. Notice the basic asymmetry of the situation: A write step *can* be interchanged with a subsequent read on the same entity.

Example 3.5: Recall the schedule

$$s = \begin{matrix} A_1 : R(x)W(x) & & R(y)W(z) \\ A_2 : & R(x)W(y) & \end{matrix}$$

This schedule is conflict multiversion serializable. To see this, let us try to transform it to A_1A_2 by legal interchanges. First, we interchange the steps $A_2 : W(y)$ and $A_1 : R(y)$; by our rules, this is allowed (although the inverse transformation is not). Next, we switch $A_2 : W(y)$ with $A_1 : W(z)$—certainly there are no conflicts here. Finally, we switch $A_2 : R(x)$ with $A_1 : R(y)$ and $A_1 : W(z)$, in that order, to arrive at the serial schedule A_1A_2. □

Proposition 3.2: *Every conflict multiversion serializable schedule is multiversion serializable.*

Proof: Suppose that s is a conflict multiversion serializable schedule. That is, s can be transformed to a serial schedule s' by a sequence of switchings that *do not* bring a write step in front of a read on the same entity. Consider the version function V which is identical to V_s (the standard version function of s) with respect to the write steps, and to $V_{s'}$ with respect to the read steps. We claim that (s, V) is a view serializable full schedule. Since it is obvious that it is view equivalent to s' with the standard version function, all we have to show is that V is a legal version function for s, that is, if $V_{s'}$ maps a read step a of s' to the preceding write step b on the same entity, then a comes after b in s as well. But this is immediate, because no switchings that could bring a after b in s' were allowed. □

There are multiversion serializable schedules that are not conflict multiversion serializable. Take, for example,

$$s = \begin{array}{ll} A_1 : & R(x)W(y) \\ A_2 : R(y) & \qquad\qquad W(x) \\ A_3 : & R(z)W(x) \end{array}$$

This schedule is multiversion serializable. An appropriate version function maps each read step to the latest previous write step on the same entity, except for $A_\infty : R(x)$, which is mapped to $A_3 : W(x)$ instead of $A_2 : W(x)$. This version function makes s view equivalent to $A_2A_3A_1$, as can be easily checked.

Nevertheless, s is *not* conflict multiversion serializable. To see this, just notice that there is no way that transactions A_1 and A_2 can escape the "deadly embrace" they seem to be in. The step $A_2 : W(x)$ cannot come in front of $A_1 : R(x)$, since such a move would be disallowed under conflict multiversion serializability. For the same reason, the step $A_2 : R(y)$ cannot come after $A_1 : W(y)$. Hence, no serial schedule can be reached from s using legal interchanges of steps, and thus s is not conflict multiversion serializable. □

We can test efficiently whether a schedule is conflict multiversion serializable. This is done by further exploiting the analogy with conflict serializability. Given a schedule s, we define a graph $G'(s)$ as follows: G' has the transactions of s as nodes, and it has an arc from transaction A to transaction B if there is a read step of A followed by a write step of B on the same entity. That is, $G'(s)$ is the graph $G(s)$ used for conflict serializability, restricted to the arcs that are the real conflicts in the presence of multiple versions. We can show the following:

Theorem 3.3: *A schedule s is conflict multiversion serializable if and only if $G'(s)$ is acyclic.*

Proof: Suppose that s is indeed conflict multiversion serializable. Then, it is transformable to a serial schedule s' via interchanges of steps *which do not erase any arcs from $G'(s)$*. Thus, $G'(s')$ is a supergraph of $G'(s)$. However, it is easy to see that all arcs of $G'(s')$ are compatible with the serial order of the transactions in s', and thus $G'(s')$ is acyclic. It follows that $G'(s)$ is acyclic as well.

Conversely, suppose that $G'(s)$ is acyclic. Consider a total order of the transactions compatible with $G'(s)$, and the serial schedule s' defined by it. Notice that, by the choice of s', $G'(s')$ is a supergraph of $G'(s)$. Let k be the number of pairs of steps of the two schedules which occur in different order in s than in s'. We shall show, by induction on k, that s can be turned into s' by interchanges between pairs of steps other than reads followed by a write in the same entity; this would imply that s is conflict multiversion serializable. Our claim is clearly valid for $k = 0$, as in the case the two schedules are identical. Suppose now that $k > 0$. This means that there are at least two steps out of order in s'. Among the pairs of steps which are out of order in s, we can choose a pair of steps which are consecutive in s. This is proved exactly as in the proof of Theorem 2.9: If the two steps in hand are not consecutive, then there is a step in between them that is out of order with one of them. So, we can replace this pair with two steps that are closer, and this cannot go on indefinitely.

Since $G'(s)$ is a subgraph of $G'(s')$, these two adjacent steps of s which are out of order cannot be a read step followed by a conflicting write step. Therefore, we can switch them, and obtain a schedule s''. However, s'' differs from s' in at most $k - 1$ pairs of steps, and thus, by induction, it can be transformed to s'. It follows that s is indeed conflict multiversion serializable. $\square$

Example 3.6: The graph $G'(s)$ for the schedule s following Proposition 3.2 is shown in Figure 3.1. It does have a cycle involving A_1 and A_2, as the discussion of that example seemed to indicate. $\square$

Multiversion Serializability and Special Cases

What if the transactions of a schedule are all in the *restricted model* of the previous section, that is, no transaction writes an entity without first reading it? It turns out that, as with ordinary (single version) view serializability, the picture becomes much simpler. In particular, we can prove the following variant

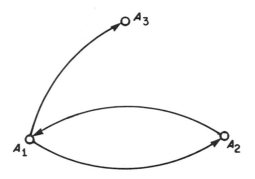

Figure 3.1. The Graph $G'(s)$.

of Theorem 2.11:

Theorem 3.4: *If the transactions are in the restricted model, then a schedule is conflict multiversion serializable if and only if it is multiversion serializable.*

Proof: One direction is trivial, as it holds for general transactions (Proposition 3.2). For the other direction, consider a multiversion serializable schedule s. Presumably, there is a version function V such that (s, V) is view serializable, that is, for some serial schedule s' the standard version function of s' agrees with V on all read steps. Let a be a read step followed in s by a write step b on the same entity; we shall show that these steps have the same order in s'. If this is so, then the graph $G'(s)$ is a subgraph of $G'(s')$, and therefore acyclic; so s is conflict multiversion serializable by Theorem 3.3.

We shall prove this claim by induction on the order in which a appears in s' (it clearly holds if a is the first read step on the entity). Suppose, for the sake of contradiction, that b comes before a in s'. Then, since V was assumed to agree on the read steps with the standard version function of s', we must have another write step c between b and a in s', namely $c = v(a)$. Consider the read step d that precedes c in its transaction (here we used the restricted model assumption). d is a read step prior to a in s', which also conflicts with b, and which comes before b in s, but after it in s'. This contradicts our induction hypothesis. $\square$

How about the action model, in which steps always come in pairs of "twin" consecutive read and write steps on the same entity called actions (recall Section 2.7)? The result here is stronger, if not a little disappointing: The multiversion approach does not buy us anything new in the action model. The basic reason for this can be stated as follows:

Lemma 3.1: *If s is a schedule in the action model, the graphs $G(s)$ and $G'(s)$ are identical.*

Proof: Recall that the graph $G(s)$ captures the order in which all conflicting steps of s occur, whereas $G'(s)$ records those write steps that are subsequent to conflicting read steps. Naturally, $G'(s)$ is a subgraph of $G(s)$; we have to show the inverse containment. Consider any arc of $G(s)$, say from transaction A to B. It implies that there is a step a of A which conflicts with a subsequent step b of B. If a is a read step and b a write step, then the arc (A, B) is already in $G'(s)$. If a and b are both write steps, then consider the "twin" read step on the same entity that comes immediately before a in A (and s). This step comes before b, and thus it again causes the arc (A, B) to appear in $G'(s)$. Finally, if a is a write step and b is a read step, then again the twin read step of a comes before the twin write step of b, and thus the arc (A, B) is in $G'(s)$. $\square$

Theorem 3.5: *In the action model a schedule is multiversion serializable if and only if it is view serializable.*

Proof: One direction is trivial (all view serializable schedules are conflict serializable). For the other direction, if s is multiversion serializable, then, by Theorem 3.4, it is conflict multiversion serializable, or, equivalently, $G'(s)$ is acyclic (Theorem 3.3). However, by Lemma 3.1 $G'(s) = G(s)$, and thus $G(s)$ is acyclic, which means that s is conflict serializable, and thus view serializable. $\square$

3.2 RELIABILITY

We have examined in great detail what it means for schedules to be correct. Alas, not all misfortunes in a database are due to incorrect schedules. Even if the scheduler does a superb job of keeping the schedule correct, certain failures will occur routinely. Such faults are usually categorized in terms of the subsystem that caused them.

1. First there are *transaction failures*. They occur as a result of exceptional conditions that originate either from the application (e.g., a fund transfer that discovered insufficient funds) or from the programming language (e.g., numerical overflow). A third important source of such failures is, interestingly, concurrency control itself. The scheduler may choose to *abort* a transaction, if this is the only way to produce a correct schedule. For example, if the transaction has caused a deadlock, or if it has read data from another transaction, which has already failed, then this may be the only way out.

2. Then there are *CPU failures*. Naturally, all transactions that were active at that time fail with the computer system. As a consequence, this type of failure can be considered as an occurrence of multiple failures of the previous kind.

3. Finally, we have *storage failures*. There is little that can be said here about them. Storage reliability is an important problem that proceeds along lines orthogonal to our concerns in this book. It is best at this point to assume

that it has somehow been solved, and catastrophes such as unrecoverable disk crashes happen with extremely low probability (lower, for example, than the probability of a theorem in this book being wrong).

It follows from this preliminary analysis that it suffices to focus on failures of the first type, that is, transaction failures. Such faults interact in a very important and interesting way with concurrency control.

A transaction is subject to a possible failure at all times, *as long as it is active*. Once it has completed its interaction with the database, once it has executed all of its steps, a transaction has terminated, and must be considered immune to failures. For one, since its execution has completed, the transaction is unable to generate a reason for its own failure. Besides, a CPU failure will not affect it. Finally, there are sound reasons why the scheduler should not be allowed to "undo" such a transaction: Other parts of the system (for example, the user who initiated the transaction) are aware of the fact that the transaction has run successfully; as a result, actions outside the database system may be initiated (mailing a check, for example), and the scheduler has no way of undoing those!

For all these reasons, we must assume that the last step of the transaction, once executed, signals the irrevocable termination of a transaction. This last step is therefore called the *commit step* of the transaction.[1] At any time after this last step, the the transaction is considered *committed* and safe from all failures. In contrast, all transactions which have executed their first step, but not yet executed their last step, called *uncommitted* or *active*, are subject at any time to the risk of abnormal termination. Formally, if s is a schedule and p a prefix of s, we say a transaction is *committed* at p (or at a, where a is the last step of p) if the last step of the transaction is contained in p; it is *uncommitted* or *active* if its first step is contained in p, but its last step is not.

Transaction failures add a new dimension to our quest for correctness in concurrent execution of transactions. In this subsection we re-examine our notions of correctness of schedules, in the light of this important issue. In fact, we shall address the problem in the more general setting of *full schedules*. It turns out that this is the most appropriate framework for discussing issues of reliability, since known techniques for ensuring reliability in the face of transaction failures use in some way or another multiple versions of data.[2]

---

[1] In much of the literature on the subject, the commit step is considered (and denoted) as a new kind of database step, neither read nor write. We chose to have it coincide with the last ordinary step of the transaction mainly for avoiding the notational inconvenience of adding a new kind of step. Naturally, there is no loss of generality here, since we can always represent the commit step as the write step on an entity particular to this transaction, not written by any other transaction. In fact, this may be the more realistic way to represent commits.

[2] Sometimes this is not very explicit. For example, many models of database reliability

Reliable Full Schedules

Transaction failures impose new restrictions on schedules. It is no more enough for a full schedule to be view serializable. A schedule is acceptable in the context of transaction failures if, intuitively, it has the property that, if a transaction fails at any moment, we can somehow pick up the pieces and continue.

Example 3.7: Consider the following schedule s, with the standard version function:

$$s = \begin{array}{llll} A_1 : & W(y) & & W(x) \\ A_2 : & & R(y) & & W(z) \end{array}$$

It is conflict serializable, and thus correct beyond doubt. Once we start thinking about failures, however, we might look even at this schedule with some suspicion. Imagine that transaction A_1 fails immediately after the first step of transaction A_2 (as it may, since it is uncommitted at that point). What are we now to do? We must somehow continue from the point of failure, and produce a full schedule that has the overall effect of A_2 —the only serial schedule of the remaining transactions. This is, however, impossible, for two reasons. First, the initial value of y has been lost, overwritten by A_1. Second, transaction A_2 has read a value of y which is no longer valid. We must conclude that s *is not reliable.* $\square$

Schedule s above exemplifies two simple sources of unreliability. The first one is the problem of *unsafe writes*, that is, write steps which overwrite the last available committed version of an entity. (We call a version committed if it is either the initial version, or a version written by a committed transaction.) The second problem is that of *unsafe reads*; an unsafe read is a read step which reads a version written by a transaction which is uncommitted at the time.

Unsafe reads can sometimes be remedied by aborting all transactions that have (unsafely) read from a failed transaction. Of course, new transactions may have to be aborted as a result of the new failures, and so on. This phenomenon is known in the literature as *cascading aborts*. In our discussion we shall at first assume that aborting a transaction in response to a transaction failure is not an option. Under this assumption, unsafe reads cannot occur in a reliable full schedule. We shall return in the next section to examine the usefulness of transaction aborts (in fact, a more general operation called rollback) as a tool for ensuring reliability.

Unfortunately, as we shall see immediately, unsafe reads and writes are not the only sources of unreliability.

---

employ a *journal* or *audit trail*, that is, stable storage in which old and new versions of the entities, among other book-keeping information, are stored. At any time, there is a single *current version* of each entity, stored in the database proper. This is the version which is presented to read requests, and may be copied back and forth to the audit trail. In our model, we somehow blur the distinction between the two kinds of versions, as it does not seem to be fundamental.

Example 3.8: Consider the following schedule, with the standard version function:

$$s' = \begin{array}{llll} A_1 : & W(x) \\ A_2 : & & R(x) & W(y) \\ A_3 : & & R(y) & & W(x) \\ A_4 : & & & & W(x) \end{array}$$

This full schedule has no unsafe reads and writes. Also, it is easy to check that it is view equivalent to $A_3 A_1 A_2 A_4$, and thus view serializable. There is, however, a serious problem with this full schedule. If transaction A_4 is aborted (at the very last step), then the remaining schedule is no more view serializable! (The reason is that, without the transaction A_4 which overwrites x, the schedule "remembers" that A_1 wrote x before A_3.) In some sense, the correctness of this full schedule depends critically on the completion of A_4. We could say that s', with the standard version function, is *unreliable*, although otherwise correct. $\square$

The above example motivates our definition of a full schedule which behaves satisfactorily in the face of transaction failures. In this definition we use the notion of a projection of a schedule to a set of transactions (recall Definition 2.8), extended in the obvious way to prefixes of schedules.

Definition 3.3: First we must define a continuation of a full schedule after a transaction failure. Let (s, V) be a full schedule involving a set τ of transactions, p a prefix of s, and $A \in \tau$ a transaction of s active at p (that is, p contains the first but not the last step of A). An *A-continuation* of (s, V) after p is a full schedule (s', V') involving the transactions in $\tau - \{A\}$ such that

(1) $p_{\tau - \{A\}}$ is a prefix of s',
(2) for all steps v of $p_{\tau - \{A\}}$ $V'(v) = V(v)$, unless v is a write step and $V(v)$ is a step of A, in which case $V'(v) = V(V(v))$, and
(3) for all read steps v of s' but not of p, and all write steps u of A in p, $V'(v) \neq V(u)$.

That is, an A-continuation of a full schedule after a prefix p (where it is implied that transaction A failed at the end of p) is a full schedule which has the same sequence of steps up to the point of failure (except, of course, that the steps of the failed transaction are missing), and a version function which is compatible with the given version function up to the point of the failure. Part (1) of the definition simply guarantees that the order of steps up to the failure does not change in the continuation; part (2) that no steps already executed at the point of failure are "redone" in a different way; and part (3) says that no write steps already overwritten by A at the time of failure are read by subsequent steps of the continuation. Notice that, if a read step of p is mapped by V to a step of an uncommitted transaction A (i.e., it is unsafe), or if a step of A except for the last overwrites the last available version of an entity (unsafe write), then no A-continuation after this step exists.

Definition 3.3 (Continued):   Now, for our definition of reliable full schedules: Let (s, V) be a full schedule and p a prefix of s. We shall define what it
means for (s, V) to be *reliable after p*. First, if $p = s$, then (s, V) is reliable
after p if it is view serializable. In all other cases, (s, V) is reliable after p if
it is view serializable, and furthermore the following is true for each prefix p'
extending p: For each transaction A which is uncommitted at the end of p',
there is an A-continuation of (s, V) after p' which is (recursively) reliable after
$p'_{\tau - \{A\}}$. A full schedule which is reliable after the empty prefix is called simply
reliable. $\square$

Example 3.9: This recursive definition appears to be necessary. One attempt
to simplify it would be to require that the continuation be simply view serializable (and thus get rid of the recursion). This is not enough. Consider the
schedule

$$
s = \begin{array}{ll}
A_1 : W(x) & \\
A_2 : \quad\quad R(x) & \quad\quad\quad R(y)W(y) \\
A_3 : \quad\quad\quad\quad W(y)W(x) & \\
A_4 : \quad\quad\quad\quad\quad\quad W(x) & \\
A_5 : & \quad\quad\quad\quad\quad W(x)
\end{array}
$$

with the version function V which agrees with the standard version function
in all steps, except that it maps $A_3 : W(y)$ to ν (thus rendering it safe). This
full schedule is equivalent to $A_3 A_4 A_1 A_2 A_5$ with the standard function, and is
consequently view serializable. It furthermore appears to be reliable: If any
transaction except for A_4 fails, then the projection of the full schedule to the
remaining transactions, with the standard version function, is a view serializable
continuation. If A_4 fails, then we can extend the rest of the schedule to the
following view serializable continuation (again, with the version function V'
which is identical to the standard one, except that it maps $A_3 : W(y)$ to ν)

$$
s' = \begin{array}{ll}
A_1 : W(x) & \\
A_2 : \quad\quad R(x) & \quad\quad\quad R(y)W(y) \\
A_3 : \quad\quad\quad\quad W(y)W(x) & \\
A_5 : & \quad\quad\quad W(x)
\end{array}
$$

In fact, (s', V') is essentially the only such continuation (we said "essentially"
because the variants in which the order of the last three steps is changed are
also view serializable continuations). The problem is that (s', V') *itself is not
reliable!* If *now* we abort A_5, then no view serializable continuation exists. In
fact, we can construct full schedules which are correct after some fixed number
of failures and continuations, but are unreliable in the next round (see Problem
3.4). Thus, the recursive nature of the definition appears to be inherent. $\square$

3.3 THE COMPLEXITY OF RELIABILITY

If the definition is any indication, reliability is probably a criterion even more involved and difficult to check than view serializability. Indeed, we shall prove in this section that testing whether a schedule is reliable is a problem complete for a complexity class even broader than NP, namely, the class PSPACE containing all computational problems that can be solved using a polynomial amount of space.

Let us first convince ourselves that this class is indeed very broad. It clearly contains P, since in a polynomial amount of time it is impossible to use up more than a polynomial amount of space. But PSPACE also contains NP. To see this, recall that NP is the class of all computational problems which, given some input, ask about the existence of some "certificate" related to the input in a way that can be checked in polynomial time. The idea is that, in polynomial space, we can test all possible such objects, one after the other, reusing the space required (this argument can be made rigorous, see the References).

Thus, $P \subset NP \subset PSPACE$. In fact, there is a strong belief that both inclusions are strict. Typical members of PSPACE that are not known or believed to be in NP are certain computational problems related to *two-person games*. In these problems we are given an initial game configuration, more or less like a position in chess, and two players are to take turns making moves, according to some rules. The rules guarantee that the game lasts only for a number of moves which is at most a polynomial in the size of the input (the initial configuration). The question is whether, say, the first player has a winning strategy. Such a problem is in PSPACE because in polynomial space we can check all possible plays and decide whether a winning strategy for the first player exists. However, generally speaking this strategy is in general an exponentially long object, as it must contain replies to exponentially many possible positions, and thus cannot serve as a proof that the problem is in NP.

We call a problem PSPACE-complete, in analogy with NP-completeness, if it belongs in PSPACE, and all problems in PSPACE can be reduced to it. A particular problem that is known to be PSPACE-complete is the problem of *quantified satisfiability* or QSAT. In this problem we are given a *quantified Boolean formula*, that is, an object of the form $\forall x_1 \exists x_2 \forall x_3 \ldots \exists x_{2n} B(x_1, \ldots, x_{2n})$, where $B(x_1, \ldots, x_{2n})$ is a Boolean formula in conjunctive normal form. We are asked whether the whole formula is satisfiable, that is, whether for all choices of truth values for x_1 there is a choice of truth value for x_2, such that for all choices for x_3, etc., and finally there is a choice for x_{2n} which leaves all clauses of F with at least one true literal. QSAT can indeed be thought as a two-person game, played between an EXISTENTIAL player and a UNIVERSAL player, who take turns setting the values of even and odd variables, respectively. The EXISTENTIAL player tries to make the formula true, while UNIVERSAL tries to make it false. The question is whether EXISTENTIAL has a winning strategy. As mentioned above, this problem is known to be PSPACE-complete.

Interestingly, we can also think of reliability as a two-person game. The board is now a schedule. An EVIL player tries to harm the correctness of the schedule by selectively aborting transactions, while a GOOD player tries to reinstate correctness, by finding appropriate continuations. This connection can be made rigorous, as the following result, our main result in this section, implies.

Theorem 3.6: *The problem of determining whether a full schedule is reliable is PSPACE-complete.*

The balance of this section is devoted to the proof of Theorem 3.6. It is quite simple to argue that the reliability problem can indeed be solved using only a polynomial amount of space: Given a schedule, all possible "plays" of the game between GOOD and EVIL can be examined one by one, reusing space after each play. Having examined all plays, we can determine which of the two players has a winning strategy. It is easy to se that the necessary bookkeeping requires only polynomial space.

The "Gadget"

In the course of this proof, we shall need the notion of the *polygraph associated with a full schedule* (s, V) *at time* t. Recall that a polygraph is a set of nodes, together with a set of *arcs* (ordered pairs of distinct nodes) and a set of *choices* (ordered triples of distinct nodes). Let (s, V) be a full schedule. As usual, we identify "time" with the steps of s (i.e., the first step takes place at time 1, the second at time 2, etc.). The polygraph of (s, V) at time t, $P_t(s, V)$, where t is an integer, has as its nodes the transactions that have started (and possibly finished) by time t. Let s_t be the prefix of s up to time t, and V_t be the version function V restricted to the steps of s_t. By a *completion* of (s_t, V_t) we mean any full schedule which agrees with (s, V) up to time t, and then executes in some order the remaining steps of the transactions that are active at t, assigning some legal version to each step. We have an arc from A to B in the polygraph $P_t(s, V)$ if A must come before B in *any* serial schedule which is view equivalent with some completion of (s_t, V_t). There are three types of arcs (A, B) (see Figures 3.2 and 3.3 for an example of a schedule s and the polygraph $P_t(s, V_s)$):

(1) If B reads an entity x from A, then clearly there is an arc (A, B) in the polygraph (example: arc (F, G) in Figure 3.3).

(2) There is also an arc (A, B) if A reads or writes x, B subsequently writes x, and furthermore the version written by B is the only one available at time t, and no other tran(saction writes x later on (example: arc (C, D) in Figure 3.3, because of entity f).

(3) If A reads the initial value of an entity, and B writes the entity, then there

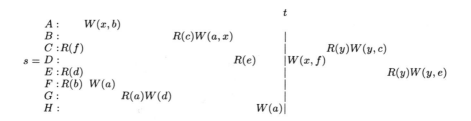

Figure 3.2. The Schedule s.

must be an arc (A, B).

Note that one of the steps that gives rise to an arc may not have occurred at time t. For example, the arc (C, D) is present because no other transaction besides D will write entity f after time t. On the other hand, there is no arc between C and E, because at time t we do not know which will read and write y last. However, since C and E both read and write y, we know that at least one of the arcs (C, E) and (E, C) will be added (this is denoted by the undirected edge with the question mark). Also, notice that there is no arc (A, B), as D may overwrite x and destroy this precedence.

The choices of $P_t(s, V)$ are triples, such as (G, B, F) in Figure 3.3, such that, in any serial schedule view equivalent to some continuation of (s, V) after t, G must come after F, and B either before F or after G (since G reads a from F, and B writes a). Choices are shown as pairs of dotted arcs, as in Figure 3.3).

In Figure 3.3 we show $P_t(s, V_s)$, where s is as in Figure 3.2. For clarity we have omitted node H (a sink with no outgoing arcs or choices, and thus irrelevant to the argument that follows). We have also used the notation $W(x, y, z)$ for consecutive write steps of the same transaction.

The issue of reliability for the schedule s in Figure 3.2, with the standard version function, is worth explaining, because it seems to encapsulate the difficulty of reliability, and lies at the heart of the argument in the proof. By inspecting the polygraph associated with (s, V_s) at time t we can conclude the following:

(1) If D is aborted, then the arc (A, B) is added to the graph (D may no longer overwrite x). This forces the choice (G, B) (that is, G must come before B), and thus the write step of C must come *after* that of E in any view serializable continuation.

(2) If D is not aborted, then the choice (B, F) is the only one that leaves the graph acyclic, and thus the write step of C must come *before* that of E. As a consequence, the right order of the write steps of C and E depends

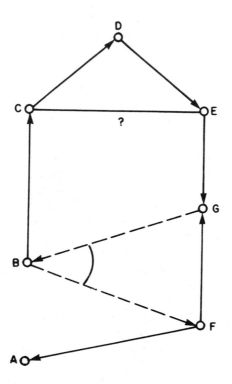

Figure 3.3. The Polygraph $P_t(s, V_s)$.

on whether D will abort or not; there is no continuation good for both eventu-
alities. Let us note, for future reference, that, up to the dotted line (i.e., until
transaction D starts) the full schedule has a conflict multiversion serializable
completion.

Our proof relies heavily on a "gadget" which is an elaboration on that in
Figures 3.2 and 3.3. In Figure 3.4 we show a schedule s_1 of 15 transactions. We
assume the standard version function, except that at each transaction all write
steps except for the last one are mapped to ν (this is necessary for reliability);
we call the resulting version function *quasi-standard*, and denote it by V'_{s_1}. The
transactions D, C, and E are "distinguished", in that they shall play a central

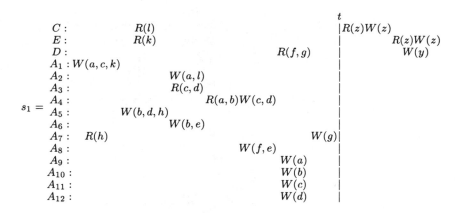

$$
s_1 =
\begin{array}{ll}
C: & R(l) & \hspace{4cm} t \\[-0.3ex]
 & & \hspace{4cm} |R(z)W(z) \\
E: & R(k) & \hspace{5cm} R(z)W(z) \\
D: & & R(f,g) \hspace{3cm} W(y) \\
A_1: W(a,c,k) & & \\
A_2: & W(a,l) & \\
A_3: & R(c,d) & \\
A_4: & & R(a,b)W(c,d) \\
A_5: & W(b,d,h) & \\
A_6: & W(b,e) & \\
A_7: R(h) & & W(g)| \\
A_8: & & W(f,e) \\
A_9: & & W(a) \\
A_{10}: & & W(b) \\
A_{11}: & & W(c) \\
A_{12}: & & W(d) \\
\end{array}
$$

Figure 3.4. The Schedule s_1.

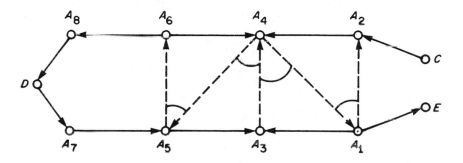

Figure 3.5. The Polygraph $P_t(s_1, V'_{s_1})$.

role in the argument that follows. Notice that after time t, the transactions C and E read and write a common entity, not accessed by any other transaction. Steps which are in the same vertical line in Figure 3.4 may take place in any order, as they do not conflict. In Figure 3.5 we show the polygraph of this full schedule at the time indicated by the broken line. We have labeled the arcs and the choices by the entities that caused them. We have omitted from this figure transactions A_9, A_{10}, A_{11}, A_{12}. These transactions serve to overwrite the entities a, b, c, d which cause the choices; they are sinks (have no outgoing arcs), and therefore do not help create any paths or cycles on the graph. At time t (the broken line of Figure 3.4) the only active transactions are C, D, and E.

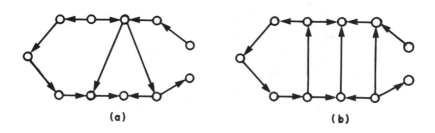

Figure 3.6. Two Orientations of the Polygraph $P_t(s_1, V'_{s_1})$.

The schedule s_1 of Figure 3.4 is view serializable. In Figure 3.6(a) we show an acyclic orientation of the polygraph in Figure 3.5. Actually, this is the only acyclic orientation: The path from A_6 to A_5 forces us to choose the arc (A_4, A_5) from choice b; then we cannot choose (A_3, A_4) in choices d and c; we must keep (A_4, A_1) and not (A_1, A_2). Note that a path from C to E is forced. Thus, in any serial schedule equivalent to s_1, C must come before E. However, there is no directed path between D and either C or E.

If transaction D is aborted, then the remaining polygraph has another acyclic orientation, shown in Figure 3.6(b). In this orientation there is no directed path between C and E, and thus either order is possible.

Furthermore, the full schedule s_1 of Figure 3.4, with the quasi-standard version function, is reliable. Until the moment that D starts, conflict serializability is observed (the acyclic conflict graph is the one shown in Figure 3.6(b)). After D starts, we can choose the orientation in Figure 3.6(a) or (b), depending on whether D aborts or not; there is no need for any rearrangement.

Our main gadget in the proof of Theorem 3.6 is a schedule s_2 composed of two copies s_1 and s'_1 of the schedule of Figure 3.4. In s'_1 we add primes to all entities and transactions, which are distinct from those of s_1, except that $C' = E$ and $E' = C$. The two copies run in parallel. At the end of s_2, the only active transactions are D, D', C, and E. We assume that none of the entities that have been accessed so far are written by any of these transactions, with the important exception that entity e' is in the write set of D. As a consequence, the polygraph does not have an arc (A'_6, A'_8) labeled e' (the final value of e' is written by D', not A'_8), but rather has arcs (A'_6, D) and (A'_8, D) labeled e'. The polygraph at the end of s_2 is shown in Figure 3.7 (again, omitting the transactions A_9 to A_{12}, and A'_9 to A'_{12}).

Schedule s_2 is also view serializable. As we explained before, we have to choose for the unprimed (left-hand) copy the orientation of Figure 3.6(a) for the choices. This causes the path from C to E, and forces the orientation of Figure 3.6(b) for the primed (right-hand) copy. Note that this is possible because the

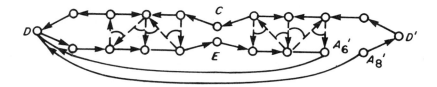

Figure 3.7. The Polygraph $P_t(s_2, V'_{s_2})$.

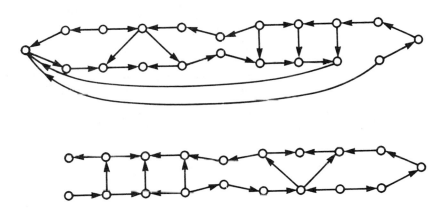

Figure 3.8. Two Orientations of the Polygraph $P_t(s_2, V'_{s_2})$.

right-hand copy does not have the arc (A'_6, A'_8). Thus, the overall polygraph has only one acyclic orientation as shown in Figure 3.8(a). In this forced orientation there is a path from C to E. The only other path between the distinguished nodes D, D', C, and E is from D' to D.

If transaction D aborts, the polygraph acquires an arc (A'_6, A'_8), because A'_8 writes the final value of e'. Thus, the right-hand copy of s_1 is "turned on," while the left copy is "turned off". The right copy must choose the orientation of Figure 3.6(a), and the left that in 3.5(b). In Figure 3.8(b) we show the overall orientation that is forced if D is aborted. Notice that there is no path between D' and either E or C. If both D and D' abort, then both parts must choose the orientation in Figure 3.6(b), and there is no path between C and E. Thus, s_2 is reliable.

To summarize, s_2 has the following properties:
(1) If D is not aborted, then there is a path from C to E.
(2) If D is aborted and D' is not, then there is a path from E to C.
(3) If both D and D' are aborted, then either order between C and E is possible.
Because of these properties, in order to ensure reliability, the write step of

D must come before the read-write steps of C and E (assuming no transaction has been aborted). Recall that C and E read and write a common entity which no other transaction writes; thus the order of these steps determines whether C must come before E or vice-versa. If the write step of C comes before those of D and E, then EVIL can abort D after the write step of C (without aborting D') and win. If the write step of E comes before those of C and D, then EVIL does not have to do anything; the schedule is not view-serializable.

Schedule s_2 will be our workhorse in the PSPACE-completeness proof of reliability. We call D and D' the *input terminals* of s_2; C and E are the *output terminals*.

The Reduction

We shall next reduce to reliability the PSPACE-complete problem QSAT. Suppose that we are given a formula of the form

$$F = \forall x_1 \exists x_2 \ldots \exists x_{2n} [C_1 \wedge C_2 \wedge \ldots \wedge C_m],$$

where the C_j's are the clauses of the Boolean formula, each containing three literals, and we are asked whether the formula F is true.   From the formula F we shall construct a schedule $s(F)$ such that $(s(F), V'_{s(F)})$ is reliable if and only if F is true.

For every variable x_i we have two transactions D_i and D'_i. A move of the EVIL player in the reliability game will correspond to a move of the UNIVERSAL player in the QSAT game as follows: Setting a universal variable x_i to **true** corresponds to abortion of D_i, while setting x_i to **false** corresponds to an abortion of D'_i (at a certain appropriate time). We shall have a device to ensure that EVIL aborts exactly one of D_i, D'_i for all odd i (otherwise GOOD wins regardless of whether F is true or not).

A move by EXISTENTIAL in QSAT is simulated by GOOD in the reliability game as follows. For each even i (existential variable x_i) transactions D_i and D'_i read and write a common entity which no other transaction writes. Thus, the order of those write steps determines the final value of this entity. After EVIL aborts D_{i-1} or D'_{i-1}, GOOD can rearrange the order in which D_i and D'_i read and write; D_i before D'_i corresponds to $x_i = $ **true**, and the opposite order corresponds to $x_i = $ **false**.

The schedule $s(F)$ has a large initial portion which "sets the stage" for the reliability game. During that portion, if EVIL makes a move (i.e., aborts a transaction) then GOOD has a guaranted win. We shall first describe the schedule by its polygraph after the stage has been set. The schedule and its polygraph are composed of several parts:

(1) A part that forces EVIL to abort D_i or D'_i for each odd i.
(2) A part for each clause, such that a cycle will be formed if all literals are false.

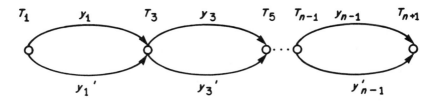

Figure 3.9. The Potential Path from T_1 to T_{n+1}.

(3) "Fan-out" gadgets for each variable x_i, which distribute the truth value from D_i, D_i' to the occurrences in the clauses.

(4) "Precedence" gadgets, which force the right order of play.

Let us now describe each part separately. For part (1), we have transactions $T_1, T_3, \ldots, T_{n-1}$ corresponding to the universal variables, and a transaction T_{n+1}. There is a *potential path* from T_1 to T_{n+1}, as in Figure 3.9 (read on why it is "potential"). The arcs of the figure are write-write, that is, T_1 reads y_1 and y_1', then T_3 writes y_1, y_1', y_3, y_3', T_5 writes y_3, y_3', y_5, y_5', and so on. These arcs, however, are not present in the polygraph, for the following reason: For each odd i, the final value of y_i is finally overwritten by D_i, and that of y_i' by D_i'. Thus, if for some odd i EVIL does not abort one of D_i, D_i', then the path from T_1 to T_{n+1} is broken; and EVIL needs this path inorder to win (create a cycle).

In (2), for each clause we have a potential path back from T_{n+1} to T_1, as shown in Figure 3.10. The path is composed of four arcs and three undirected edges; each undirected edge corresponds to a literal in the clause. For each arc and edge, the entity labeling it is unique to its endpoints, that is, no other transaction reads or writes it. Each arc is a read-write arc, that is, the tail of the arc reads the initial value of the entity, and then the head writes a new value of the entity. The undirected edges correspond to write-write conflicts that take place at the final part of the schedule, and are resolved in a way that reflects the truth values of the variables. Eventually, all edges will be directed one way or the other. If they all become directed in the direction from T_{n+1} to T_1, corresponding to all literals in the clause being false, then a path from T_{n+1} to T_1 will result. This path, together with the potential path from T_1 to T_{n+1} path from part (1), will form a cycle.

For part (3), we have different fan-out gadgets for universal and existential variables. For a universal variable x_i we use schedule s_2. That is, for every occurrence of x_i or $\bar{x}_i$ in a clause C_j, we have a distinct copy of s_2. Nodes D and D' of s_2 are identified with nodes D_i and D_i', and nodes C and E of s_2 are identified with the endpoints of the undirected edge that corresponds to the occurrence of x_i in C_j. For a positive occurrence, C is identified with the

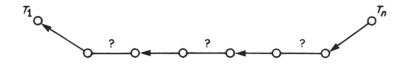

Figure 3.10. The Path Corresponding to a Clause.

node that is closer to T_{n+1}, and for a negative occurrence it is identified with the endpoint that is closer to T_1. In either case, when EVIL chooses a truth value for x_i (aborts D_i or D_i'), GOOD is forced to give a consistent direction to all edges, in order to keep the graph acyclic: If the literal is false, then the edge is directed towards T_1; if it is true, the edge is directed away from T_1, thus breaking this potential path from T_{n+1} to T_1.

For existential variables, we use a variant of s_1 as our fan-out gadget. In this variant, denote it $\bar{s}_1$, the read set of D is empty; the entities f and g are in the write set of D, the broken line is moved right after transactions A_9 through A_{12} write, and the order in which D and A_7 write their common entity is left unspecified (refer to Figure 3.4). The polygraph of $\bar{s}_1$ at its broken line is almost identical to that of s_1 (Figure 3.5). There is still an arc (A_8, D) labeled f (now it is a write-write arc). The only difference is that we do not have the arc (D, A_7). Instead, there is an undirected edge, the orientation of which is to be determined by the order in which D and A_7 write g. If D writes g before A_7, then the gadget is "turned on" and C must precede E (as in Figure 3.6(a)). However, if A_7 writes g before D, then the gadget is "turned off"; we can choose the acyclic orientation in Figure 3.6(b), which does not force an order between C and E. Notice that, in either case, there are no paths from D to A_7 and from C to E.

For each occurrence of an existential variable x_i (i even) or its negation in a clause, we have a distinct copy of $\bar{s}_1$ connecting nodes D_i and D_i' to the nodes of the edge that corresponds to the literal occurrence in the clause part. Node C of $\bar{s}_1$ is identified with that node of the edge which is closer to T_{n+1}, whereas node E with the other one. For a positive occurrence of x_i node D of the copy of $\bar{s}_1$ is identified with D_i' and node A_7 of $\bar{s}_1$ with D_i; for a negative occurrence, D is identified with D_i and A_7 with D_i'.

Suppose that GOOD sets x_i to **true**, that is, orders the write step of D_i before D_i'. Then, for every occurence of $\bar{x}_i$, the copy of $\bar{s}_1$ will be turned on and force C before E; i.e., the corresponding edge in the clause part will be directed from T_{n+1} to T_1. The gadgets corresponding to the positive occurrence will be turned off, this means that GOOD may choose to direct the corresponding edges so that the potential path from T_{n+1} to T_1 is broken. The case in which

GOOD sets x_i to **false** is symmetric.

Finally let us specify (4), the precedence gadgets. For every pair of consecutive variables x_i, x_{i+1} we have gadgets which force the write steps of D_i and D_i' to come before the write steps of D_{i+1} and D_{i+1}', if the schedule is to be reliable. For example, to force the write step of D_i to come before that of D_{i+1}, we have a copy of s_2 (with a small alteration to be described in a moment) whose node D is identified with D_i and node C with D_{i+1}. The other two terminals of s_2 are ordinary transactions, but D' has empty write set, and E has in its write set one entity which is also written by D_{i+1} (terminal C), and no other transaction. We have similar copies of s_2 for the other three pairs $(D_i, D_{i+1}'), (D_i', D_{i+1}), (D_i', D_{i+1}')$. The purpose of these gadgets is to place restrictions on the ways that GOOD can rearrange after an abort, so that the rules of the QSAT game are not violated. To illustrate this point, suppose that our formula F is $\forall x_1 \exists x_2 \forall x_3 \exists x_4 B$, where B is a conjunction of clauses. After EVIL chooses a value for x_1, GOOD could rearrange the schedule to in effect transform the formula to $\forall x_1 \forall x_3 \exists x_2 \exists x_4 B$, that is, allow herself to look at EVIL's next move. These last gadgets prevent GOOD from cheating in this way; if she does, EVIL wins right away, even if F is true.

We will describe now how the various parts are put together in the schedule $s(F)$. First let us summarize the transactions in $s(F)$. We have transactions $T_1, T_3, \ldots, T_{n+1}$ from part (1), and transactions belonging to various gadgets—copies of s_2 or $\bar{s}_1$. The various gadgets use distinct entities and transactions unless we have specified otherwise. Each gadget communicates with the rest of the world only through its terminals D, D', C, E for s_2, and D, A_7, C, E for $\bar{s}_1$. Note that the terminals perform only read-steps in s_2 or $\bar{s}_1$.

The first portion of $s(F)$ executes all the steps of all the gadgets from parts (3) and (4), and also the read steps that are responsible for the arcs on the clause paths of part (2). The only nodes that belong to more than one gadget are the transactions D_i, D_i' corresponding to the variables; note that each intermediate node in a clause path belongs to exactly one fan-out gadget. Nodes D_i and D_i' belong to several fan-out and precedence gadgets. Once we synchronize the read-steps of the D_i's and D_i''s, then we can add easily (and independently of each other) the steps of the other transactions in the different gadgets. From Figure 3.4 we see that in s_2, the read steps of C and E come before the read steps of D and D'. Therefore, because of the precedence gadgets, we must have the read steps of D_n, D_n' before those of D_{n-1}, D_{n-1}' before .... the read steps of D_1, D_1'. This is the only restriction: In s_2, either order between the read steps of D and D' is permitted; in $\bar{s}_1$, D does not read anything. Thus, the fan-out gadgets do not require any particular order between the read steps of D_i and D_i'.

Thus, in the first portion of $s(F)$, we execute in a consistent order all the copies of s_2 and $\bar{s}_1$, and then T_{n+1} executes its read step. At this point, parts

(2), (3), and (4) have been formed.

In the second portion of $s(F), T_1, T_3, T_5, \ldots, T_{n+1}$ execute their write steps in this order. Now, part (1) is also formed, and the stage is ready for the game.

In the third portion of $s(F)$ we execute the write steps of the transactions D_i, D'_i in order of increasing i's, with D'_i immediately preceding D_i. After this, we execute the write steps of the dummy (output) terminals of the precedence gadgets.

Finally, in the fourth and final portion of $s(F)$, the transactions that correspond to literal occurrences (intermediate nodes on the clause paths) execute their write steps in an order consistent with a truth assignment that sets all variables to false. The construction of $s(F)$ is thus complete. It remains to be shown that $(s(F), V'_{s(F)})$ is reliable if and only if F is true.

First, we shall show that $s(F)$ is view serializable. That is, the polygraph of the whole schedule has an acyclic orientation. Since all transactions D_i, D'_i are present, there is no path from T_1 to T_{n+1} in part (1). Therefore, the clause paths cannot form a cycle. This means that the formula F plays no role, and the various gadgets are completely decoupled. (Note how crucial it is here that there are no directed paths between the input and the output terminals of the gadgets.)

In each gadget s_2, the fact that the input terminal D is present forces the order C, E; this is the reason that we placed the dummy outputs of the precedence gadgets after the D_i's and D'_i's, and also that we use a default value of **false** (D_i present) for universal variables x_i. For existential variables x_i, we have D'_i before D_i, corresponding to $x_i = $ **false**, and this is correctly distributed to the clause parts.

Schedule $s(F)$ is reliable during the first two portions, in the sense that, if EVIL makes a move (aborts a transaction) before the end of the second portion, then GOOD can find a reliable continuation; and this, regardless of the truth value of F. The reason is that until the second portion, there is no potential path from T_1 to T_{n+1}. Thus, again, the paths of the clauses cannot close a cycle, and the different gadgets are completely decoupled. GOOD can win, because each individual gadget is reliable.

The third portion of the schedule is the crucial one. We shall show that $(s(F), V'_{s(F)})$ is reliable if and only if F is true.

First for the *if* direction, suppose that F is true, i.e., the existential player has a winning strategy in QSAT. We shall show that GOOD has a winning strategy in the reliability game. Throughout the game, the current schedule resulting from GOOD's moves (rearrangements) has the following invariant:

(i) For each copy of s_2 and $\bar{s}_1$, the order of the write steps of the output terminals satisfies the serializability constraints, and

(ii) For each copy of s_2, the reliability constraints are satisfied.

In (i), by "serializability constraint" we mean the ordering that may be forced between the output terminals. In case of s_2, these are given by properties (1)-(3); for example, if D is present then C must be before E. In case of $\bar{s}_1$, the constraint is that if the write step of D comes before that of A_7) then the read-write steps of C must come before those of E. By "reliability constraints" in (ii), we mean that the write step of the input terminal D of s_2 comes before the write steps of the output terminals. Note that the invariant is true of our initial schedule $s(F)$.

After every move of EVIL, GOOD will do whatever rearrangements are necessary to restore the invariant. In particular, if EVIL aborts a transaction D_i, then GOOD will move the write steps of the dummy output terminals of the precedence gadgets for the pairs (D_i, D_{i+1}), (D_i, D'_{i+1}) right before the write steps of D_{i+1} and D'_{i+1} respectively. In addition, if x_i is a universal variable, GOOD will reorder the write steps of the transactions corresponding to the occurrences of x_i and $\bar{x}_i$ in the clauses, to be consistent with $x_i = $ **true**. At all times, the write steps of all the nodes on the clause paths will be in the final (fourth) portion of the schedule. Similar rearrangements will be made by GOOD if a D'_i is aborted. Note that after the end of the second portion, all dummy input terminals of the precedence gadgets have terminated, and therefore, cannot be aborted anymore.

Given this invariant, the only cycle that EVIL can possibly force is one involving a path from T_1 to T_{n+1} of part (1) and a path from T_{n+1} to T_1 resulting from some clause of part (2). Therefore, if EVIL wants to have a chance at winning, he cannot pass up a chance of choosing a truth value for a universal variable. That is, if for some odd i, both D_i and D'_i perform their write steps, without EVIL having aborted either of them, then GOOD has won: The path from T_1 to T_{n+1} of part (1) is broken, and cannot be restored any more.

We will describe now how GOOD responds to EVIL's moves before the write steps of D'_i and D_1 take place. As we mentioned before, there is no danger during the first two portions. After that, the only active transactions are the ones corresponding to the variables (D_i, D'_i), the ones corresponding to literal occurrences and the dummy output terminals of the precedence gadgets. In fact, we can assume that EVIL does not abort a transaction except D_1, D'_1. Here is why: If EVIL aborts a transaction corresponding to a literal occurrence, then what he has done is to effectively forfeit the possibility of creating a cycle at the clause of the occurrence. Clearly this is a suboptimal move for EVIL, and we can assume it is not made. If EVIL aborts a dummy terminal, then he has destroyed the functionality of a precedence gadget. This implies that GOOD has the opportunity to rearrange future moves at will, a possibility that is also against EVIL's interests. If EVIL aborts some D_i or D'_i for $i \neq 1$, then GOOD restores the serializability and reliability constraints for the gadgets that are affected, as we described before, and does nothing else. This has the effect of EVIL committing to a subsequent move beforehand (i odd), or allowing GOOD to satisfy all clauses in which either x_i or $\bar{x}_i$ appear (i even). Thus, we can assume that EVIL aborts either D_1 or D_1'.

Suppose EVIL aborts D_1, corresponding to $x_1 = $ **true**. GOOD sets the truth value of the existential variable x_2 according to the move of the existential player in response to the value of x_1, That is, GOOD possibly switches the write steps of D_2' and D_2 (if $x_2 = $ **true**); she also fan-outs the truth values to the clauses, and restores the serializability and realiability constraints of the affected gadgets. If EVIL aborts D_1', then GOOD responds in a symmetric way.

Subsequently, GOOD moves in exactly the same way: If x_i is the earliest universal variable whose value is still undetermined (both D_i and D_i' are present), GOOD waits until EVIL sets the value of x_i, making sure in the meantime only that the invariant is preserved. When EVIL sets the value of x_i, GOOD sets appropriately the value of x_{i+1} and continues similarly. Since F is true, all clauses will be eventually satisfied, and therefore no cycle will be formed.

Now for the *only if* direction: Suppose that F is false; i.e., the universal player has a winning strategy in QSAT. First, we observe that GOOD must move so that the invariant is continuously satisfied: If the serialibility constraint of some gadget is violated, then the schedule is not serializable (the graph has a cycle) and EVIL has won; if a reliability constraint is violated, then EVIL can win in one more step (the schedule is not reliable, as we explained earlier).

EVIL follows the moves of the universal player. He starts by aborting D_1 or D_1' (according to whether $x_1 = $ **true** or **false**) right before the write step of D_1'. The precedence gadgets force GOOD to retain the order between transactions corresponding to different variables. GOOD has the freedom to switch any number of adjacent pairs of write steps of transactions D_i', D_i. Now, EVIL observes the value of x_2 chosen by GOOD, and correspondingly sets x_3, by aborting D_3 or D_3' right before they finish.

Note that now the values of x_1, x_2, x_3 have been set once and for all; GOOD cannot switch the write steps of D_2 and D_2' any more. Because of the serializability constraints, GOOD must propagate the values to the clauses in a consistent way.

EVIL continues playing in this way until he sets properly all universal variables. Since F is false, some clause is not satisfied. The path from T_{n+1} to T_1 of this clause, together with the path from T_1 to T_{n+1} of part (1) forms a cycle. $\square$

When interpreting a PSPACE-completeness result such as Theorem 3.6, one should not forget that NP-complete and PSPACE-complete problems have an important property in common: The best algorithm known for either kind of problems is exponential. Thus, there is no immediate sense in which the

PSPACE-complete problems are harder than the NP-complete ones. Of course, there is always the theoretical possibility that all NP-complete problems can be solvable in polynomial time, whereas PSPACE-complete problems cannot; but the first part of the statement is considered so unlikely that this point is of no real interest. Still, Theorem 3.6 does imply that, in some sense, reliability is "harder" than view serializability. We have been interpreting NP-completeness as evidence that the problem is "nasty," and mathematically "ill-behaved." Well, PSPACE-completeness is considered much stronger such evidence. A PSPACE-complete problem is equivalent to any two-person game, and these games comprise some of the most intricate and puzzling mathematical objects ever studied, and therefore conceptually even nastier and more opaque than the NP-complete problems. In Chapter 6 we shall see another example of PSPACE-completeness this time related to *distibuted* concurrency control.

Conflicts and Reliability

It turns out that even reliability becomes considerably simpler in the context of conflict serializable schedules. As a result, in practice schedulers can ensure the reliability of their output without dealing with the complexities of PSPACE-completeness. We discuss this issue next.

Let us call a full schedule *conservative* if it has no unsafe reads or writes (recall the discussion after Example 3.7). More formally, a full schedule (s, V) is conservative if for each read step r, $V(r)$ belongs to a transaction committed at r; and for each $W(x)$ step w which is not the last step of its transaction, $V(w) = w'$ implies that there is another $W(x)$ step w'' coming after w' in s whose transaction has committed at w, and such that no other write step before w is mapped by V to w''. In other words, a schedule is conservative if all read steps read committed versions, and no write step overwrites the latest committed version of an entity. Notice that if a schedule contains a transaction with more than one write step, then automatically its standard version function is not conservative (but its quasi-standard version function may be). It turns out that not all reliable schedules are conservative (Problem 3.4). Also, we noticed in Example 3.8 that a conservative schedule may not be reliable. On the other hand, it is easy to see that schedule s' in Example 4.8 is not conflict serializable either. As we shall see next, for conflict serializable schedules, being conservative is enough to guarantee reliability.

Theorem 3.7: *Let s be a conflict serializable schedule, and V a version function which agrees with the standard one V_s on all read steps. Then (s, V) is reliable if it is conservative.*

Proof: The proof is by induction on the cardinality of the set τ of transactions of s. The statement is trivial when τ contains just one transaction. Suppose now that s has at least two transactions. For each prefix p of s and a transaction

$A \in \tau$, uncommitted at p, we can define the A-continuation of (s, V) from p to be (s', V'), where $s' = s_{\tau - \{A\}}$, the projection of s on the remaining transactions, and V' is defined as follows: For r a read step of s' but not of p, $V'(r) = V_{s'}(r)$; for w a write step of s' not in p, $V'(w) = \nu$. For a read step r of s' and p, $V'(r) = V(r)$ (since (s, V) is conservative, we know that $V(r)$ is not a step of A). Finally, for a write step w of s' and p, $V'(w) = V(w)$, unless the latter is a step of A, in which case $V'(w) = V(V(w))$.

To check that (s', V') is an A-continuation of s after p, condition (1) of Definition 3.3 is trivially satisfied, and condition (2) is a consequence of the definition of V'. To show that the continuation is reliable, notice that s' is conflict serializable (since it is the projection of a conflict serializable schedule, recall Theorem 2.10 and the preceding discussion), and that V' agrees with $V_{s'}$ on the read steps. It follows from our induction hypothesis that (s', V') is reliable. $\square$

In some of the earlier literature on concurrency control, a somewhat restricted model of transactions and schedules was assumed. In this model, each transaction consists of a sequence of (zero or more) read steps, followed by an *atomic write step*. This step writes several entities *simultaneously*, in an indivisible manner. A typical schedule in this model looks like this:

$$
\begin{array}{lll}
A_1 : R(x) & R(y)W(x, y) & \\
A_2 : & R(y) & R(x)W(x, z) \\
A_3 : & & W(y)
\end{array}
$$

We denote by $W(x, y)$ the atomic write step on entities x and y. As usual, we call a transaction in a schedule in the atomic write model *committed* at some step of the schedule if it has executed its last (write) step at this point. The interesting observation is that in the atomic write model *all schedules are conservative* when considered as full schedules with the standard version function. This is because every read step reads from committed transactions (since uncommitted transactions are those which have written nothing at all), and no write step is unsafe (because each write step *is* the last step of its transaction).

Corollary: *In the atomic write model, (s, V_s) is reliable if it is conflict serializable.* $\square$

As we shall see in the next chapter, Theorem 3.7 and its corollary are very helpful in designing reliable schedulers, that is, algorithms which transform any input schedule into a reliable output schedule. The point is that, in practice, schedulers output only conflict serializable schedules anyway. Thus, if such a scheduler only outputs conservative schedules, or schedules of transactions in the atomic write model, then it is guaranteed to be reliable as well.

3.4 ROLLBACK RELIABILITY

When a transaction fails, we must somehow pick up the pieces and continue. So far we have assumed that the only possible reaction to a transaction failure is to rearrange the as of yet unscheduled steps of the active transactions in order to produce a correct schedule. Suppose, however, that we also have the option to rearrange steps that have *already been scheduled*. Of course, for this to be possible, the corresponding transactions must be active at the time of failure. This is tantamount to *rolling back* these transactions before the corresponding steps, presumably in order to redo them in a manner that is more correct, in the light of the new situation. As an extreme case, the scheduler might even *abort* a transaction in response to another abort; this is equivalent to rolling back the transaction to its beginning, in order to redo it in the end of the schedule.

The rollback option is potentially very costly, as such rollbacks and aborts can cascade, and necessitate similar rollbacks on other transactions (for example, if a transaction has already read the value written by an undone step). On the other hand, if rolling back active transactions is among the possible responses to a transaction failure, this would presumably relax our notion of reliable full schedules. In this section we study this new concept of reliability.

Example 3.10: Consider the following schedule

$$s = \begin{array}{l} A_1 : W(y) \qquad\; W(x) \\ A_2 : \qquad R(y) \qquad\quad W(z) \end{array}$$

with the version function which agrees with the standard one in everything, except that it maps $A_1 : W(y)$ to ν thus rendering this write step safe. The read step $A_2 : R(y)$ is still unsafe. This, however, is no problem, if rolling back transactions is among our options. If A_1 fails after the first step of A_2, we can now respond by redoing the read step of A_2 as well, assigning to it the original version of y (which is available, since $V(A_1 : W(y)) = \nu$). The corresponding full schedule, consisting only of the transaction A_2, is certainly correct.

The same cannot be said of the following variant of s

$$s' = \begin{array}{l} A_1 : W(y) \qquad\qquad\; W(x) \\ A_2 : \qquad R(y)W(z) \end{array}$$

The problem is that, if A_1 aborts after the second step of A_2, the latter transaction has already committed, and there is no way that we can abort it as well. In s' transaction A_2 is committed at a time at which A_1, from which A_2 has read an entity, is not yet committed; we call this an *unsafe commit*. Evidently, unsafe commits are sources of unreliability, even when we are allowed to redo and/or abort transactions in response to failures. □

We shall next define our notion of reliability when transaction aborts are allowed.

Definition 3.4:   Let (s, V) be a full schedule involving a set τ of transactions, p a prefix of s, and $A \in \tau$ a transaction of s uncommitted at the end of p. Let σ denote the set of all transactions in τ committed at the end of p. A *rollback A-continuation of* (s, V) *after* p is a full schedule (s', V') involving the transactions in $\tau - \{A\}$, such that there is a prefix p' of s' which is a subsequence of p, and satisfies the following properties:

(1) $p_\sigma = p'_\sigma$,

(2) for all steps v of p' $V'(v) = V(v)$, unless v is a write step and $V(v)$ is a step not in p' or the initial transaction A_0, in which case $V'(v) = V(V(v))$, or $V(V(V(v)))$, and so on, until the image is λ, ν, or a step of p' or A_0, and

(3) for all read steps v of s' but not of p', and all write steps u in p, $V'(v) \neq V(u)$.

In other words, committed transactions are not rolled back, but all others may, and p' contains all steps that are not redone. p' is called *the stable part* of the continuation. We next define what it means for a full schedule to be *rollback reliable*, that is, to be resilient to failures, when transaction rollbacks are an option. Let (s, V) be a full schedule involving a set τ of transactions and p a prefix of s. We say that (s, V) is *rollback reliable after* p if it is view serializable, and, for each prefix p' of s that extends p, and each transaction A which is uncommitted at the end of p', there is a rollback A-continuation of (s, V) which is (recursively) rollback reliable after its stable part. A full schedule is called rollback reliable if it is rollback reliable after the empty prefix. $\square$

The similarity with Definition 3.3 is remarkable. Still, it turns out that rollback reliability is a simpler concept than reliability. To understand why, let us define the *standard continuation* (s', V') of a full schedule (s, V) after a prefix p of s, as follows: s' is p with all steps of transactions uncommitted at p omitted. V' agrees with V on all read steps and write steps, except when, for some write step w of s', $V(w)$ is a step of a transaction uncommitted at p, in which case $V'(w) = V(V(w))$, or $V(V(V(w)))$, and so on, until the result is a step of s', or a step of A_0, or ν, or λ. Notice that the standard continuation may not exist (if, for example, the schedule contains an unsafe commit).

Theorem 3.8: *A full schedule (s, V) is rollback reliable if and only if for each prefix p of s the standard continuation exists and is view serializable.*

Proof: If the standard continuation of every prefix p exists and is view serializable, then it can play the role of the stable part of the rollback A-continuation in any possible failure of a transaction A at p, followed by a serial execution of all other transactions, except for A. Therefore, (s, V) is rollback reliable.

Conversely, if (s, V) is rollback reliable, then choose a prefix p of s, and abort all transactions that are active at the end of p; at the end, if A is the last such transaction to be aborted, the only possible rollback A-continuation is the standard continuation of p, which must therefore exist and be view serializable.$\square$

Based on this result, it can be shown that telling whether a full schedule is rollback reliable is an NP-complete problem (see Problem 3.5); this is almost good news, in view of Theorem 3.6. Finally, it turns out that, once more, the situation is far simpler when we deal with conflict serializable schedules:

Theorem 3.9: *If s is a conflict serializable schedule, and V agrees with V_s on all read steps, then (s, V) is rollback reliable if and only if it contains no unsafe commits.*

Proof: If (s, V) contains an unsafe commit, then we have already argued in Example 3.10 that it cannot be rollback reliable. For the other direction, suppose then that s contains no unsafe commits. We shall show that (s, V) is rollback reliable. Since (s, V) contains no unsafe commits, it follows that for any prefix p of s, V maps all read steps of transactions committed at the end of p to write steps of transactions that are also committed at the end of p. Thus, the standard continuation of (s, V) at p indeed exists, and is in fact a conflict serializable schedule, by Theorem 2.10. $\square$

Aborting all active transactions whenever a transaction fails, as suggested by Theorem 3.8, is clearly an extreme measure. One expects that, usually, there should be a way to remedy a failure by just rolling back a few steps. This gives rise to some interesting optimization problems (see Problem 3.6).

PROBLEMS

3.1 Show that the schedule s below is multiversion serializable, itself and its projections, but it is not conflict multiversion serializable (compare with Theorem 2.10).

$$
\begin{array}{llll}
A_1 : W(y)R(x) & & W(z) & \\
s = A_2 : & R(y) & & W(x) \\
A_3 : & & R(z) & W(y)
\end{array}
$$

*3.2 Describe a test of view serializability for full schedules which is analogous to Theorem 2.4. Define a reasonable analogue of conflict serializability for full schedules.

3.3 Given a full schedule (s, V) we can define a polygraph $P(s, V) = (V, A, C)$. V contains all transactions in s, plus the two auxiliary ones. A contains arcs from each transaction to A_∞, from A_0 to each transaction, and all arcs (A_1, A_2) if V maps a read step of A_2 to a write step of A_1. Finally, C contains (A_1, A_2, A_3) for each arc (A_3, A_1) and each transaction A_2 also writing the entity that caused the arc to be in A. Show that $P(s, V)$ is acyclic if and only if (s, V) is view serializable.

3.4 Give an example of a reliable schedule that is not conservative.

3.5 Show that it is NP-complete to tell whether a schedule is rollback reliable. (*Hint:* Use the proof of Theorem 2.6.)

**3.6 Formulate the problem of restoring the correctness of a schedule by rolling back as few transactions as possible. What is the complexity of this problem? Is it in NP, for example?

NOTES AND REFERENCES

The idea of using multiple versions in order to facilitate access to data has been quite old, see for example [Reed 1978]. It was proposed as part of the concurrency control techniques of [Bayer et al. 1980] and [Stearns and Rosenkrantz 1981]. "Thomas' write rule," an idea from [Thomas 1979], was formulated in [Bernstein and Goodman 1981]. The concept of multiversion serializability was formally developed independently by several researchers, including [Lausen 1981], [Ibaraki and Kameda 1983], and [Papadimitriou and Kanellakis 1984]. Theorems 3.2 and 3.5 were shown in the latter paper. Theorem 3.3 on conflict multiversion serializability is from [Hadzilacos and Papadimitriou 1985].

Reliability has always been a major concern in database systems—see for example [Verhofstad 1978]. A formal framework for understanding the reliability of schedules was first developed in [Hadzilacos 1984]; see also [Hadzilacos 1986]. The definitions of reliability used here and Theorems 3.6 through 3.9 are from [Papadimitriou and Yannakakis 1985].

4

SCHEDULERS

4.1 INTRODUCTION

Once we have settled upon some notion of correctness (such as view serializ-ability, conflict serializability, multiversion serializability, or any subset thereof), we have to design an algorithm for *implementing* it. This algorithm examines the arriving steps, originating from different transactions, and for each step it decides whether to grant it immediately, or delay it (recall Figure 1.1). If the notion of correctness adopted necessitates multiple versions, the algorithm maintains and administers the versions appropriately. The desired effect is that the algorithm lets through *all* schedules in the class being implemented, *and just these*. Such algorithms are called *schedulers*. In this chapter, we introduce and study certain important examples of schedulers. Most known concurrency con-trol systems and algorithms, proposed in the literature or actually implemented in practice, are based more or less closely on one or more of the schedulers de-scribed here.

We present all our schedulers in a stylized, unified framework, which, neces-sarily, suppresses many of the potentially interesting implementation details and idiosyncracies of each scheduler, as originally proposed and/or implemented. In Section 4.6 we shall extend slightly our framework in order to describe certain interesting schedulers which maintain multiple versions of entities. Through-out this discussion, we shall disregard two important issues: deadlocks (that is, instances in which the scheduler introduces indefinite waiting to certain trans-actions) and reliability (the problems associated with transaction failures and aborts). These problems are resolved in ways more or less independent of the specific scheduler; in Sections 4.7 and 4.8 we introduce and discuss the neces-

```
algorithm scheduler;
newstep: step, Q: queue of steps;
begin
Q := ∅;
state := initial-state;
repeat
on arrival(newstep) do
  begin
  update-state;
  schedule(newstep);
  for each qstep ⇐ Q do schedule(qstep)
  end
forever
end

  procedure schedule(s: step);
  if test(state, s) then output(s)
    else Q ⇐ s
```

Figure 4.1. A General Scheduler.

sary additions to the schedulers described up to that point, in order for them
to cope with the realities of deadlocks and failures.

A General Scheduler

Schedulers can generally be cast in the "standard" form shown in Figure 4.1. A
typical scheduler loops *ad infinitum* awaiting for a new step to arrive. Whenever
a step arrives, the algorithm updates the "state" of the scheduler to record the
information obtained from the arrival of this particular step, and *schedules*
the step. This entails submitting the step to a *test*, which is the heart of the
algorithm. If the step passes the test, this means that it can be output as the
next step of the output schedule. If not, it joins a *queue* of awaiting steps. Once
a new step arrives and is scheduled, the resulting situation and new information
may render unnecessary any further waiting for certain steps in the queue. For
this reason, all steps in the queue are scheduled.

   This "generic" scheduler has a number of unspecified parts:

The Information available to the scheduler about the transactions that it is
supposed to handle. This information is denoted in the algorithm by the global
variable *state*. In the beginning, the scheduler has some initial information
about the transactions, contained in *initial-state*. As steps arrive, the scheduler
learns more and more about the transactions. This dynamic acquisition of

information is implicit in the procedure *update-state*.

The Test. This is by far the most important part. Depending on how restricted or relaxed is the test to which we submit the arriving steps, we get schedulers which output smaller or larger classes of correct schedules—and we shall see that this is an important measure. Naturally, the sophistication of the tests that can be performed is delimited by the amount of available information.

Another unspecified part is the **Queuing Discipline** implicit in the **for each** loop of the algorithm. This choice very rarely makes a difference. In all schedulers introduced in this chapter we assume the queuing discipline is first-come, first-served. Finally, we have not specified whether a step of a transaction can arrive while the previous step is waiting in the queue (recall Problem 1.3). Again, little depends on this. It seems more realistic to assume that the next step can arrive when the previous step in the queue is a write step, but not when it is a read step.

As we are going to see in the rest of this chapter, by varying these unspecified parts, we can obtain a wealth of different schedulers.

Information

How can we measure or classify information? We shall attempt a rigorous treatment of the subject in the next chapter. But first, let us examine exactly how information is *acquired* by the scheduler. To begin, we shall assume that all schedulers keep adequate information concerning their own operation, namely the input schedule seen so far, the schedule output so far, and the contents of the queue. What can vary considerably, however, is the precise way whereby the scheduler acquires, either initially or from the arriving steps, information concerning the transactions appearing in the input schedule. There are many possible such modes of information acquisition. Three of these, however, are most common in database systems.

Dynamic Mode. Initially the scheduler has no information whatever (i.e., *initial-state* is some constant, independent of the transactions or the schedule to be input). Each time a step arrives, the scheduler acquires some information *concerning the particular step only* (e.g., the name of the entity read or written). We also assume that, when the last step of a transaction arrives, the scheduler is informed that this is the last step.

Declaration Mode. We assume that the *first* step of each transaction carries information concerning the rest of the transaction. For example, it could be the case that, whenever a new transaction starts, its first step declares upon arrival the names of the entities read or written by each of the subsequent steps of the transaction. Notice that, for this mode to be practically attainable, the underlying programs must have very poor control structure, so that their execution path can be adequately predicted in the beginning.

Static Mode. Here information concerning all transactions appearing in the input is available in the beginning—that is, it is contained in *initial-state*. For example, we might start knowing the number of steps in each transaction, and the name of the entity read or written by each step. As it should be clear, only in very special database environments is it realistic to assume that information is available in this way. One such example is the distributed database system SDD-1, in which the set of entities accessed by a transaction is known to be one of a finite selection of sets (see the references).

Notice that the mode simply determines the *timing* of the acquisition of information, not the *amount* of information finally acquired. This amount may vary tremendously. We could end up knowing next to nothing (e.g., just the number of steps in each transaction) or everything (the transactions, their interpretations, and the integrity constraints). The most common and interesting situation, however, is the one in which we acquire *syntactic information* about the transactions. This means that all we know is the name of the entity read or written by each step. The methodology of concurrency control and the correctness criteria discussed in the previous chapter are most relevant exactly in those situations in which only syntactic information is available.

4.2 LOCKING

In this section we shall introduce our first examples of schedulers. What these diverse schedulers have in commom is that they can all be implemented by an important concurrency control method called *locking*. For simplicity of notation and concept, for most of this section we shall assume the action model of transactions, in which each access to an entity x is a combined read-write operation denoted $A(x)$ (recall Section 2.7). All our locking schedulers can be extended in a more or less straightforward way to the general model; this is usually left as a problem. After introducing the example schedulers of this section, we develop in Chapter 6 an interesting theory for the study of the general properties, the power, and the limitations of locking schedulers.

Static Two-Phase Locking

During the operation of a scheduler, we say that a transaction is *active* if its first step has been output, but its last hasn't. Two transactions are said to *conflict* if there are two steps, one in each, that conflict in the sense of the previous chapter (that is, they act on the same entity.) Consider now the scheduler with the following test:

   "*A step can always proceed, unless it is the first step of a transaction, and*

> *this transaction conflicts with an active transaction."*

Let us first examine which mode and amount of information is needed by this scheduler. It should be clear that only syntactic information is required—that is, names of entities acted upon by the transactions. We are supposed to have this information for all transactions whose first step has arrived, and therefore the declaration mode is appropriate. The queuing discipline is first in-first out, say.

Example 4.1: Once we have decided on a test and a queuing discipline (and the information acquisition structure necessary to support them) the *input-output behavior* of the scheduler is completely specified. Suppose that the schedule

$$s = \begin{array}{llll} A_1 : & A(y) & & A(z) \\ A_2 : & & A(x) & \\ A_3 : & & A(w) & A(y) \end{array}$$

is submitted to the scheduler. The output is the following schedule:

$$s' = \begin{array}{lll} A_1 : & A(y) & A(z) \\ A_2 : & A(x) & \\ A_3 : & & A(w)A(y) \end{array}$$

Here is what happened: The first step of transaction A_1 easily passed the test, since there are no active transactions at its arrival. Then the step A_2 : $A(x)$ arrives. Since transaction A_2 does not conflict with A_1, the only active transaction at the moment, the step is output as well. Then the step $A_3 : A(w)$ arrived. Although this step does not conflict with any other step in the schedule, it *is* the first step of a transaction (A_3) which conflicts with an active transaction (it acts on y, as does A_1). Step $A_3 : A(w)$ fails the test, and joins the queue.

Next, the second step of A_1 arrives. However, the test only restricts first steps of transaction, and so this step passes the test as well. We now have to go through the contents of the queue (just $A_3 : A(w)$) and reschedule the steps in it. We immediately notice that $A_3 : A(w)$ is no longer the first step of a transaction that conflicts with an active transaction, because A_1 *is no longer active*. It is therefore output, and so is the last step $A_3 : A(y)$ which arrives next. $\Box$

Is this scheduler *safe?* That is, does it output only correct schedules? This is a question of obvious importance, which we shall be asking of all our schedulers.

Theorem 4.1: *The schedules output by the scheduler described above are serializable.*[1]

---

[1] Since final-state serializability, view serializability, and conflict serializability (even multiversion serializability) coincide in the action model, we use the term *serializable* for all three.

Proof: Let s be a schedule output by the scheduler. We shall exhibit a serial schedule s' which is conflict-equivalent to s. The order of the transactions in s' is determined as follows: Transaction A comes before B in s' if the first step of A comes before the first step of B in s. It remains, of course, to show that s and s' are conflict equivalent. Suppose that a step a of A conflicts with a step b of B that comes later in s. The first step of B comes after a in s, because otherwise transactions A and B would be active simultaneously, contrary to the policy of the scheduler. Thus, the first step of A comes before the first step of B in s, and therefore A comes before B in s'. It follows that a comes before b in s', and the proof is complete. $\square$

Implementation. What we have described is a relatively simple and unsophisticated scheduler, known as *static two-phase locking*. The unexpected name comes from the fact that the easiest way to implement this scheduler is by a very important concurrency control method called *locking*. In locking, new kinds of steps are inserted in the transactions, namely steps of the form $L(x)$ (pronounced "lock x"), and $U(x)$ ("unlock x"), where x is an entity. The insertion of these steps to transactions follows one simple ground rule: For each entity x, there is at most one $L(x)$ step in a transaction and at most one $U(x)$ step; if one of them exists, then so does the other. The $L(x)$ step precedes the $U(x)$ step in the transaction, and there is at least one $A(x)$ step in between the two. The resulting object is called a *locked transaction*. For example, $L(x)A(x)L(y)A(y)U(y)U(x)$ is a locked transaction, resulting from the transaction $A(x)A(y)$ by inserting lock and unlock steps. During the execution of a transaction A, we say that A *is holding a lock* on entity x if $L(x)$ has been executed, but not $U(x)$.

Locked transactions can shuffle their steps to form schedules too, for example

$$s = \begin{array}{ll} A_1: & L(x) \qquad L(y)A(y)A(x)U(x)U(y) \\ A_2: L(x) \qquad A(x) \qquad\qquad\qquad\qquad\quad U(x) \end{array}$$

A schedule of locked transactions is called *legal* if, at all times, no two different transactions are holding two conflicting locks. For example, the schedule s above is not legal, since, after the second step, A_1 holds a lock on x at the same time that A_2 is holding a lock on x.

If from a schedule of locked transactions we delete all lock steps, the remaining schedule is called the *reduction* of s, $\rho(s)$. For example, the reduction of the above schedule s is

$$\rho(s) = \begin{array}{ll} A_1: & A(y)A(x) \\ A_2: A(x) \end{array} \quad .$$

Many schedulers can be implemented by locking. This means that, instead of writing a program which enforces the test of the scheduler, we can do something else: We can insert lock and unlock steps in the transactions according to

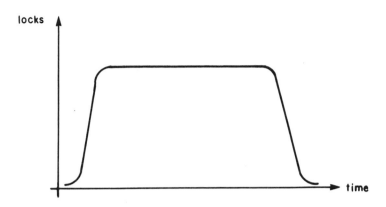

Figure 4.2. Static Two-Phase Locking.

a certain set of rules, called a *locking protocol*, so that *the set of reductions of the legal schedules coincides with the set of schedules which are output by the scheduler.* For example, it turns out that the static two-phase locking scheduler discussed above has the same effect as the following *static two-phase locking protocol*:

"*Lock all entities accessed by the transaction before the first step of the transaction. Unlock everything immediately after the last step.*"

That is, in this protocol we are holding all locks throughout the duration of the transaction, in the manner depicted in Figure 4.2. For example, the transaction $A(x)A(y)$ would be locked under the static two-phase locking protocol thus: $L(x)L(y)A(x)A(y)U(y)U(x)$. We next prove that the static two-phase locking protocol is equivalent to the two-phase locking scheduler described above.

Theorem 4.2: *A schedule is output by the static two-phase locking scheduler if and only if it is the reduction of a legal schedule of the transactions locked under the static two-phase locking protocol.*

Proof: Suppose s is output by the scheduler. This means that, in s, no first step of a transaction in conflict with an active transaction is ever output, and thus no two conflicting transactions are active simultaneously. Let us now insert to s all relevant locking steps immediately before the first step of each transaction, and the corresponding unlocking steps after the last one. The resulting schedule is legal, because no two conflicting transactions are active simultaneously, and thus no two transactions hold conflicting locks simultaneously. It follows that s is the reduction of a legal schedule of the same transactions, locked under the static two-phase locking protocol.

Conversely, if s is the reduction of a legal schedule of transactions locked under the protocol, then no two conflicting transactions are active simultaneously because, if they were, we would have two transactions holding conflicting locks simultaneously in the original schedule. Therefore, if s is input to the static two-phase locking scheduler, at no time will the first step of a transaction arrive, while a conflicting transaction is active. So, no step of s will ever be delayed, and therefore s will be output unchanged. $\square$

In general a *locking protocol* is a set of rules to be obeyed by locked transactions. Alternatively, the protocol can be seen as a set of locked transactions; a locked transaction is considered to be in the set if it obeys the protocol. A third way of viewing a locking protocol is as an algorithm which, given a transaction without locks, inserts lock and unlock steps in such a way that it produces a locked transaction in the protocol. As we shall see later in this chapter, for certain protocols there may be more than one way of doing this, and for certain protocols and transactions there may be no way at all. A protocol (or, more generally, a set of locked transactions) is termed *safe* if the reduction of any legal schedule of its transactions is serializable. By Theorems 4.1 and 4.2, the static two-phase locking protocol is our first example of a safe locking protocol.

Dynamic Two-Phase Locking

Suppose now that our scheduler has the following test:

> "A step can always proceed, unless it conflicts with a previous step of an active transaction (other than its own)."

This scheduler again needs only syntactic information. The mode, however, can now be dynamic, because we only need information concerning steps that have already arrived. (Recall that, in the dynamic mode, the scheduler knows the last step of a transaction, once that step has arrived.)

Example 4.2: Suppose that the following schedule is input to this scheduler:

$$s = \begin{array}{lll} A_1: A(y) & & A(z) \\ A_2: & A(x) & \\ A_3: & & A(w)A(y) \end{array}$$

All steps would pass the test, until the last step of A_3, which indeed conflicts with a previous (the first) step of an active transaction (A_1). Thus $A_3 : A(y)$ joins the queue. Next $A_1 : A(z)$ arrives and is output; since at this point A_1 is no longer active, $A_3 : A(y)$ is output. The following schedule results:

$$s' = \begin{array}{lll} A_1: A(y) & & A(z) \\ A_2: & A(x) & \\ A_3: & & A(w) \qquad A(y) \end{array}$$

Notice that the output schedule would not be allowed under static two-phase locking (recall Example 4.1). $\square$

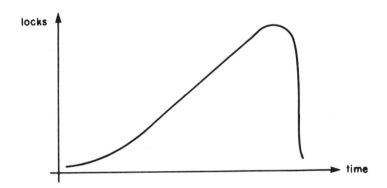

Figure 4.3. Dynamic Two-Phase Locking.

Theorem 4.3: *The schedules output by the scheduler described above are serializable.*

Proof: The proof is similar to that of Theorem 4.1. The order in our serial schedule s' is now determined by the order of the *last* steps of the transactions. To show that s and s' are conflict equivalent, take a step a of transaction A which conflicts with a subsequent step b of transaction B. When b was output, A was not active, because otherwise our test would not have allowed b to be output. Therefore, the last step of A comes before the last step of B, and thus a comes before b in s', as required by conflict serializability. $\square$

It is easy to see that the set of schedules output by this scheduler is strictly a subset of the conflict serializable schedules, although it properly contains the corresponding set for the static two-phase locking scheduler of the previous subsection (Problems 4.1 and 4.2).

Implementation. This scheduler is known as *dynamic two-phase locking*, because it can be implemented by the following locking protocol:

> *"Lock each entity accessed by the transaction immediately before the corresponding action; release all locks immediately following the last step of the transaction."*

The idea can be depicted graphically as in Figure 4.3. For example, the transaction $A(x)A(y)A(z)$, if locked according to this protocol, would result in the following locked transaction: $L(x)A(x)L(y)A(y)L(z)A(z)U(x)U(y)U(z)$.

Theorem 4.4: *A schedule is output by the dynamic two-phase locking scheduler if and only if it is the reduction of a legal schedule of transactions locked by the dynamic two-phase locking protocol.*

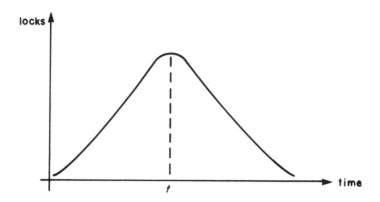

Figure 4.4. Two-Phase Locking.

Proof: The proof is analogous to that of Theorem 4.2 (see Problem 4.3). ☐

Two-Phase Locking

The safe locking protocols described in the two previous subsections allow locked transactions with the following properties:

1. *Whenever a transaction acts on an entity, it is holding a lock for this entity.*
2. *In each transaction, no lock step follows an unlock step.*

If we intuitively interpret a lock on x as the "right" of a transaction to act on x, we might have expected the first property. The second property, however, is quite interesting. It asserts that lock acquisition and release proceeds as shown in Figure 4.4, in *two phases*. In the first phase, locks are acquired but not released. In the second phase, locks are released but not acquired. For example, the transaction $A(x)A(y)A(z)$ can be locked according to rules (1) and (2) in the following ways, among others: $L(x)A(x)L(z)L(y)U(x)A(y)U(y)A(z)U(z)$, or $L(x)L(y)A(x)A(y)L(z)U(y)U(x)A(z)U(z)$.

Quite interestingly, these simple rules, a generalization of the two protocols examined previously, are enough to guarantee correctness.

Theorem 4.5: *Let s be a legal schedule with transactions locked according to rules (1) and (2) above. Then $\rho(s)$ is serializable.*

Proof: For each transaction A of s, define the *phase transition* of A to be the last locking step of A in s (point t in Figure 4.4). Let now s' be the serial schedule of the transactions of s, with the lock steps removed, in which transactions are ordered in increasing phase transitions in s. We claim that s' is conflict equivalent to $\rho(s)$. To show this, suppose that a step a of a transaction A of $\rho(s)$ conflicts with a subsequent step b of transaction B. By rule (2), transaction A released its lock pertinent to a after its phase transition, and transaction B acquired the lock pertinent to b before its own phase transition. By rule (1), transaction A was holding the lock on the entity of a at the time a was executed, and so did transaction B for b. It follows that the phase transition of A occurred before the phase transition for B, and therefore a comes before b in s', as required by conflict equivalence. $\Box$

Exclusive and Shared Locks

In the read-write model of transactions we can define a variant of locking that is a little more sophisticated and effective. In particular, a transaction can acquire either an *exclusive* or a *shared* lock on the entity. Many transactions can hold a shared lock on an entity, but no two transactions can hold an exclusive lock on the same entity, nor one an exclusive and the other a shared lock. A schedule is legal if at no time in it two transactions are simultaneously holding a lock on the same entity, one of them an exclusive lock.

The safe, two-phase locking protocols introduced in this section can be generalized in a straightforward manner to yield safe locking protocols in this more general model. Typically, instead of requiring that the transaction is holding a lock for each entity acted upon, we now insist that transactions hold an exclusive lock for each entity written, and a shared lock *or* an exclusive lock for each entity read (notice the parallel with the definition of what constitutes a conflict in the read-write model). See Problem 4.4 and 4.5.

Granule Locks

Suppose that we now allow whole sets of entities to be locked at once. This is not just a theoretical possibility. In practice, data are seldom a flat set of entities, as we have viewed them so far. Usually, there is a whole hierarchy of different *granules* of data. For example, if our entities are fields of records, a possible hierarchy of coarser and coarser granularities would be fields, whole records, blocks of records, files, and the whole database. Now, it may be physically possible to acquire locks not only on fields (entities), but also on records, blocks, etc., in other words, whole sets of entities. Locking a set of entities is equivalent to locking each of the entities in the set individually.

To formally define the situation, suppose that we have fixed a *granularity hierarchy*, that is, a class Γ of subsets of E, called *granules*, satisfying the following properties: First, $E \in \Gamma$; also, for each $e \in E$, $\{e\} \in \Gamma$. Also, for any two granules $G_1, G_2 \in \Gamma$ either $G_1 \cap G_2 = \emptyset$, or $G_1 \subset G_2$, or $G_2 \subset G_1$. Finally, we require that for each granule $G \in \Gamma$ there is a *chain* $\langle E = G_1, G_2 \ldots, G_{l-1}, G_l = G \rangle$ of granules in Γ, such that for each $i = 1, \ldots, l-1$, $G_{i+1} \subset G_i$, and there is no other $G' \in \Gamma$ such that $G_{i+1} \subset G' \subset G_i$ (the previous rules guarantee that a chain exists, but possibly an *infinite* one). The *length* of such a chain is l. Finally, the *depth* of Γ is the length of the longest chain in Γ. The depth of a granule hierarchy is typically fairly small; in our example of database, files, blocks, records, and fields, the depth is five, and in the example of Figure 4.5 the depth is 4.

Suppose that we are given a granularity hierarchy, such as our running example of files, blocks, etc., and the ability to lock whole granules, instead of individual entities. This may have very beneficial effects on the performance of the concurrency control system. For example, if most fields in a block are to be accessed and locked, it is far simpler (and faster) to lock the whole block. Furthermore, it can be argued that coarser granularity of locks reduces the danger of *deadlocks* (see Section 4.7). Thus, it seems important to consider the new possibilities offered by granule locks for improved safe protocols.

Unfortunately, we must also deal with a serious implementation problem particular to granularity locks. In ordinary locking, when only entities are locked, it is easy to make sure that no two transactions hold a lock on the same entity. We simply maintain for each entity an entry indicating the transaction which is holding a lock on the entity, if any. For shared locks we just maintain a *list* of such transactions. When whole granules are locked, however, it is non-trivial to design similar data structures for making sure that no two transactions are holding locks on granules that have entities in common (and this is the important question). For example, when a transaction attempts to lock a file, there is no obvious way to make sure that no block, record, or field in this file is locked by another transaction, short of examining each block, record and field. This method may involve for each granule lock a number of operations which is comparable to the number of entities in the database. We wish to devise granule-locking protocols which are far more efficient to implement.

One such protocol uses, besides ordinary locks on granules (called *access locks* in the sequel, for clarity), a new kind of lock on granules called *intention lock*. Intention locks on granules behave very much like shared locks. As usual, no two transactions hold an access lock on the same granule; however, two or more transactions may hold an intention lock on the same granule. Finally, it is not permitted for a transaction to hold an intention lock on a granule, on which another transaction is holding an access lock.

The protocol is defined by the following rules:

$1'$. *Whenever a transaction acts on an entity, it is holding an access lock on at least one of the granules in the chain to this entity.*

$2'$. *Whenever a transaction is holding an access lock or an intention lock on a granule, it must be holding an intention lock or an access lock on all other granules in the chain to this granule.*

$3'$. *In each transaction, no lock step (access or intention) follows an unlock step.*

A transaction obeying this protocol starts by obtaining an intention lock on E,

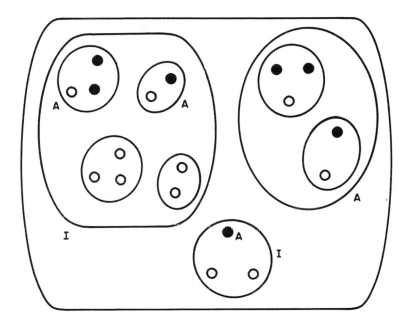

Figure 4.5. Granule Locking.

the coarsest granule. It continues obtaining intention locks on chains leading to granules for which it needs to acquire access locks. When it arrives in this way at such a granule, it obtains an access lock, and possibly accesses several entities in it. Once all the necessary granules are locked, the transaction may start releasing access and intention locks, from the finer granules up. Figure 4.5 shows a typical snapshot during the execution of such a transaction. Entities to be accessed are represented by full little circles, granules for which the transaction is holding an intention lock are marked by an I, and access locks by an A.

Theorem 4.6: *If transactions are locked according to these rules, then all legal schedules are serializable.*

Proof: We shall first show that, if transactions are locked according to this protocol, then no two transactions can hold access locks on granules which share an entity. Suppose that two transactions A_1 and A_2 are holding access locks on two granules G_1 and G_2, respectively, sharing an entity. First, we know that $G_1 \neq G_2$ (otherwise the two transactions cannot hold an access hold to the granule). By the structure of the granularity hierarchy, we know that either $G_1 \subset G_2$ or the opposite; by symmetry, assume that $G_1 \subset G_2$. Thus, G_2 lies on the chain to G_1. By rule (2′) above, A_1 must be holding an access lock or an intention lock on G_2. This, however, contradicts our assumption that A_2 is holding an access lock on G_2.

Since this property holds, it follows that for any transaction system locked using granule locks according to the three rules, we can define an equivalent transaction system in which each lock or unlock step on a granule G is replaced by a sequence of ordinary lock or unlock steps on all entities in G. It is easy to see that the legal schedules would remain the same. It follows from rules $(1')$ and $(3')$, however, that the resulting transctions would be locked according to the two-phase protocol. $\square$

The above protocol may lock up to d granules for each granule accessed, where d is the depth of the hierarchy. This is a considerable improvement over the obvious method of implementing granule locks, which requires a number of operations per access lock equal to the number of entities in the database.

4.3 STRUCTURED LOCKING

We saw in the previous section that rules (1) and (2) of two-phase locking are sufficient for safety. Are they also necessary, or are there locking protocols which are even more relaxed than this general two-phase locking protocol?

In this section we are going to introduce some interesting safe protocols that do not obey the two rules. These protocols, however, are not "general-purpose" protocols like the ones we have seen so far. By this we mean that they cannot be applied to produce safe locked transactions by inserting lock and unlock steps to any possible (unlocked) transaction. They can only be applied to transactions that possess a certain structure. To better understand what we mean by "structure" in this context, and the importance of structured sets of transactions, we shall first prove a result suggesting that, if the transactions have no special structure, then two-phase locking is necessary.

The Need for Two-Phase Locking

Let us call a set τ of locked transactions *unstructured* if the following is true: If we take any transaction in τ and permute the names of the entities (in both the actions and the lock-unlock steps), then the new transaction is also in τ. In other words, τ is unstructured if it is closed under renamings of the entities. Our intention is to show that, if we wish our locking protocol to be safe when applied to arbitrary unstructured sets of transactions, the rules of two-phase locking must be obeyed if the protocol is to be safe.

There are certain trivial cases in which we can violate the rules of two-phase locking with impunity. For example, if each transaction accesses just one entity (and thus has one step), then no locks are necessary—all schedules are serial. For a more complicated, but equally trivial, example, suppose that we have a finite set of entities, and each transaction starts by locking *more than half of the entities*, and holds these locks until the end (although it may lock and unlock other entities in between as well). Any such protocol is safe, because no two transactions can run concurrently, and the reductions of all legal schedules are serial. Still, the protocol could very well fail to be two-phase (for example, by releasing and acquiring locks besides the original ones). For our proof of necessity we must therefore rule out such absurd cases. The precise statement is the following:

Theorem 4.7: *Suppose that τ is a safe set of unstructured locked transactions. Then any transaction of τ which accesses more than one entity and locks no more than half of all the entities, is locked according to rules (1) and (2).*

Proof: Suppose not, that is, suppose that there is a transaction A in τ which accesses at least two entities, locks no more than half of the entities, and violates two-phase locking. This can mean one of two things: Either there is an entity accessed in A which is not locked (violation of rule (1)), or A has a lock step after an unlock one (rule (2)). In the first case, suppose that A accesses x without locking it, and let y be another entity accessed by A. For concreteness, let $A = \cdots A(x) \cdots A(y) \cdots$; the case in which $A(y)$ precedes $A(x)$ is symmetric. By our assumption that τ is unstructured, there is a transaction $B \in \tau$ which results from A by interchanging x and y, and mapping all other entities locked in A to new entity names (since A locks at most half the entities, this will always be possible). Since x is not locked in A and y is not locked in B, it follows that all schedules involving A and B are legal. However, there is one legal schedule involving A and B whose reduction is not serializable, namely

$$s = \begin{array}{ll} A: & \cdots A(x) \qquad \cdots \qquad A(y)\cdots \\ B: & \quad \cdots A(y) \quad \cdots \quad A(x) \; \cdots \end{array}$$

Suppose now that, for some entities x and y, A releases its lock on x before it acquires its lock on y. Let us map the names of all entities besides x and y to entities not locked in A (by our assumption, enough entities must exist). We thus obtain a new transaction $B \in \tau$. Now, the schedule

$$\begin{array}{ll} A: & \cdots A(x)U(x) \qquad\qquad \cdots \qquad\qquad L(y)A(y)\cdots \\ B: & \qquad\quad \cdots \quad L(x)A(x)\cdots U(y)A(y) \quad \cdots \end{array}$$

is legal, although its reduction is not serializable. $\square$

The Path Protocol

What kind of structure would allow us to design safe protocols more relaxed than two-phase locking? Here is an example. Suppose that we have fixed a linear order on the entities $\langle x_1, x_2, \ldots, x_n \rangle$. Furthermore, suppose that we are only interested in transactions that access *consecutive sets of entities, in the given order*. $A(x_2)A(x_3)$ and $A(x_3)A(x_4)A(x_5)A(x_6)$ are examples of unlocked transactions of this kind. Obviously, this is not an unstructured set of travery nsactions, because arbitrary renamings of the entities can produce transactions not in this set. Also notice that this is not a far-fetched example; such a set of transactions could arise in an environment of sequential storage structures, such as linked lists and files.

The structure defined by a linear order on the entities can be the basis of an interesting protocol called the *path protocol*. A locked transaction in this protocol accesses the entities as outlined above, in order of increasing i's and without gaps. As for lock steps, the following rules are observed: When an entity is accessed, a lock must be held on it. When an entity x_i is locked, the transaction must be holding a lock on x_{i-1}, unless x_i is the first entity accessed. We can lock the first entity at any time, and we can unlock entities at any time, subject to the above rules. For example, the following locked transaction obeys the path protocol: $L(x_3)A(x_3)L(x_4)U(x_3)A(x_4)L(x_5)U(x_4)A(x_5)L(x_6)U(x_5)A(x_6)U(x_6)$. It is clear that the path protocol does not obey the rules for two-phase locking. For example, x_5 is locked after x_3 is unlocked. Still, we can show the following result:

Theorem 4.8: *The path protocol is safe.*

In the proof of the theorem, we shall make use of the following lemma:

Lemma 4.1: *Suppose that two transactions A and B, locked according to the path protocol, both access entities x_i and x_j, $i \le j$. Then in any legal schedule involving A and B, if A accesses x_i before B does, then it also accesses x_j before B.*

Proof of the Lemma: The proof is by induction on $j - i$. If the difference is zero, then the result is trivial. Suppose then that it holds for entities with distance up to k, and that $j = i + k + 1$. Since transactions access whole intervals of the path, it is immediate that both A and B access x_{j-1}. By induction hypothesis, A accesses it first. At the time it does so, A is holding a lock on x_{j-1}, and, by the path protocol, it holds this lock until after it acquires the lock on x_j. Since the schedule is legal, B locks x_{j-1} after A locks x_j, and it locks x_j even later. The lemma now follows. $\square$

Proof of the Theorem: Suppose that a schedule s is legal but not serializable. This means that there is a cycle in the conflict graph $G(s)$ (Theorem 2.8). In fact, let us pick the *shortest* cycle $(A_1, A_2, \ldots, A_k, A_1)$ of $G(s)$. We distinguish between three cases, depending on the length k of the shortest cycle.

Case 1. $k = 2$. Both A_1 and A_2 access two entities x and y; A_1 accesses x before A_2 does, and y after A_2 does. This, however, contradicts Lemma 4.1.

Case 2. $k = 3$. Any two of the three transactions A_1, A_2, A_3 share an entity. Among these entities, consider the one that is neither larger nor smaller than the other two in the linear order of the entities; call it x. x is accessed by two of the three transactions, and the third accesses one entity before x in the order, and one after x. It follows that x is accessed by all three transactions. Consider now the order in which the three transactions access x. The accesses of at least one of the remaining entities by the corresponding two transactions must be in the reverse order, otherwise there would be no cycle. But this contradicts the fact that the cycle is shortest.

Case 3. $k \geq 4$. Let y_i be the entity accessed by both A_i and A_{i+1} (addition of indices modulo k). First, we claim that the y_i's are all distinct. If not, then there is an arc in $G(s)$ between two non-consecutive transactions on the cycle. This arc forms a shorter cycle, a contradiction. Next, we claim that some transaction on the cycle accesses three y_i's. If not, all k transactions access two y_i's that have no other y_i between them in the order of the entities; however, there are only $k-1$ such pairs. Finally, there is an arc between the transaction that accesses three y_i's and a transaction on the cycle not adjacent to it; but, again, this arc forms a shorter cycle, a contradiction. $\square$

What we have shown in this proof is that the underlying undirected graph of $G(s)$, for any legal schedule s of transactions locked according to the path protocol, has the following remarkable property: Any cycle longer than three contains a shorter cycle. Such graphs are called *triangulated* or *chordal*.

We next describe an important generalization of the path protocol. In the path protocol, entities are arranged in a *path* (directed acyclic graph with all in-degrees and out-degrees equal to one, except the first node that has in-degree zero, and the last with out-degree zero), and transactions access whole *subpaths* (subgraphs that are themselves paths). In our generalization, called *the tree protocol*, entities are arranged in a *tree*. A tree is a directed acyclic graph (V, A) such that all vertices have in-degree one, except for one (the *root*) that has in-degree zero. If (x, y) is an arc of the tree, then x is called the *father* of y; if there is a directed path from x to y, then x is an *ancestor* of y. An example of a tree is shown in Figure 4.6. A *subtree* is a subgraph of the tree that is itself a tree (that is, it has one root).

In the tree protocol the entities are nodes of a tree. Transactions access *whole subtrees*, and an entity is accessed after all of its ancestors in the subtree have been accessed. The rules for the locking steps are the following: First, no entity is accessed unless a lock on this entity is held. Then, to lock any entity we must hold a lock on the father of the entity, unless this entity is the root of the subtree accessed by the entity. Finally, the root of the subtree accessed by the entity can be locked at any time, and all entities can be unlocked at any time, subject to the above rules. Notice that these rules are relaxations of the corresponding ones for the path protocol. Examples of transactions in this protocol, for the rooted tree in Figure 4.6 are: $L(x_2)A(x_2)L(x_5)U(x_2)A(x_5)U(x_2)$, and $L(x_3)L(x_7)A(x_3)A(x_7)L(x_6)A(x_6)U(x_3)L(x_{10})U(x_6)A(x_{10})U(x_{10})$.

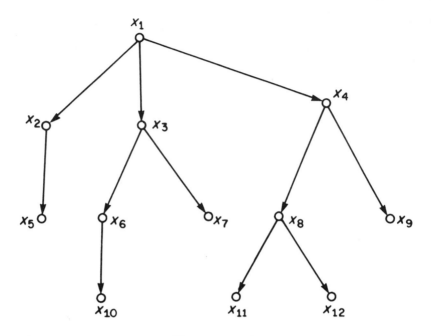

Figure 4.6. A Tree.

It is clear that the tree protocol is a generalization of the path protocol (as a tree is a generalization of a path).

Theorem 4.9: *The tree protocol is safe.*

Proof (Sketch):   First we show that Lemma 4.1 holds for the tree protocol as well. Since transactions access whole subtrees, if A and B access two entities in common, they also access the entity which is the *lowest common ancestor* of the entities in the tree. Thus, we can assume that x_i is an ancestor of x_j, and use the proof of the lemma. Next, we have to show that the underlying undirected graph of the conflict graph of any legal schedule is chordal. The proof proceeds along similar lines as that of Theorem 4.8 (see Problem 4.6—this is also a well-known result in Graph Theory—see the references). $\square$

The tree protocol is one of practical importance, because in many situations the entities of the database naturally form a tree. Examples are databases in the hierarchical model, and databases using physical storage organizations such as B-trees (see the notes and references).

4.4 TIMESTAMP SCHEDULERS

Next we turn to schedulers that are based on techniques other than locking.

In this discussion we shall return to the read-write model of transactions. To introduce our first non-locking scheduler we need a definition: If the first step of transaction A has arrived before the first step of transaction B, we say that transaction A is *older* than B, and B is, naturally, *younger*. Consider then the scheduler with the following test:

> "*A step can proceed if all conflicting steps of older active transactions have already been output.*"

Syntactic information is needed for this scheduler, and it must be gathered in declaration mode. The reason is that, otherwise, there is no way of knowing whether there are conflicting steps of older active transactions, which have not arrived yet.

Example 4.3: Suppose that the following schedule is submitted to this scheduler:

$$s = \begin{array}{llll} A_1 : & R(y) & & W(x) \\ A_2 : & & W(x) & \\ A_3 : & & W(y) & W(x) \end{array}$$

The first step is immediately output. When the step of A_2 is subjected to the test, it joins the queue, as it conflicts with a subsequent step of the (older) transaction A_1. The step $A_3 : W(y)$ is output, since the conflicting step $R(y)$ of the older active transaction A_1 has already been output. Then $A_1 : W(x)$ arrives and is output immediately, since it only conflicts with steps of younger transactions. Step $A_2 : W(x)$ can now be output, since $A_1 W(x)$ has been output; notice that A_3 is younger than A_2 because its first step arrived after the first step of A_2 (although it was executed before the first step of A_2). Next, $A_3 : W(x)$ arrives and is output, since the conflicting step of the active older transactions $A_1 : W(x)$ and $A_2 : W(x)$ have been output. The schedule output is:

$$s = \begin{array}{llll} A_1 : & R(y) & W(x) & \\ A_2 : & & & W(x) \\ A_3 : & W(y) & & W(x) \end{array}$$

We can show that this scheduler is safe:

Theorem 4.10: *The schedules output by the scheduler described above are conflict serializable.*

Proof: Let s be a schedule output by the scheduler. We must exhibit a serial schedule s' which is conflict equivalent to s. As the reader may have guessed, this time the right serial schedule is the one that orders transactions according to the time that their first step was output. Suppose that step a of transaction A in s conflicts with a subsequent step b of transaction B. When a was output, it evidently passed the test, and yet b was not yet output. This means that transaction B is younger than A, and thus b follows a in s' as well. $\square$

It can be shown that the set of schedules output by this scheduler is a superset of that of static two-phase locking, but is incomparable to that of dynamic two-phase locking (Problem 4.7).

Implementation. The scheduler described above is called the *timestamp scheduler*. The reason is that it can be implemented by using a simple device called a *timestamp*. Each active transaction is assigned a number (its timestamp), which is the time at which its first step was received.[2] Since we have adopted the convention that "time" is measured by the steps of the output schedule, the timestamp of an active transaction is defined to be the number of steps that have been output at the time at which the first step of the transaction arrived, plus one. It will soon become clear that the first step of a transaction is never delayed, and thus this number is unique and identifies the transaction. It is immediate that transaction A is older than B if and only if the timestamp of A is smaller than the timestamp of B, so the timestamps represent useful information for implementing the test of the scheduler.

We can also assign timestamps to *entities*. For each entity x, the *read timestamp of x* is the timestamp of the youngest transaction that has read x. The *write timestamp* of x is the timestamp of the youngest transaction that wrote it. Initially, both timestamps of each entity are zero. The test can then be rewritten as follows:

"A $R(x)$ *proceeds if the timestamp of its transaction is larger than the write timestamp of x. A $W(x)$ step proceeds if the timestamp of its transaction is larger than both the read and write timestamps of x."*

It is not hard to show that the set of schedules output by the timestamp implementation is the same with the set of schedules output by the original scheduler (Problem 4.8). Consequently, it may seem rather curious that the timestamp implementation does not require declaration information, as does the original scheduler. Unfortunately, this weaker mode of information may result in steps joining the queue *indefinitely*.

Example 4.3 (continued): In the case of Example 4.3, initially all timestamps of the entities are zero. When $A_1 : R(y)$ arrives, its timestamp (one) is larger than the write timestamp of y, and so it is output. The read timestamp of y becomes 1. Then $A_2 : W(x)$ arrives. Its timestamp, 2, is greater than the read and write timestamp of x (both are zero), so it is output; the write timestamp of x is now 2. $A_3 : W(y)$ arrives next. It is also output immediately, because the timestamp of A_3, which is 3, is greater than the read and write

---

[2] In practice, the first step of a transaction is neither a read nor a write step, but one of a different kind called "begin transaction step". The timestamp of a transaction is usually defined as the time at which this step was executed. In our presentation, we have chosen once more to avoid the complications of a new kind of step.

timestamp of y (one and zero, respectively). $A_1 : W(x)$ arrives now, however, and it must join the queue. The reason is that the timestamp of A_1 (one) is no greater than the write timestamp of x (two)—although it is greater than the read timestamp. Then $A_3 : W(x)$ arrives, and is output, as the timestamp of A_3 is three. Notice that $A_2 : W(x)$ ended up joining the queue indefinitely. Theorem 4.10 is not contradicted, however, since no schedule that is not conflict serializable was output; the scheduler simply produced no output at all! We shall see in Section 4.7 how such *deadlocks* can be prevented, or at least cured. □

4.5 CONFLICT GRAPH SCHEDULERS

So far, all schedulers that we have examined output schedules belonging in various subsets of the conflict serializable schedules. It turns out that we can design a scheduler whose output set is all of conflict serializable schedules. Recall that, by Theorem 2.8, a schedule s is conflict serializable if and only if its conflict graph $G(s)$ is acyclic. The latter is a directed graph with the transactions of the schedule as nodes, and an arc from A to B if a step of A conflicts with a subsequent step of B. The notion of a conflict graph of a schedule can be extended in the obvious way to prefixes of schedules: The conflict graph of a prefix p, also denoted $G(p)$, contains as nodes the transactions that appear in p, and an arc from A to B whenever a step of A in p conflicts with a subsequent step of B, also in p.

Our scheduler in this section guarantees that the output schedule is conflict serializable by maintaining the graph $G(p)$, and making sure it is acyclic. Whenever the first step of a new transaction arrives, a new node is added to the graph. Whenever a step a of a transaction A is output, then we add to the graph an arc from B to A if a conflicts with an already output step of B. It is easy to see that, indeed, the graph thus maintained is $G(p)$, where p is the prefix output so far. How do we decide, however, whether we should output a particular step? The test is simply the following:

> "A step can proceed if the new arcs that would be added to $G(p)$ if it were output do not create a cycle."

Evidently, dynamic acquisition of syntactic information is needed for this scheduler, which is called the *conflict graph scheduler*.

Theorem 4.11: *The set of schedules output by the conflict graph scheduler is precisely the set of conflict serializable schedules.*

Proof: Suppose that schedule s is output by this scheduler; we shall show that it is conflict serializable. It is easy to argue that the graph maintained by the scheduler is the graph $G(p)$ of the prefix that has been currently output. Thus, at completion the graph is $G(s)$. Since all steps of s passed the test and no arcs are ever deleted, $G(s)$ is acyclic, and thus s is conflict serializable.

For the other direction, we have to show that every conflict serializable schedule can potentially appear on the output of the conflict graph scheduler. To prove this, we imagine that a conflict serializable schedule s is fed as input to the scheduler. Consider a step a of s ($s = paq$). We shall show, by induction on the length of p that (a) the graph maintained when p has been output is $G(p)$, and (b) a will pass the test. For empty p both statements are trivial, because the graph constructed is empty. For the induction step, (a) follows immediately from the induction hypothesis and the observation that the arcs added at this step are precisely the arcs of $G(pa)$ that are not arcs of $G(p)$. Finally (b) is implied by (a) and the fact that s is conflict serializable. $\square$

The efficient implementation of the conflict scheduler gives rise to interesting algorithmic problems (see Problem 4.9).

Deleting Transactions

Many transactions appear in the output schedule, adding a node and possibly arcs to $G(p)$, and eventually terminate and commit. As the operation of the scheduler continues indefinitely, the graph $G(p)$ may end up containing many nodes which correspond to terminated transactions. At which point can the conflict graph scheduler delete the node corresponding to a transaction that has already terminated? It is a question of obvious importance to the implementation of the conflict graph scheduler, and the answer is surprisingly involved and elegant. Notice that such question did not arise in the previous schedulers we have examined, because the corresponding tests involved only active transactions.

First, let us notice that if an arc (A, B) is added to $G(p)$, this means that transaction B is currently active. A terminated transaction which has no active predecessors (nodes from which it can be reached by a path) will never acquire any new predecessors, and hence such a transaction cannot participate in a cycle in the future. Thus, a terminated transaction with no active predecessors can always be deleted from the conflict graph, as it will never be involved in a cycle. In fact, there is a sort of converse to this: If a transaction A has an active predecessor B, for all we know B may next issue a step conflicting with an already output step of A, and thus create a cycle. So, it may superficially appear that the necessary and sufficient condition for deleting a terminated transaction is that it should have no active predecessors. This condition is indeed sufficient, as we argued above, but not necessary, as the following example demonstrates:

Example 4.4: Consider this prefix of a schedule

$$
p = \begin{array}{lll}
A_1 : R(y) & & \\
A_2 : & W(y)W(x) & \quad \cdots \\
A_3 : & & W(y)W(x)
\end{array}
$$

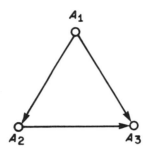

Figure 4.7. The Conflict Graph $G(p)$.

Assume that both transactions A_2 and A_3 have terminated, but A_1 is active. $G(p)$ is shown in Figure 4.7. Notice that both A_2 and A_3 have an active predecessor, A_1, and thus presumably could participate in a cycle in the future (for example, if A_1 should attempt to write x in the future). Notice however that, although it would be a mistake to delete both A_2 and A_3, *one of them can be safely deleted*. The reason is that for any extension pr of p for which A_2 participates in a cycle in $G(pr)$, there is another cycle in $G(pr)$, involving A_3 and not A_2; and vice-versa for the other transaction. The situation is similar in the prefix

$$
\begin{array}{lll}
 & A_1 : R(y) & \\
p' = & A_2 : \quad W(y)W(x) & \quad \cdots \\
 & A_3 : \qquad\qquad\quad W(y)R(x) &
\end{array}
$$

but now A_3 can be deleted and not A_2. The reason is that A_2 writes x, whereas A_3 only reads it, and thus has fewer possibilities for creating potential cycles. $\square$

Let p be a prefix such that $G(p)$ is acyclic and A a transaction that has terminated at the end of p. Suppose that we decide to delete transaction A from the conflict graph, at the time at which the last step of p has been output. This entails deleting A from $G(p)$, as well as any arc incident upon A; besides, we add all arcs (B, C) such that (B, A) and (A, C) are both arcs of $G(p)$. These latter arcs are useful for remembering paths which involve A after A has been deleted, and, as we shall see, are crucial. The resulting graph is called the *reduced conflict graph* $R(p, A, e)$ (e is the empty extension, see below). Suppose now that new steps arrive and are output, forming an extension pr of p. We update $R(p, A, e)$ in exactly the same way that $G(p)$ is updated to form $G(pr)$, except that we omit arcs out of A. The resulting graph is denoted $R(p, A, r)$. We call an extension r *relevant* if $G(pr)$ can be submitted to the test of the conflict graph scheduler; this means that either $G(pr)$ is acyclic, or $G(ps)$ is, where $r = sa$ and a is a step.

We can now formalize what it means for the conflict graph scheduler to be able to delete transaction A with no loss of information. Namely, A can be deleted at p if the acyclicity of $G(pr)$ is exactly the same as the acyclicity of $R(p, A, r)$, for all possible relevant extensions r. The next theorem states a precise graph-theoretic condition for this to be the case.

Theorem 4.12: *Suppose that p is a prefix with $G(p)$ acyclic, and A a transaction terminated at the end of p. Then the following are equivalent:*

(a) For each relevant extension r of p $G(pr)$ is acyclic if and only if $R(p, A, r)$ is acyclic.

(b) For each active predecessor B of A in $G(p)$ and each entity x accessed by A, there is a successor C of B, other than A, which accesses x at least as strongly[3] as A.

Proof: Suppose that condition (b) holds; we shall show (a) by induction on the length of r. The statement when r is the empty extension is immediate from the construction of $R(p, A, r)$. So, let $r = sa$ where a is the last step of r and $G(ps)$ is acyclic. By induction, $R(p, A, s)$ is acyclic as well. First, suppose that some arc (B, C) is in $R(p, A, r)$. Either it was added because of a step in pr, in which case it is also an arc of $G(pr)$, or it was added because (B, A) and (A, C) are arcs of $G(p)$, in which case there is a path of length two from B to C in $G(pr)$. It follows that, if $R(p, A, r)$ has a cycle, then so does $G(pr)$.

Conversely, suppose that a creates a cycle in $G(pr)$. If the cycle does not involve A then the same cycle exists in $R(p, A, r)$, so assume that it does. Starting from A, go backwards until the first transaction B that was active at the end of p is found; such a transaction exists, because otherwise no cycle could be created. We claim that B was an active predecessor of A at the time of p, since all intermediate transactions had appeared (in fact, completed) at the end of p. In proof, consider the transaction D in the path from B to A which is closest to A and is not in p. D first appeared in r, and has an arc to its successor D' in the path. However, D' was active at the time the arc was added, and thus also at the end of p. This is absurd, because B was assumed to be closest to A among all such transactions.

Consider now the transaction A' which comes after A in the cycle, and suppose that arc (A, A') was in $G(p)$. Then it is easy to see that $R(p, A, s)$ has a cycle, the one involving the same arcs as that in $G(pr)$, plus the arc from the immediate predecessor of A in the cycle to A'. So, assume that (A, A') was added to $G(pr)$ after p, and suppose that it was due to a conflict on entity x. Since B was an active predecessor of A at the time A was deleted, there is a transaction C, with a path from B to C in $G(p)$, which accesses x in p at least as strongly as A does. Hence, there is a path in $R(p, A, r)$ from B to C, from

---

[3] Writing an entity is termed a *stronger access* than reading it.

there via an arc to A', and from that, following the arcs of the cycle, back to B. Hence, $R(p, A, r)$ contains a cycle. This completes the proof of the direction from (b) to (a).

To show that (a) implies (b), suppose that (b) does not hold. That is, there is an active predecessor B of A and an entity x such that no successor of B other than A accesses x at least as strongly as A does. Consider now the continuation r of p which consists of the single step $B : W(x)$ if A reads x, or $B : R(x)$ if A writes x. $G(pr)$ contains a cycle, namely from B to A via the existing path, and back to B by the newly added arc. Suppose that $R(p, s, r)$ also contains a cycle. Since $R(p, s, e)$ is acyclic, this cycle must involve a newly added arc (C, B) from a transaction C conflicting with the last step of B. Besides, there must be a path from B to C to close the cycle. It follows that C is a successor of B which accesses x in p at least as strongly as A, contrary to our assumption. $\square$

It is immediate that it can be tested in polynomial time whether a transaction is "obsolete", in the sense of Theorem 4.12, with respect to a prefix (see Problem 4.10 for the precise complexity of the test). A simpler condition, sufficient for deleting a transaction, is given by the following corollary.

Corollary: *A transaction A which has been completed and has neither written nor read the current value of any entity can be deleted.*

Proof: For any active predecessor B of such a transaction and any entity x read or written by A, B has a successor which accesses x at least as strongly as A (namely the transaction that overwrote the value read or written). $\square$

The condition of the corollary can be tested easily, by keeping a tally of entities the current values of which each transaction has read or written. The precise condition becomes even more complex when transactions can be aborted; in fact, it is complex to the point that it is NP-complete to decide whether a transaction A can be safely deleted, although the corresponding condition for the *two-step model* can be checked efficiently, even in the face of aborts (Problem 4.11). Furthermore, if we have neglected to delete all transactions we are entitled to by Theorem 4.12, we may wish to find the largest set of transactions to delete at some point; this problem is also NP-complete (Problem 4.12). Also NP-complete is the problem of determining which transactions to delete when we have declaration syntactic information about the future steps of the transactions (Problem 4.13). Finally, a very interesting result is that the condition in Theorem 4.12 holds even when the starting graph is not $G(p)$, *but the result of deleting one or more transactions by applying the same condition at earlier times*; this is not as automatic as it may seem at first. As a consequence of this result, the condition of Theorem 4.12 can be the basis of a sound, realistic policy for deleting obsolete transactions from the data structure of conflict graph schedulers (see Problem 4.14). The same holds for the condition in the corollary.

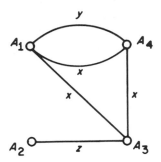

Figure 4.8. A Conflict Multigraph.

Schedulers Requiring Static Information

We shall next describe the main ideas behind a class of schedulers operating in the static mode of information acquisition. Such a scheduler has in the beginning of its operation complete syntactic information about all transactions that are going to appear in the schedule. Based on this information, the scheduler can construct the *conflict multigraph* of the transactions. A *multigraph* (not to be confused with a polygraph) is a graph in which possibly more than one copy of each edge is present. The conflict multigraph for a set of transactions has as nodes the transactions in the set, and contains a copy of the edge between two transactions for every pair of conflicting steps belonging to the two transactions. For example, the conflict multigraph $M(\tau)$ of the transaction set $\tau = \{A_1 : R(x)W(x)W(y), A_2 : R(z), A_3 : R(x)W(z), A_4 : W(x)R(y)\}$ is shown in Figure 4.8.

The definition of the conflict multigraph is such that each arc of the conflict graph $G(s)$ of any schedule s involving the transactions of τ corresponds to one or more edges of $M(\tau)$. If there is a cycle in $G(s)$ (that is, if s is not conflict serializable, recall Theorem 2.8) then there is an undirected cycle in $M(\tau)$ involving the same transactions (notice that in a multigraph, a cycle may involve only two nodes, and two copies of the same edge). We can therefore correspond to each cycle of possible conflict graphs $G(s)$ a cycle of $M(\tau)$—the correspondence does not quite go the other way, see Problem 4.15. Now, to see why the information in the conflict multigraph is valuable to the scheduler, take the simple special case in which $M(\tau)$ has no cycles. The above argument implies that for all schedules s there are no cycles in $G(s)$. Hence, the transactions can be left to run at will, without scheduling. *All* schedules are conflict serializable!

It turns out that the scheduler can make profitable use of the information in M even if the latter does have cycles. The idea is that the scheduler can now apply any of the previous tests *selectively*, only to steps that are in danger of creating cycles in $G(s)$. We shall describe here a very straightforward way of taking advantage of this. We define a *bridge* of a multigraph to be an edge which does not participate in any cycle. For example, in the multigraph of Figure 4.8, edge $[A_2, A_3]$ is a bridge. Let us say the two steps of different transactions *conflict severely* if they conflict in the ordinary sense, and furthermore the edge of $M(\tau)$ corresponding to the conflict is not a bridge. Then we can improve upon any of the schedulers studied in this chapter by modifying their test, so that the word "conflicts" is replaced by "severely conflicts". This is bound to give more relaxed tests, and thus larger output classes for the corresponding schedulers. For example, the static two-phase locking scheduler now becomes

> "A step can proceed unless it is the first step of a transaction, and this transaction severely conflicts with an active transaction."

The test of the timestamp scheduler becomes

> "A step can proceed if all steps of older transactions which severely conflict with it have already been output."

And so on. It is clear that the tests become more relaxed, and the sets of schedules output by the scheduler richer. What is more important, the output schedules are still correct:

Theorem 4.13: *The schedulers described above output only conflict serializable schedules.*

Proof: The tests of the schedulers, before the modification, were designed to guarantee that the directed graph $G(s)$ with an arc for each pair of conflicting steps is acyclic. It follows that the modified schedulers guarantee that the directed graph with arcs corresponding to *severe conflicts* is acyclic. If however this is so, it follows immediately that $G(s)$ itself is acyclic, since the arcs corresponding to non-severe conflicts cannot by definition participate in cycles of $G(s)$. $\square$

If our transaction set is such that $M(\tau)$ has many bridges, then the proposed schedulers produce more potential output schedules than their counter parts without static information. However, it can be argued that such circumstances are extremely rare (see Problem 4.16). For more sophisticated ways of taking advantage of static information see the references.

4.6 MULTIVERSION SCHEDULERS

Certain important schedulers enhance concurrency control by making use of the idea of multiple versions discussed in Section 3.1. These schedulers keep more than one version of each entity, and assign to each read step one of the available versions. The schedule output by the scheduler, together with the

```
procedure schedule(s: step);
if test(state, s) then
   begin
   output(s);
   if s is a read step then
      assign-version(state,s)
   end
else Q ⇐ s
```

Figure 4.9. Scheduling with Multiple Versions.

version function implicit in the assignment of a version to each read step, define a full schedule which can be considered to be the output of the scheduler. This full schedule must be view serializable. To describe multiversion schedulers, we must specify not only the *update-state, initial-state* and *test* features of the generic scheduler of Figure 4.1, but also the scheduler's policy for supplying versions to the read steps; this is the procedure *assign-version* in the modified scheduler shown in Figure 4.9. Of course, we must also specify which version, if any, is overwritten at each write step. However, in order to simplify matters, in the multiversion schedulers which we shall describe in this section *all* versions of each entity are kept. Naturally, in any implementation we would like to keep as few versions as possible. In all schedulers presented here, finding the optimal overwriting policy is not particularly hard, and is left as an exercise (see Problem 4.17). Finally, the scheduler must at the end proclaim one version from each entity to be the *final* version, (this can be thought of as executing *assign-version* for the read steps of A_∞). In all, the response of the multiversion scheduler to an input is a full schedule (s, V), where s is the schedule output, and V is the version function defined by running *assign-version* on the read steps output, and on the read steps of A_∞; as mentioned above, we shall assume for simplicity that $V(w) = \nu$ for all write steps w of s. We say that the scheduler *outputs* the full schedule (s, V).

It is this added complexity of assigning versions to read steps that makes the subject of multiversion schedulers so interesting (this subject is examined in its generality in Section 5.3). In the present section we shall present the principal examples of multiversion schedulers.

Multiversion Timestamps

One immediate improvement to the timestamp scheduler that can be brought about by the multiversion philosophy is *Thomas' write rule*, discussed briefly in Section 3.1. This strategy produces full schedules with a version function which agrees with the standard one in all steps, except that certain write steps are mapped to λ, that is, they are ignored. Thus, subsequent read steps on the same entity are mapped to the previous write step on the same entity. In Thomas' write rule a write step is ignored because, intuitively, it arrived "too late"; it should have been overwritten by a preceding write step on the same entity, if the overall schedule were to be equivalent to the serial schedule in which transactions are ordered in increasing timestamp. The modified rule for the timestamp scheduler is:

"A $R(x)$ proceeds if the timestamp of its transaction is larger than the write timestamp of x. A $W(x)$ step proceeds if the timestamp of its transaction is larger than both the read and write timestamps of x. If the timestamp of the transaction of $W(x)$ is larger than the read timestamp of x, but smaller than the write timestamp of x, then $W(x)$ is ignored."

Theorem 4.14: *Any full schedule output by the timestamp schedule described above is view serializable.*

Proof: The proof is identical to that of the Theorem 4.10; the only write steps that are ignored are write steps which are dead in s'. $\square$

For example, this scheduler would output the schedule shown below with no changes, except that it would ignore the write step of A_1.

$$A_1 : R(x) \qquad W(x)$$
$$A_2 : \qquad W(x)$$

It turns out that multiple versions can be employed to enhance timestamp schedulers in a much more effective way. Assume that we are keeping all versions of each entity, each with its write timestamp (the timestamp of the transaction that created it) and its read timestamp (the timestamp of the youngest transaction that read this particular version; 0 if none). Given a transaction A, the appropriate version of x for A is the version of x whose write timestamp is (a) smaller than the timestamp of A, and (b) as large as possible, subject to (a). When a read step $A : R(x)$ arrives, we always output it. As for versions, we present it with the version of x which is appropriate for A. When a $W(x)$ step of A arrives, we simply execute it and keep its version. There is, however, a case in which we cannot output the write step. Suppose that another version, with smaller write timestamp, has already been read by a transaction younger than A. Intuitively, this means that the order of transactions in increasing timestamps has been violated, and the write step cannot proceed. The rule is:

"An $A : R(x)$ step always proceeds; it is presented with the version of x appropriate for A. An $A : W(x)$ step proceeds if the timestamp of A is larger than the read timestamp of the version of x appropriate for A."

In a multiversion scheduler, we must also specify which, among all versions of the entities, is the final one (we can think this as defining the value of the version function for the steps of A_∞). In the multiversion timestamp scheduler, the final version of an entity is the one with the largest write timestamp.

Theorem 4.15: *The full schedules produced by the scheduler above are view serializable.*

Proof: Let (s, V) be a full schedule produced by this scheduler. We shall show that it is view equivalent to the serial schedule s' of transactions in A ordered in increasing timestamps, with the standard version function. Consider a read step $A : R(x)$ in $\hat{s}$. We shall show that V maps this step to the last $W(x)$ step of $\hat{s}'$ before $A : R(x)$, call it $B : W(x)$. This is immediately true for $A = A_\infty$. If $A \neq A_\infty$, suppose, for the sake of contradiction, that V instead maps $A : R(x)$ to $C : W(x)$. This means that, at the time that $A : R(x)$ is executed in s, the appropriate version of x for A is the one written by C. Thus, C must be older than B, and $B : W(x)$ must come after $A : R(x)$ in s. However, once A read x from C, the second part of the test guarantees that no $W(x)$ steps of transactions (such as B) with timestamps between those of C and A can proceed. $\square$

Notice that we did not show that all schedules are conflict multiversion serializable, and for a good reason: The multiversion timestamp scheduler would output without any rearrangements the following schedule, which is not conflict multiversion serializable:

$$
\begin{array}{lll}
A_1 : R(x) & & W(y) \\
A_2 : & W(y) & \\
A_3 : & & R(y)W(x)
\end{array}
$$

Multiversion Locking

One interesting class of multiversion schedulers is very much in the spirit of locking algorithms. We present here an abstraction of the ideas involved. As before, we assume for simplicity that we are keeping all versions of entities ever written. Certain versions were written by transactions that are presently committed, that is, they have already executed their last step. We call these the *committed versions*. Among the committed versions of an entity, the *current* version is the one whose transaction has finished last. If no committed transaction has yet written this entity, the current version is the initial one. A version that is not committed is called *uncommitted*. Our scheduler guarantees that, at any moment, there is at most one such uncommitted version of each entity. Read steps are presented either with the current version of the corresponding entity, or the uncommitted version; the precise strategy for choosing among the two distinguishes several possible variants of this scheduler.

Our scheduler treats the last step of a transaction very differently from other steps. We shall first describe how the scheduler reacts to a step that is not the last of its transaction. A read step which is not the last of its transaction is never delayed; it is presented with either the current version or the uncommitted version, depending on the particular variant being implemented. For write steps, however, we must make sure that no other uncommitted version of this entity currently exists:

> "Any read step which is not the last step of its transaction can proceed; the version read is either the current one for the entity read, or an uncommitted one. Any write step which is not the last step of its transaction can proceed only if the last transaction that wrote this entity has committed. If it proceeds, the version written is kept."

It is clear that the test for write steps guarantees that there is only one uncommitted version of each entity available at any time. If the step is the last one in its transaction, a more strict protocol must be observed.

> "Any step which is the last step of its transaction cannot proceed, until the following two categories of transactions have committed: (a) Transactions which have read the current version of an entity this transaction writes, and (b) Transactions from which the present transaction has read a version."

Notice that a write step does not have to wait for the transaction that wrote the same entity last to commit if it is the last step of its transaction. Also, once the last step is output, the handling of versions is done in exactly the same way as with steps that are not last. Finally, the final version of each entity is the current version for that entity at termination. This concludes our description of the *multiversion locking scheduler*.

Example 4.5: Suppose that the following schedule is submitted to the multiversion locking scheduler.

$$s = \begin{array}{ll} A_1: & R(x)W(x) \qquad\qquad R(y) \qquad W(y) \\ A_2: & \qquad\qquad R(x)W(y) \qquad W(x) \end{array}$$

First $A_1 : R(x)$ arrives, and is presented with the only version of x available, the initial one. Then $A_1 : W(x)$ arrives, and, since there is no previous write on x, is also output. Then, $A_2 : R(x)$ arrives; it can be given either the initial version or the one written by A_1; suppose it is given the latter. Next, $A_2 : W(y)$ writes a new version; it is not delayed because no other uncommitted transaction has written y. Then $R(y)$ arrives; it can also be given either the initial version of y or that written by A_2; suppose that it is given the former. Then $A_2 : W(x)$ arrives. If it were not the last step, it would have to wait for A_1, the transaction that wrote x last, to commit. It is, however, the last step of A_2; as a result, it has to wait for A_1 to commit, but for two new different reasons: A_2 has read x from A_1; and besides, A_1 has read the current version of y. So, $A_2 : W(x)$ joins the queue. Then $A_1 : W(y)$ arrives, and it is output immediately, since A_2, the only other active transaction, has not read the current version of an entity A_1 wrote (A_2 read the uncommitted version of x), neither has A_1 read a version that A_2 wrote (it read the initial versions of both x and y). Finally $A_2 : W(x)$ is removed from the queue and scheduled. $\square$

Theorem 4.16: *The full schedules output by the multiversion locking scheduler are view serializable.*

Proof: Suppose that s is a schedule output by the scheduler, and that V is the version function defined by the function *assign-version*. We shall show that (s, V) is view equivalent to the serial schedule s' defined by the order of the last steps of the transactions, with the standard version function. We must show that each transaction reads each entity from the same transaction in both full schedules. In (s, V), transaction A reads x either from the transaction that writes x and was the last to terminate before the $R(x)$ step of A, or from another transaction, uncommitted at the time of the $R(x)$ step of A. On the other hand, in s' A reads x from the last transaction writing x that terminates, in s, before A's last step. We claim that the two transactions coincide. In proof, by the rule for last steps, no transaction which writes x can terminate in the interval between the $R(x)$ and the last step of A, by (a), unless it is the transaction whose version $R(x)$ read, in which case it *must* terminate before the termination of A, by (b). If the transaction from which A reads x in s had terminated before the $R(x)$ step in s (i.e., A read the current version of x), then no other transaction could have terminated between this and the $R(x)$ end of A, since then *its* version would be current, or between the $R(x)$ step of A and the termination of A, by (a). It follows that A reads the same version of x in both schedules. Showing that the views from A_∞ coincide is very similar. $\square$

Implementation. To implement any multiversion scheduler, first we must have a data structure that maintains the various versions of each entity; this can be achieved by employing any one of several standard data structures.

To implement the tests for write steps and for last steps, we use locking in a rather interesting way. If a transaction reads the current version of an entity x, it acquires a lock on entity x immediately before the $R(x)$ step. This is a kind of a shared lock, called *read lock*, and is released (like all other locks in this method) after the termination of the transaction. A read lock on x can co-exist with other read locks on the same entity. If a transaction writes a new uncommitted version of entity x then it acquires immediately before the write step another kind of lock on *this version* of x, called a *version lock*, also kept until after the last step of the transaction. Notice that the version lock is a lock on the uncommitted version of x, not on the entity x, and thus it can co-exist with a read lock on x, but not with another version lock on the same version of x.

Finally, before a transaction executes its last step, it must acquire several

	$RL(x)$	$VL(x_1)$	$CL(x)$	$CL(x_1)$
$RL(x)$			X	
$VL(x_1)$		X		X
$CL(x)$	X			
$CL(x_1)$		X		

Figure 4.10. Lock Compatibility in Multiversion Locking.

new locks, again to be released immediately after the last step is executed. For each entity x the transaction wrote, it acquires a *commit lock* on x. Also, for each entity x, of which it read the uncommitted version, it acquires a commit lock *on the version read*. Neither version locks, nor read locks can co-exist with a commit lock on the same version or, respectively, entity, although two commit locks on the same entity or version can. In all, the compatibility of the three kinds of locks is shown schematically in Figure 4.10. Conflicting pairs of locks are marked with an ×.

Example 4.5 (continued): According to this protocol, the schedule s in Example 4.5 would be modified by insertions of lock steps as shown below. We use $RL(x)$ for the read lock on entity x, $VL(x_1)$ for version lock on the version of entity x written by transaction A_1, and $CL(x)$ for commit lock on x; similarly for unlocks.

$A_1 :RL(x)R(x)VL(x_1)W(x)$ $\qquad\qquad RL(x)R(y)CL(x)W(y)$
$A_2 :$ $\qquad\qquad R(x)VL(y_2)W(y)$ $\qquad\qquad\qquad CL(x_1)CL(y)W(x)$

The "legal" schedules under this protocol are precisely the schedules output by the multiversion locking scheduler (see Problem 4.18).

Multiversion Conflict Graph Schedulers

We developed in Section 4.4 a single-version scheduler, based on conflict graphs, which outputs all conflict serializable schedules. Can we design a multiversion scheduler (presumably based on conflict multiversion graphs) which outputs all conflict multiversion serializable schedules? As we shall see in the next chapter, there are compelling mathematical reasons why it is not possible for any one multiversion scheduler to output all conflict multiversion serializable schedules. Instead, we shall see that there are endlessly many possible multiversion schedulers, each implementing a different subset of the conflict multiversion serializable schedules, and which collectively exhaust all conflict multiversion serializable schedules. We shall present here a *general framework* for such schedulers, based on multiversion conflict graphs. By fixing certain *nondeterministic steps* in our framework, a wealth of multiversion schedulers results.

Our scheduler maintains an acyclic directed graph G, with nodes the transactions appearing in the input schedule, plus the initial transaction A_0. Initially G contains arcs from A_0 to all other transactions. In the end, after the processing of the input schedule is complete, G contains all arcs of the multiversion conflict graph of the output schedule, plus some other arcs, depending on the nondeterministic choices made by the scheduler. The intended meaning of an arc (A, B) of G is that A preceeds B in the serial schedule which is view equivalent to the full schedule resulting from the algorithm.

We shall first examine how the scheduler assigns a version to each read step. To choose a version for $A : R(x)$ to read, we examine all transactions B such that $B : W(x)$ has already appeared in the output—and also A_0. We call these the *candidate* transactions. Among all the candidate transactions, there are two kinds of transactions from which A should not read x. First, all transactions B such that there is a directed path in G from A to B should be excluded (after all, such a B must come after A in the equivalent serial schedule); these are called the *late* transactions. Also, suppose that there are two candidate transactions B and C such that there is a directed path from B to C, and another from C to A. If this is the case, B obviously is a poor choice for a transaction from which A reads x, because in the equivalent serial schedule it cannot be the last transaction that writes x and comes before A— C must come in between. We call transactions like B in this example *early* transactions. The algorithm allows us to choose the version of x to be read by A among those written by all candidate transactions that are neither early nor late. This is one of the two nondeterministic steps of the algorithm.

Example 4.6: Suppose that G is the graph shown in Figure 4.11 (arcs from A_0 to all nodes omitted), transaction A is to read an entity x, and suppose that all transactions B, C, D, E, F, and H have written x (and are therefore candidate transactions, together with A_0). Transactions B and C are late, and transactions A_0 and D are early; this leaves us with the following three options: E, F, and H. $\Box$

Lemma 4.2: *If G is acyclic, then at least one candidate transaction exists which is neither late nor early.*

Proof: Since G is acyclic, and there are candidate transactions with a path to A (A_0 is such a transaction), not all transactions are late. Among those that

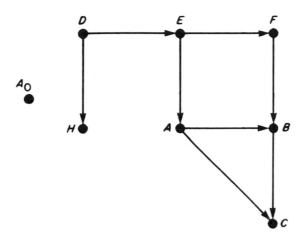

Figure 4.11. Example for Assigning a Version.

are not, choose one with no paths to other candidate transactions that are not late; this transaction is not early either. □

The graph G is maintained as follows: First, when a step $A : W(x)$ is output, we add to G the arc (B, A) for each step $B : R(x)$ that has already been output (this keeps G a supergraph of the conflict multiversion graph). If a cycle in G results, the step is rejected. If the write step is output, the version written is always kept. If a step $A : R(x)$ is output and assigned the version written by $B : W(x)$, we add an arc (B, A) to G. Since B is not late, this does not create a cycle. Then we do the following: For each step $C : W(x)$ that has already been output, we add to G one of the arcs (C, B) or (A, C).

Example 4.6 (continued): Suppose that among the three options in the example of Figure 4.11 we chose the version written by H. Then the arcs (H, A), (E, H) and (A, F) (or, for the other possibility, (F, H)) are added. □

Lemma 4.3: *There is a way to add one of the two arcs (C, B) or (A, C) for each C that has already written x so that G remains acyclic.*

Proof: If a path from C to A exists in G, then we choose the arc (C, B). It does not create a cycle, because, if it did, there would be a path from B to C and another from C to A; thus B was an early candidate transaction, mistakenly chosen for A to read from. If no path from C to A exists, we choose (A, C). It is easy to see that this can be repeated for all C's, leaving G acyclic. □

To determine the final versions of the entities, we may process the steps of A_∞ as ordinary read steps, and choose any transaction that wrote the entity considered and is not early. We call any scheduler which follows the rules of the framework explained above (and resolves in an arbitrary way the nondeterministic decisions) a *conflict multiversion scheduler.*

Theorem 4.17: *If a full schedule* (s, V) *is output by a conflict multiversion graph scheduler, then it is multiversion serializable.*

Proof: Consider the graph G at the end of the processing of the input; by Lemmas 4.2 and 4.3 G is acyclic. Consider a serial schedule s' of the same transactions, arranged in a way compatible with G. We claim that (s, V) is view equivalent to $(s', V_{s'})$. In proof, consider any read step $A : R(x)$ of $\hat{s}'$; we claim that its image under V is the same as that under $V_{s'}$. In proof, suppose that the scheduler assigned to $A : R(x)$ the version written by B. Then (B, A) is in G, and for each other C that had written x at the time, one of the arcs C, B or A, C was added to G. Thus, C is not the last transaction to write x before A in $\hat{s}'$. If C wrote x after A read x, then again there is an arc from A to C in G, and C comes after A in s'. It follows that the last transaction to write x before A in $\hat{s}'$ is B. $\square$

What we have described is a surprisingly rich class of schedulers. We can show that, by fixing a particular policy for implementing the nondeterministic steps of the scheduler, several schedulers result, such as the (single-version) conflict graph scheduler, two-phase locking, and the multiversion locking scheduler.

4.7 DEADLOCKS

The alert reader has noticed that none of the schedulers that we have introduced in this chapter has been proven to be correct. All we have shown in each case is that the scheduler does not output incorrect schedules; also, we have at times argued that, if the input schedule belongs to a particular class of correct schedules, it will be output without changes. This, however, is not enough. A scheduler must also be in a position to rearrange the steps of *any* input schedule, so that the resulting output schedule is correct. Unfortunately, many of the schedulers introduced so far do not have this property. It is possible that, in response to an input schedule, the scheduler has a step join the queue *forever.* This phenomenon is called *deadlock.* The problem of deadlocks has been studied extensively in the context of operating systems, where deadlocks are considered a disaster to be avoided at all costs. Deadlocks are undesirable in databases as well, since they block indefinitely further execution of some of the transactions involved. However, the nuisance of deadlocks pales in comparison to the true horrors that we try to avoid in database concurrency control, namely, *incorrect completions* of schedules, and the resulting *erroneous data.* In this section we study the possibility of deadlocks in the various schedulers introduced so far in this chapter, and outline the necessary modifications to the various schedulers so that the problem of deadlocks is dealt with somehow.

Deadlock Graphs

Let us recall the scheduler that we called dynamic two-phase locking, with the following test:

> "A step can always proceed, unless it conflicts with a previous step of an active transaction (other than its own)."

Suppose that the following schedule is submitted to this scheduler:

$$A_1 : A(x) \qquad A(y)$$
$$A_2 : \qquad A(y) \qquad A(x)$$

The first two steps easily pass the test, but after this the next two steps join the queue. We have a deadlock. Formally, we say that a scheduler *is in deadlock* while processing a schedule, if at least one step of the schedule remains in the queue after all steps of the remaining transactions (that is, transactions with no steps in the queue) have been processed by the scheduler. Schedulers that are never in deadlock are called *deadlock-free*.

The above problem is best understood in the locking interpretation of this algorithm. Recall that a transaction requests new locks as needed, and releases all locks after it has terminated. In the above schedule, transaction A_1 starts by locking x and acting on it, transaction A_2 does the same on y, and then A_1 waits for A_2 (to unlock y), while A_2 is waiting for A_1 (to unlock x). This *cyclical waiting* is at the root of the deadlock that we observed above (in fact, this connection is soon to be made formal). It should be clear that more complex deadlock situations are possible, in which A_1 waits for A_2, A_2 for A_3, and so on, and finally A_k waits for A_1.

Once a deadlock has occurred, the only sensible reaction is to abort an appropriate set of transactions, so that there is no deadlock in the remaining ones. The only question is, how do we know that a deadlock has occurred, and, if it has, which transaction or transactions to abort.

Detecting deadlocks requires some cleverness. In the context of locking, let us say that a transaction A *is waiting* for transaction B at some time during the processing of a schedule if B is holding a lock conflicting with a lock currently requested by A. Now let us define a directed graph, called the *deadlock graph*. This graph evolves with the processing of the schedule by the scheduler. Its vertices are the transactions of the schedule, and there is an arc from node A to node B if transaction A is waiting for B. Thus, arcs are both added and deleted from this graph. It is quite easy to see that we have a deadlock if there is a cycle in the graph.

Theorem 4.18: *A scheduler implemented by locks is in deadlock if and only if the deadlock graph has a cycle.*

Proof: It should be clear that, if a cycle exists in the deadlock graph, no transaction on the cycle can proceed, as it waits for the one following it in the cycle. Thus, each of the steps involved will remain in the queue indefinitely, causing a deadlock. Conversely, suppose that a deadlock occurs. That is, we have processed all steps of the schedule except for the remaining parts of the transactions with steps in the queue, and still there are certain steps in the queue. Looking at each step in the queue, it is clear that it is waiting for another transaction. Since all other transactions have terminated, the waited-for transaction must have a step in the queue. Thus, if we restrict the deadlock graph to transactions with a step in the queue, all transactions will have out-degree of at least one. However, such graphs always contain a cycle (recall Proposition 1.1). $\square$

Using the deadlock graph, we can detect deadlocks on-line by updating the deadlock graph and testing it for acyclicity each time a step is scheduled (but see Problem 4.9 for the interesting algorithmic issues involved). We then abort the transaction that caused the cycle—naturally, we have to know how to implement aborts, but this is the subject of the next section. A simpler idea is to periodically suspend the execution of the scheduler, and construct the deadlock graph by inspecting the steps in the queue. If cycles are found, we abort an appropriate set of transactions that renders the remaining graph acyclic. This again gives rise to a number of non-trivial issues (see Problem 4.19).

Deadlock Prevention

Deadlocks can be prevented. In locking, a simple idea for preventing deadlocks is to keep the deadlock graph *empty* of arcs. One way of doing this is by aborting one of the two transactions involved every time a transaction requests a lock which conflicts with a lock held by another. Which of the two transactions is to be aborted can be an interesting subject (see Problem 4.20 for several ideas related to this).

Another, quite different, method of deadlock avoidance in locking schedulers involves restricting the transactions allowed. In this method, we arrange the entities in some partial order, and require transactions to lock entities in an order compatible with the partial order. More specifically, imagine that we have defined a directed acyclic graph $P = (E, A)$ with the entities as nodes, and that our locking protocol also obeys the following additional rule:

"If a transaction requests a lock on y while holding a lock on x, then there is a path from x to y in P."

Theorem 4.19: *The schedulers implemented by protocols obeying the above rule are deadlock-free.*

Proof: Suppose, for the sake of contradiction, that a deadlock occurs. By Theorem 4.18, the deadlock graph contains a cycle $(A_1, A_2, \ldots, A_k, A_1)$ such that A_i waits for A_{i+1}, $i = 1, \ldots, k$, addition modulo k. Now, with any arc (A_i, A_{i+1}) of the cycle, we can associate an entity x such that A_{i+1} is holding x_i and A_i is requesting it. This, however, means that $(x_1, x_2, \ldots, x_k, x_1)$ is a closed walk in P, contradicting the fact that P is acyclic. $\square$

Corollary 1: *The path and tree protocols are deadlock-free.*

Proof: These protocols do obey the rule above, where graph P coincides with the path (respectively, tree) of the protocol. $\square$

Corollary 2: *The static two-phase locking protocol is deadlock free.*

Proof: Since all locks of a transaction are requested simultaneously at the beginning of the transaction, we can request them according to some fixed linear order of the transactions. $\square$

Of all the schedulers (equivalently, protocols) based on locking, this leaves us with the multiversion locking scheduler (Section 4.6) and the granule locking protocol (Section 4.2). Let us note at this point that deadlocks are possible in multiversion locking. The counterexample here is the following schedule:

$$A_1 : \ R(x) \qquad W(y)$$
$$A_2 : \qquad R(y) \qquad W(x)$$

It is easy to check that, if this schedule is input to the multiversion locking scheduler, the last steps of both transactions join the queue waiting for the other transaction to commit, and a deadlock results. Naturally, the above methods for deadlock prevention and detection are applicable to this scheduler as well. It turns out that deadlocks are possible in granule locking too (see Problem 4.21).

Single Transaction Deadlocks

Our definition of deadlocks as an instance in which a step joins the scheduler's queue indefinitely, also allows for deadlocks involving a single transaction[4]. Consider, for example, the basic timestamp scheduler (Section 4.4). Its test is the following:

> "*A step can proceed if all conflicting steps of older transactions have already been output.*"

It is quite easy to see that this scheduler is deadlock-free. The argument is that a transaction can "wait" (in the intuitive sense, since our formal definition of

---

[4] Such situations would not be called deadlocks in the traditional literature

waiting applies only to schedulers implemented by locking) for older transactions, and thus no cyclic waiting is possible (Problem 4.22). Things are very different, however, if we consider the "equivalent"[5] timestamp implementation of this scheduler:

> "An $R(x)$ step proceeds if the timestamp of its transaction is larger than the write timestamp of x. A $W(x)$ step proceeds if the timestamp of its transaction is larger than both the read and write timestamps of x."

The application of this rule may result in a step joining the queue forever. For example, in the schedule

$$A_1 : R(x) \qquad W(y)$$
$$A_2 : \qquad R(y) \qquad W(z)$$

once the second step of A_1 arrives, it is noticed that the timestamp of A_1 is smaller than the read timestamp of y, and thus the step cannot proceed. Unfortunately, it will never be enabled, since the read timestamp of y can only increase. We have a deadlock involving only one transaction! Notice that the same deadlock situation would arise in the variant of timestamp scheduler in which Thomas' write rule is used (Section 4.6). Finally, we have a similar kind of deadlock in the multiversion timestamp scheduler, if the read timestamp of the appropriate version is larger than the transaction's; the above input schedule provides a counterexample here as well. It is simple to show that no other kinds of deadlocks are possible in the timestamp schedulers.

Deadlocks are possible also in the conflict graph scheduler (Section 4.5). To see this, consider the schedule:

$$s = \begin{array}{l} A_1 : R(x) \qquad W(y) \\ A_2 : \qquad R(y) \qquad W(x) \end{array}$$

The first three steps of this schedule pass the test, and a conflict graph with only an arc from A_2 to A_1 results. Next, however, the last step of A_2 cannot proceed, since it would add an arc from A_1 to A_2, and therefore create a cycle. It must join the queue, and, since the situation concerning the two transactions cannot change in the future, a deadlock results.

How can we prevent single transaction deadlocks? The example of the timestamp scheduler provides a hint: Deadlocks become a problem in the variant in which only dynamic information is available. In contrast, the variant which uses declaration information is free of deadlocks. It is quite natural to

---

[5] The timestamp implementation is equivalent to the original rule only in the sense that the same set of schedules are output. Evidently, the two implementations vary considerably with respect to how they treat schedules which are not output, an issue that we had been ignoring up to this section.

expect that, using advance information, the scheduler should be able to antici-
pate deadlocks, and therefore improve the deadlock situation.

For another example, if the conflict graph scheduler had declaration information, then the deadlock in the schedule in the previous paragraph would be
prevented[6]. We can design a variant of the conflict graph scheduler which uses
declaration information. This scheduler adds an arc from transaction A to B
not only when the currently scheduled step of B conflicts with a previous step
of A, but also whenever it becomes apparent that the currently scheduled or
already output step of A conflicts with an as yet unscheduled step of B. As
before, a step proceeds only if the arcs added would not create a cycle. Notice
that, in the case of the schedule in the previous paragraph, the second step
would already be delayed, since the cycle (A_1, A_2, A_1) is already detected.

Dealing with single transaction deadlocks, once they have occurred, is in
some sense simpler, since they leave us with no options: Whenever a transaction
is involved in such a deadlock, it must be aborted. In the next section, we discuss
the modifications needed so that our schedulers can support aborts, which are
so useful in our treatment of deadlocks.

4.8 RELIABLE SCHEDULERS

A scheduler is called *reliable* if all full schedules produced by it are reliable (recall
the definition in Section 3.2). A reliable scheduler, therefore, can recover from
transaction failures, and can implement aborts, whenever the deadlock situation
calls for such a measure. Needless to say, the schedulers described thus far in
this chapter are, as a rule, not reliable. In the balance of the chapter we shall
discuss three general methods for modifying these schedulers so as to make
them reliable.

Conservative Schedulers

One technique for rendering reliable any one of the single version schedulers examined in this chapter would be to employ Theorem 3.7. This result states that
reliability is guaranteed if we only allow conservative and conflict serializable
schedules. Since all schedulers that we have seen (with the exception of multiversion schedulers) output only conflict serializable schedules, this seems an
attractive approach. (For ways of making reliable the multiversion schedulers
introduced in Section 4.6, see Problem 4.23.)

To turn any of the single-version schedulers that we have examined so far
into one that outputs only conservative schedules, we have to add the following

---

[6] A variant of a scheduler which requires declaration information for the purpose of
preventing deadlocks is sometimes called a *conservative version* of the scheduler (see
the references; we use the term with a different meaning in the next Section). The
original timestamp scheduler, and the conflict graph scheduler proposed now are both
conservative.

two clauses to the test:

> "A read step $R(x)$ cannot proceed if the transaction that wrote x last has not yet committed; if it does proceed, it reads the last version of x written. A write step $W(x)$ which is not the last step of its transaction may only overwrite a version of x which was written before the latest committed version."

Notice that multiple versions must now be supported (this requirement is typical of reliability mechanisms), and thus the scheduler has become a multiversion one. It is immediate that any scheduler whose test includes the two clauses above outputs only conservative full schedules.

Example 4.7: Let us apply this methodology to the timestamp scheduler. Recall that the test of that scheduler is

> "An $R(x)$ step proceeds if the timestamp of its transaction is larger than the write timestamp of x. A $W(x)$ step proceeds if the timestamp of its transaction is larger than both the read and write timestamps of x."

To make the scheduler reliable, we add to this test the two clauses above. Also, recall that if a step joins the queue because its timestamp is too small, its transaction must be immediately aborted, as it is involved in a single-transaction deadlock. Since the schedules output are conservative, aborting a transaction entails no action on the scheduler's part. We have thus a description of a full-blown scheduler, complete with its strategy for avoiding deadlocks and coping with transaction failures and aborts.

Suppose that the following schedule is submitted to this scheduler.

$$s = \begin{array}{llllll} A_1: & W(x) & & W(y) & & \\ A_2: & & R(x) & & W(x) & \\ A_3: & & & R(y) & & W(x)W(y) \\ A_4: & & & & R(y) & & W(y) \end{array}$$

The first step of A_1 proceeds, but the value written is kept as a separate version (each version has its own write timestamp, and the write timestamp of the entity is the largest among the versions). The next step, $A_2 : R(x)$, passes the timestamp test, but it has to join the queue because the last transaction to write x, A_1, has not yet committed. Next, $A_3 : R(y)$ is output, since it passes both the timestamp and the conservativeness test. Then $A_1 : W(y)$ arrives, and it fails the timestamp test (the read timestamp of y is larger than the timestamp of A_1). Hence, A_1 must be aborted (it was a good thing that we prevented A_1 from overwriting x), and its version of x discarded. After aborting A_1, we reconsider the step $A_2 : R(x)$ in the queue, and notice that there is no active transaction that has written x. Hence $A_2 : R(x)$ is output, presented with the initial version of x. Then $A_2 : W(x)$ arrives, and it passes the timestamp test. Since it is the last step of its transaction, the reliability clause does not apply, and the initial version of x is overwritten. Then $A_4 : R(y)$ passes the timestamp test and the reliability clause (remember, the $A_1 : W(y)$ step was never executed), and so it is presented with the initial version of y. Then $A_3 : W(x)$ arrives, passes the timestamp test, and writes a new entity of x. Next $A_3 : W(y)$ passes the timestamp test and overwrites the initial version of y (it is the last step of A_3). Finally, $A_4 : W(y)$ arrives, passes the timestamp test, and overwrites y. The schedule output is the following:

$$
\begin{array}{llll}
A_2 : & R(x) & W(x) & \\
A_3 : & R(y) & & W(x)W(y) \\
A_4 : & & R(y) & W(y)
\end{array}
$$

Example 4.8: Suppose that the two conservativeness clauses are added to any one of the locking schedulers of Sections 4.2 and 4.3. Since the two clauses state that entities are not available for access until after the previous transaction that accessed them commits, this method is equivalent to adding to the locking protocol the following clause:

"*No lock is released until after the last step of the transaction.*"

Thus, the general two-phase locking scheduler with the two conservativeness clauses is identical to the dynamic two-phase locking. Similar results are obtained with the various structured locking protocols of Section 4.3. If we apply the same idea to the case in which we distinguish between write and read steps, and as a consequence each entity is equipped by a read (shared) lock and a write (exclusive) lock (Problem 4.4), the additional restriction on the protocols becomes

"*No write lock is released until after the last step of the transaction.*"

Read locks can be released before termination, subject of course to the rules of two-phase locking. $\square$

Reliability by Atomic Writes

Another way of rendering a scheduler reliable is through the corollary to Theorem 3.7. It was pointed out there that, if all write steps of the transaction always came in the end and were executed in an atomic manner—with no other steps or, perhaps more importantly, failures happening in between them—then the schedule output would automatically be conservative. Thus, if the transactions handled by the scheduler fall into this category, reliability is automatic (assuming, of course, that our scheduler outputs conflict serializable schedules).

Even in the case in which transactions have multiple write steps, we can use the same principle to make schedulers reliable. In particular, we can modify

any scheduler to output schedules in the atomic write model by adding to the
test the following clause:

> "Any write step that is not the last step of its transaction cannot proceed.
> For the last step of a transaction, we remove all write steps of the trans-
> action from the queue, and, if all these steps pass the test, they are all
> executed as an atomic step. Otherwise, they all join the queue."

Example 4.9: We can apply this method for ensuring reliability to the conflict graph scheduler (Section 4.5), among others. Suppose that the following
schedule is input to this scheduler:

$$
\begin{array}{llll}
A_1 : R(x) & W(y) & & W(x) \\
s = A_2 : & W(x) & R(y) & W(y) \\
A_3 : & & W(y) & & W(x)
\end{array}
$$

The first step is output immediately, as there are no arcs in the conflict graph.
The second step, $A_2 : W(x)$, if output, would add an arc (A_1, A_2) to the conflict
graph, but no cycles, so it passes the test of the main scheduler. However, it is
a write step which is not the last step of its transaction, and thus it has to join
the queue. Similarly for the next two steps $A_1 : W(y)$ and $A_3 : W(y)$. Next,
the step $A_2 : R(y)$ arrives, and is also output immediately. Then $A_1 : W(x)$
arrives. This step is the last step of its transaction, and so all other write steps
are removed from the queue, and subjected to the test. If both these steps were
output, an arc (A_2, A_1) would be added to the conflict graph; since the graph is
empty of arcs, no cycle results. Hence, the two write steps $W(y)$ and $W(x)$ of
A_1 are executed as a single, uninterrupted, atomic step; arc (A_2, A_1) is added
to the conflict graph.

Next, the step $A_2 : W(y)$ arrives; it is also the last step of a transaction,
and so the step $A_2 : W(x)$ is removed from the queue, and both steps are
subjected to the test. It is noticed that, were these two steps to be output, the
arc (A_1, A_2) would be added to the conflict graph, thus creating a cycle. As a
result, both steps must join the queue forever, and we have a deadlock. We can
recover from the deadlock by aborting transaction A_2. Finally, step $A_3 : W(x)$
arrives, it passes the test with $A_3 : W(y)$, and both are output as an atomic
write step. The schedule output is

$$
\begin{array}{ll}
A_1 : R(x)W(y,x) \\
A_3 : & W(y,x)
\end{array}
$$

Implementation. In order to be able to implement the atomic write technique,
a scheduler must have the ability to execute a multiple write step such as
$W(x, y, z)$ as an atomic step. By "atomic" we mean two things. First, the
three write steps involved must be executed without any other conflicting steps

executing intermittently; the scheduler can easily achieve this by refraining from scheduling other steps during the execution of the multiple write step. The second and most important requirement is that *no transaction failures should occur* during the execution of the multiple write step. In particular, it is critical that the transaction which issued the step should not fail. Should such a failure occur at the moment at which the scheduler has written, in our example of $W(x, y, z)$, the values of x and y but not that of z, an unsafe write has been performed, with all the ensuing perils.

A scheduler can implement atomic multiple write steps by employing an important technique called *two-phase commit* (see the references). In two-phase commit, the scheduler would execute the write steps on x, y, and z in our example above without overwriting the old values. Instead, it would create new versions of the entities. After this is done, the issuing transaction is considered terminated and committed (that is, it cannot be aborted from this point on). This is the end of *phase one*. Then *phase two* starts, during which the scheduler copies the new values of x, y, and z to the locations where the entities are stored, overwriting the old values.

Should the issuing transaction fail during phase one, we simply do not execute phase two, and ignore the new versions; this way the transaction has been effectively aborted. On the other hand, if a system failure occurs during phase two, again no harm is done, since the new versions are safely stored away, and the copying process can be redone.

Optimistic Schedulers

Once we decide to use the atomic write technique in order to ensure reliability, interesting new possibilities arise for improving the scheduler even further. The atomic write technique postpones all tests of the write steps until the very end of the transaction. An intriguing idea is to postpone *all* tests until this time. Such a scheduler would let all read steps proceed, and postpone all write steps. Once the last step has arrived, the scheduler takes another look at the timing of the various steps of the transaction. If it finds that the various read steps, and the final atomic write, would pass the test of the concurrency control principle adopted by the scheduler (be it dynamic two-phase locking, conflict serializability, timestamp, etc.) then the atomic write step is granted, otherwise transaction is aborted. Such a scheduler is called *optimistic*, because it operates on the assumption that no step of the input schedule will be delayed (and pays the price if it is wrong). Another term for this kind of scheduler is a *certifier*, since such schedulers certify the correctness of the execution of each transaction *ex post facto*, instead of tersting preemptively each arriving step for correctness.

The optimistic style of concurrency control is especially attractive in environments in which the probability of conflict between two transactions is rather low, and therefore most steps would end up passing the test. It is also advantageous as a method for implementing *distributed* schedulers, as their operation (and thus the need for exchange of information between the sites) is limited to the end of each transaction.

Rollback Reliable Schedulers

Finally, suppose that we add to the test of a scheduler the following restriction:

> *"The last step of a transaction cannot proceed, until all transactions from which the current transaction has read an entity have committed."*

If this additional guideline is observed, then the full schedule output by the scheduler is guaranteed to be rollback reliable (recall Theorem 3.9). If a transaction failure occurs, the scheduler must abort all transactions that have read a version from the aborted transaction, all transactions that have read a version from these, and so on. The result is guaranteed to be a correct schedule.

PROBLEMS

4.1 Show that any schedule which passes the tests of the static two-phase locking scheduler will also pass the tests of the dynamic two-phase locking scheduler. Give another proof based on locking. Show that the converse does not hold.

4.2 Give an example of a conflict serializable schedule which would be rearranged by the dynamic two-phase locking scheduler. Find a conflict serializable schedule which would be rearranged by *any* two-phase locking scheduler.

4.3 Prove Theorem 4.4.

4.4 In the read-write model of transactions we can use exclusive and shared locks to implement two-phase locking. Suppose that we lock the transactions according to the following protocol:

> *"Lock each entity read by the transaction by a shared lock immediately before the read step; lock each entity written by an exclusive lock immediately before the write step. Release all locks immediately following the last step of the transaction."*

(We assume that a transaction may acquire an exclusive lock on an entity even though a shared lock is held *by the same transaction*.) Show that all legal schedules under this protocol are conflict serializable, by proving that the protocol implements the same test as dynamic two-phase locking (where "conflict" is interpreted as usual in the read-write model).

4.5 Generalize the rules (1), (2), and (3) of general two-phase locking for the case of shared and exclusive locks in the read-write model. Prove that your rules guarantee conflict serializability.

4.6 Prove Theorem 4.9.

4.7 Show that if a schedule is accepted without rearrangement by the static two-phase locking scheduler, then it is also accepted by the multiversion scheduler, but not vice-versa. Show that for the dynamic two-phase locking and multiversion schedulers neither direction holds.

4.8 Show that the set of schedules output by the timestamp implementation of the timestamp scheduler (Section 4.4) is the same as the set of schedules output by the original timestamp scheduler.

4.9 We are to design an algorithm which will maintain a directed graph $G = (V, A)$, and which must carry out streams of the following two types of operations: (1) Add arc (v, u) to A, for given vertices $u, v \in V$; (2) Determine whether G has a cycle.
  (a) Design an algorithm which takes $O(1)$ time to perform operation (1), and $O(n^2)$ time to perform operation (2), where n is the number of nodes in V.
  (b) Design another algorithm which takes $O(n^2)$ time for operation (1) and $O(1)$ time for (2).
 **(c) Can you design an algorithm which carries out both operations (1) and (2) in less than quadratic time? Can you prove a lower bound higher than linear for the worst-case performance per operation of any algorithm carrying out streams of operations (1) and (2)?
 **(d) Part (c) may be easier in the special case in which we have to carry out a stream of operations of the following kind: (3) Given arc (u, v), add it to A if it does not create a cycle.

4.10 Show that, given a prefix p of a schedule with $G(p)$ acyclic, and a transaction A, the condition of Theorem 4.12 can be tested in time quadratic in the length of s. Show that in the same time bound we can test whether any transaction A satisfying Theorem 4.12 exists for a given p.

4.11 Suppose that any transaction which has not terminated may abort; the problem of deleting transactions (Section 4.5) becomes considerably more complicated.
  (a) Show that it is NP-complete to determine in this case whether transaction A can be deleted (i.e., whether condition (a) of Theorem 4.12 holds).
  (b) Suppose now that transactions have atomic writes (Section 4.8). A *terminated path* from A to B in the directed graph $G(p)$ is one in which all intermediate transactions are terminated. Show that condition (b) of Theorem 4.12 is now necessary and sufficient if the paths from B to A and C are required to be terminated.

4.12 Show that it is NP-complete, given a prefix p with acyclic $G(p)$, to determine the largest k for which there is a set of transactions $\{A_1, \ldots, A_k\}$ such that transaction A_i satisfies the condition of Theorem 4.12 in the graph $G(p)$ with transactions $A_1, \ldots, A_{i-1}$ deleted, $i = 1, \ldots, k$.

4.13 Show that it is NP-complete to determine whether a transaction A can be deleted from a prefix p (i.e., whether condition (a) of Theorem 4.12 holds) if we know the continuations of all active transactions.

4.14 Show that the condition (b) is still equivalent to (a) in the case in which we have deleted some other transaction satisfying condition (b) at some previous step. Repeat for the condition in the corollary to Theorem 4.12.

4.15 Give an example of a conflict multigraph such that, for some cycle in this graph, there is no prefix p of a schedule of the transactions such that $G(p)$ contains a cycle involving the same set of transactions and in the same order.

*4.16 Show that almost all graphs with n nodes and cn^2 edges, for any $c > 0$, have no bridges.

4.17 For each of the three multiversion schedulers presented in Serction 4.6, give a reasonable policy for overwriting useless copies. If it is optimal, prove it.

4.18 Show that the set of full schedules output by the multiversion locking scheduler are precisely the same as those that are legal under the multiversion locking protocol (assuming the same choices among the current and the uncommitted version are made by all steps).

4.19 Show that, given a directed graph, it is NP-complete to find the smallest k such that, by deleting k nodes, an acyclic directed graph results.

4.20 Suppose that we are to prevent deadlocks by aborting either end of any arc that would be added to the deadlock graph. Suppose that you are to define a policy on which of the two transactions to abort, using the timestamps of the transactions as the only criterion. Define such a policy and defend it as a reasonable choicc in practice.

4.21 Give an example of a granularity structure and a schedule, for which the granularity locking scheduler would deadlock.

4.22 Show that the conservative version of the timestamp scheduler (the one based on the test which requires declaration syntactic information) is deadlock-free.

*4.23 Show that all multiversion schedulers of Section 4.6 can be made reliable if they are further restricted so that they output only conservative schedules.

NOTES AND REFERENCES

There is a great number of papers proposing concurrency control algorithms, in most cases variants of the ones described in this chapter and the problems. Two-phase locking was first formally described in [Eswaran et al. 1976], where a weaker version of its necessity (Theorem 4.7) was shown. Theorem 4.7 is from [Yannakakis 1982a]. The path protocol was apparently well-known among database practitioners for some timc, as was the two-phase principle. The tree protocol is from [Silberschatz and Kedem 1979], and new variants of this algorithm are described in [Kedem and Silberschatz 1979], [Mohan et al. 1982], and [Buckley and Silberschatz 1985]. For further generalizations see Chapter 6. [Bayer and Schkolnick 1977] describe a concurrency control mechanism for B-trees.

Timestamps were used in the concurrency control system of SDD-1 [Bernstein et al. 1978], and the abstraction described here first appeared in [Bernstein and

Goodman 1981]. SDD-1 is also an example of a scheduler based on static information (Theorem 4.13). The conflict graph scheduler is from [Papadimitriou 1979], and
Theorem 4.12 from [Hadzilacos and Yannakakis 1986], where solutions to Problems
4.11–15 can be found. Multiversion timestamps were formalized in [Bernstein and
Goodman 1983], and multiversion conflict graphs in [Hadzilacos and Papadimitriou
1985]. Multiversion locking is based on [Bayer et al. 1980]. More multiversion schedulers are described in [Buckley and Silberschatz 1983] and [Muro et al. 1984]. For a
treatise on deadlocks see [Yannakakis 1982b]. The term *conservative scheduler* for a
scheduler that prevents deadlocks by using declaration information is from [Bernstein
et al. 1986]. For more on techniques used for ensuring reliability see [Gray 1978],
[Verhofstad 1978], and [Hadzilacos 1986]. Two-phase commit is from [Gray 1978],
and optimistic schedulers were proposed in [Kung and Robinson 1981]. The atomic
write model was used in much of the early concurrency control literature, e.g. in
[Papadimitriou 1979]. Problem 4.19 is from [Karp 1972].

5

THE PERFORMANCE OF SCHEDULERS

5.1 EFFICIENCY AND CONCURRENCY

Which of the various schedulers presented in the previous chapter is the best? What are the right criteria for deciding this? What other, better schedulers are there? In the present chapter we shall develop the theory necessary for *evaluating* schedulers, as well as for determining the *inherent limitations* of all possible schedulers. We start by considering only single-version schedulers; later in the chapter we study the interesting peculiarities of the theory of multiversion schedulers.

Efficient Schedulers

When should we consider a scheduler to be "good"? Since a scheduler is first of all an algorithm, an important criterion is the time required for its operation. Recall that this operation consists of executions of two procedures: First, the procedure *test* decides whether a step will be output or will join the queue; in order to reach this decision, *test* consults a data structure called *state*. The procedure *update-state* modifies the state to reflect the information obtained from the last step to arrive; the initial value of *state* is *initial-state*.

Definition 5.1: We say that a scheduler is *efficient* if the following are true of any possible input schedule: (a) the size of the *state* data structure is at any moment bounded by a polynomial in the size of the *initial-state* and the number of steps of the schedule that have arrived so far, and (b) each call of the *test* and *update-state* procedures takes a number of steps that is polynomial in the size of the *state*. □

Notice that all schedulers introduced in the previous chapter are efficient.

It is now straightforward to show the following:

Proposition 5.1: *If a scheduler is efficient, then the total number of steps required for processing a schedule of length n are bounded by a polynomial in the size of initial-state and n.*

Proof: The total time is bounded by n times a polynomial function of n and the size of the *state*; the latter, however, is a polynomial function of n and the size of *initial-state*. $\square$

A Measure of Concurrency

Efficiency is not all, however. Recall that the main purpose of a scheduler is to output correct schedules, *while allowing as much concurrency as possible.* In the absence of this important consideration, it is trivial to construct a fast and safe scheduler, namely, the one that outputs only serial schedules. Therefore, we consider good schedulers those which support a lot of concurrency. But how can we measure concurrency?

Ideally, we would have liked to be able to evaluate the amount of concurrency of a scheduler quantitatively, by calculating a parameter such as its *throughput* (the number of transactions that the scheduler can handle in parallel without experiencing unbounded delays). Attempts at such analysis have been made in the past (see the references); unfortunately, the corresponding analytical problems turn out to be very hard, and only experimental, approximate, or empirical results are available. What is more disappointing, in order to even start towards this direction, one has to make some very strong assumptions about the structure of the transactions and the scheduler, going far beyond the simple and general model that we have used in this book. In what follows we shall define in our model a "qualitative" measure of concurrency of schedulers which is mathematically clean, intuitive, and also pragmatic, in that it gives sound insights about the performance of the various schedulers.

Let $\mathcal{H}$ denote the set of all possible schedules, and let S be a scheduler. Certain schedules in $\mathcal{H}$ have the following property: When they are submitted, step by step, as inputs of the scheduler S, none of their steps is delayed by the scheduler—that is, none fails the test of S. Call this subset of $\mathcal{H}$ *the concurrency of S*, denoted $\mathcal{C}(S)$. This set is our measure of the performance of S. If two schedulers S and S' satisfy $\mathcal{C}(S) \subset \mathcal{C}(S')$, then we say that S' "has more concurrency than S."

This measure of concurrency is quite natural. It is clear that, the more schedules S is able to output without any delay, the more "liberal" it is, the more concurrency it supports. However, this measure is only "qualitative." This is best manifested by the fact that it only *partially orders* schedulers (by the partial order induced by set inclusion of their concurrency sets), and does not order them totally, as would, for example, a single numerical performance

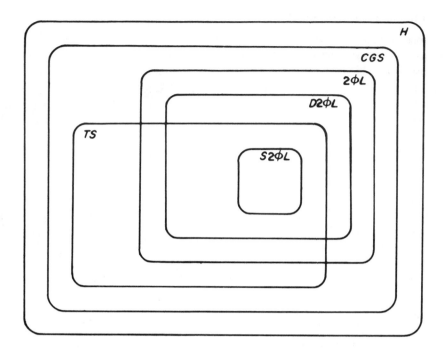

Figure 5.1. The concurrency sets of various schedulers.

parameter, such as the scheduler's throughput. Given two schedulers, we may
not be able to tell which has more concurrency. Figure 5.1 depicts the relationships among the concurrencies of the various schedulers introduced in the
previous chapter. H stands for all schedules, CGS for the conflict graph scheduler, TS for the timestamp scheduler, 2ΦL for the two-phase locking scheduler,
and S2ΦL, D2ΦL for static and dynamic two-phase locking, respectively.

   Besides $\mathcal{C}(S)$, there is another important set of schedules associated with
a scheduler S; namely, the set of schedules that are *output* by the scheduler
—with or without delays. This set, called the *output set* of S, is denoted by
$\mathcal{O}(S)$. Obviously, $\mathcal{C}(S) \subseteq \mathcal{O}(S)$, for any scheduler S. It is quite interesting to
observe that, for all schedulers introduced in the previous chapter (in fact, for
all schedulers studied in the literature) $\mathcal{C}(S)$ and $\mathcal{O}(S)$ are *identical*. There is
a simple explanation for this. Intuitively, we can think of $\mathcal{O}(S)$ as the set of
schedules that the scheduler S, in its limited sophistication, can recognize as
correct, and therefore output. It would thus appear suboptimal for a scheduler
S to purposely delay some steps of a schedule in $\mathcal{O}(S)$, as this schedule could,
under different circumstances, be output and certified as correct by the same
scheduler S.

Concurrency and Complexity

Suppose that we are to design a scheduler S, given a set C of schedules which we are to assume correct. Typically C will be a generally accepted notion of correctness, such as the set of all view serializable schedules. The set of schedules output by our scheduler S, $\mathcal{O}(S)$, must be a subset of C. Subject to this, we would like to design the scheduler S such that its concurrency set $C(S)$ is as large as possible. Ideally, since $C(S) \subseteq \mathcal{O}(S) \subseteq C$, we would like these three sets to coincide. If they do coincide, we say that S realizes C. At the same time, we wish our scheduler S to be efficient. Thus we arrive at the following important question: *Given a set C of schedules, under what conditions can we design an efficient scheduler that realizes it?*

Intuitively, the NP-completeness results of Chapter 2 seem a serious impediment here. If a set of schedules, like the set of all view serializable schedules, is $\mathcal{NP}$-complete, it is doubtful that one can design a fast scheduler for realizing it. It is therefore tempting to conjecture that *the necessary and sufficient condition for the existence of an efficient scheduler for realizing C is that $C \in P$, that is, that there be an efficient algorithm for recognizing the schedules in C.*

Example 5.1: This conjecture is false. To introduce our counterexample, we need the concept of the *concatenation* of two schedules. Let s and s' be two schedules, involving different transactions. Their concatenation ss' is the schedule which, considered as a string, is the language-theoretic concatenation of s and s'. For example, if

$$s = \begin{matrix} A_1 : & R(x) & & W(x) & \\ A_2 : & & R(y) & & W(x) \end{matrix}$$

and

$$s' = \begin{matrix} A_1' : & R(x)W(x) & \\ A_2' : & & R(y)W(x) \end{matrix}$$

then the concatenation of the two schedules is

$$ss' = \begin{matrix} A_1 : & R(x) & & W(x) & & \\ A_2 : & & R(y) & & W(x) & \\ A_1' : & & & & R(x)W(x) & \\ A_2' : & & & & & R(y)W(x) \end{matrix}$$

Consider now the set $\mathcal{V}$ of all schedules that are the concatenation of a view serializable schedule s, involving transactions $A_1, \ldots, A_n$, with a serial schedule s', involving transactions $A_1', \ldots, A_n'$, such that, transaction A_i is identical to transaction A_i', and s is view equivalent to s', if the primes are ignored. The schedule ss' above is an example of a schedule in $\mathcal{V}$.

It is quite clear that the schedules in the class $\mathcal{V}$ can be recognized in polynomial time. All we need to do is divide a schedule in half, see if both halves are schedules in themselves, and whether the second one is a serial schedule, view equivalent to the first. All this can be done in $O(n^2)$ time, where n is the length of the schedule.

Were our conjecture true, there would be an efficient scheduler S such that $\mathcal{V} = \mathcal{C}(S) = \mathcal{O}(S)$. If such a scheduler existed, how would it respond to an input starting with some schedule s? It follows easily from our definition of $\mathcal{C}(S)$ and $\mathcal{O}(S)$ that all steps of s would pass the test of S *if and only if s is view serializable*. Thus, we can test any schedule s for view serializability by submitting all of its steps to S. If S delays any of them, s is not serializable, but if all steps of s pass the test, then s is view serializable. Since S was assumed to be efficient, this is a polynomial time algorithm for view serializability. From the assumption that there is an efficient scheduler that realizes $\mathcal{V}$, we concluded that P=NP! Thus, most likely, there is no efficient scheduler that realizes $\mathcal{V}$. $\square$

Let $\mathcal{C}$ be a subset of $\mathcal{H}$, the set of all schedules. Recall that we denote by PREFIX($\mathcal{C}$) the set of all prefixes of schedules in $\mathcal{C}$. The correct necessary and sufficient condition for $\mathcal{C}$ to be realizable by some efficient scheduler is the following:

Theorem 5.1: *There is an efficient scheduler that realizes $\mathcal{C}$ if and only if* PREFIX($\mathcal{C}$) *is in P.*

Proof: *Only If.* Suppose that an efficient scheduler S exists such that $\mathcal{C}(S) = \mathcal{O}(S) = \mathcal{C}$. Using this scheduler we can test whether an arbitrary schedule prefix p is in PREFIX($\mathcal{C}$), as follows. We submit the steps of p in their right order to S; it is straightforward that $p \in$ PREFIX($\mathcal{C}$) if and only if no step of p fails the test. By Proposition 5.1 this is a polynomial-time algorithm for PREFIX($\mathcal{C}$), which implies $\mathcal{C} \in$P.

If. If we have a polynomial time algorithm to recognize PREFIX($\mathcal{C}$), we can define a scheduler S which remembers and updates the prefix p of the schedule output so far, and lets a step a proceed if and only if $pa \in$ PREFIX($\mathcal{C}$). That is, the *state* of S (recall Figure 3.1) is the prefix output so far, *update-state* simply maintains this information, and the *test* checks whether $pa \in$ PREFIX($\mathcal{C}$). It is evident that $\mathcal{C}(S)=\mathcal{O}(S)=\mathcal{C}$. $\square$

This result has the same negative implications as our original conjecture:

Corollary: *Unless P=NP, there is no efficient scheduler realizing the set of all view serializable schedules.*

Proof: The set of prefixes of view serializable schedules is as NP-complete as the set of view serializable schedules (see Problem 5.1). The corollary then follows immediately from the theorem. $\square$

Thus, there is no hope of having efficient schedulers of "maximum" concurrency. To obtain efficient schedulers we must settle for sets of schedules that are sufficiently restricted subsets of the view serializable ones, so that they have polynomially recognizable prefixes. The notion of conflict serializability and the schedulers of the previous chapter represent various compromises along these lines.

5.2 INFORMATION AND CONCURRENCY

It is clear that the performance of a scheduler is limited by the information available to it about the various transactions in the system. In this section we prove results that make this dependency explicit. The statement of the results is simplified considerably in the *action model* of transactions (Section 2.7). Consequently, in this section we shall adopt this model.

Information

A scheduler handles a transaction system τ, that is, an object comprising a set of transactions, semantics for the entities and the actions of the transactions, and the integrity constraints. This transaction system is completely specified by the number of steps in each transaction, the entity acted upon at each step (remember that our transactions are in the action model), the domains of the entities, the interpretations of the write part of the action in each step, and the integrity constraints. These parts of the specification of a set of transactions must conform to our basic assumption throughout this book, namely that each individual transaction is correct in that it maps consistent states of the database to consistent states.

If we know all these parts (number and semantics of steps, domains of entities, and integrity constraints) we can say that we have *complete information* about the transaction system τ. However, the scheduler often has less than complete information about the transactions that it handles. For example, the interpretations of the functions and the integrity constraints are usually unavailable, for reasons detailed in Section 2.1. How can we formalize this notion of incomplete information?

Definition 5.2: An *information operator* is a mapping Φ assigning to each transaction system τ a string $\Phi(\tau) \in \{0,1\}^*$. Each such image $\varphi = \Phi(\tau)$ is called the *information* available to the scheduler about τ. $\square$

Intuitively, Φ "extracts" from τ the information denoted by the string $\Phi(\tau)$. If many transaction systems are mapped by Φ to the same string φ, then the scheduler cannot distinguish among them. The more such "look-alikes" exist in $\Phi^{-1}(\varphi)$, the less information about the transaction system is contained in φ.

Example 5.2: We describe below some common examples of information operators. Perfect information corresponds to any Φ which is one-to-one (notice that, since we insist that domains are denumerable, such a mapping exists). Such an operator is called *the complete information* operator. An opposite extreme, in which hopelessly little information is available, is the case in which

$\Phi(\tau)$ encodes just the number of steps in the transactions of τ. This is the weakest information operator that we shall consider, and is called the *minimum information* operator.

A more common intermediate case is when $\Phi(\tau)$ encodes the "syntax" of τ, that is, the entity acted upon at each step; we call this the *syntactic information* operator. $\square$

Optimal Schedulers

Given a transaction set τ, complete with its interpretation $I = (\mathbf{D}, \mathbf{F})$, and integrity constraints $\mathbf{C}$, it is straightforward to define a set $C(\tau)$ of *correct schedules*. A schedule s of τ is called correct, $s \in C(\tau)$, if for each consistent state $X \in \mathbf{C}$ the state produced by the execution of s, $s(I, X)$ is also in $\mathbf{C}$. A scheduler S is correct if $\mathcal{O}(S) \subseteq C(\tau)$.

This notion of correctness is appropriate only when complete information is available. Typically, however, the scheduler will have only some partial information $\Phi(\tau)$ about the transaction system τ it is supposed to handle. What is, in this case, the appropriate definition of correctness?

Definition 5.3: A scheduler S with information $\varphi = \Phi(\tau)$ is *correct* if

$$\mathcal{O}(S) \subseteq \bigcap_{\tau' \in \Phi^{-1}(\varphi)} C(\tau'). \ \square$$

In other words, the scheduler must output schedules which are correct in the context of each possible τ' with the same information image as τ. If a scheduler S with information $\varphi = \Phi(T)$ satisfies

$$\mathcal{C}(S) = \mathcal{O}(S) = \bigcap_{\tau' \in \Phi^{-1}(\varphi)} C(\tau'),$$

then S is called *optimal* for this information.

Example 5.3: When complete information is available, then the intersection in Definition 5.3 is over only one set $C(\tau')$, and degenerates to $C(\tau)$. A scheduler with complete information is optimal if it lets through all correct schedules. $\square$

Example 5.4: For a slightly more interesting example, what is this intersection in the case of minimal information? For simplicity, we shall assume that transactions have at least two steps, as otherwise the answer is a bit more complicated (see Problem 5.2). As we shall show next, in this case the intersection in Definition 5.3 coincides with the set of all serial schedules.

First, it is easy to see that all serial schedules are correct under any possible syntax and semantics of the transactions, because of our assumption that all individual transactions are correct. Next, we show that there are no other schedules in the intersection. Suppose that a schedule s is not serial. We shall specify the syntax and the semantics of a transaction system τ, with the same number of steps in each transaction as in s, such that $s \notin C(\tau)$. Since s is not serial, there are steps a, b, of some transaction A and a', b' of another transaction A', appearing in s either in the order a, a', b', b, or in the order a, a', b, b'. We construct a τ in which a is an $A(x)$ step, b is an $A(y)$ step, a' is a $A(y)$ step and b' is a $A(x)$ step. All other steps are irrelevant (say, they act on new entities). The domains are the integers, and the integrity constraint is "$x = y$", say. By defining the semantics of the four steps a, b, a', and b' as $x{:=}x + 1$, $y{:=}y + 1$, $y{:=}1$, and $x{:=}1$, respectively, we obtain a set of correct transactions. It is also obvious, however, that s is not correct in this transaction system, since it maps a consistent state with $x = y = 0$ to an inconsistent state $x = 1, y = 2$.

This result means that, when no syntactic or semantic information is available, we have no choice but to schedule the transactions one at a time, in a serial way. □

Example 5.5: If only syntactic information is available, the intersection in the Definition 5.3 turns out to coincide with the class of serializable schedules (recall that in the action model view serializability, final-state serializability, and conflict serializability coincide, and we use the term "serializable" to denote any one of them). In proof, observe first that any serializable schedule is correct under any interpretation and integrity constraints. The reason is that individual transactions are by definition correct in any transaction system, and therefore so are serial schedules of the transactions. Since serializable schedules map any initial state to the same final state as would a serial schedule, we conclude that serializable schedules are correct in any transaction system with the given syntax.

To show that only serializable schedules are in the intersection, we shall employ the same "adversary argument" as in the previous examples: Assuming that s is not serializable, we shall construct a transaction system τ with the same syntax, such that $s \notin C(\tau)$. τ will assign to the transactions semantics similar to those in the proof of the *only if* part of Theorem 2.1. In particular, each step $A(x)$ computes a sequence of transactions acting on x, in the order in which the $A(x)$ steps occurred in s. Formally, the domains of the entities are finite sequences of transactions, and the semantics of the step $B : A(x)$ is $x{:=}xB$. Finally, the consistent states of τ are all those mappings from E to sequences of transactions that can be obtained as final states of serial schedules containing any number of copies of the transactions of τ, starting from the empty sequences.

The integrity constraints were defined in such a way that all transactions are correct, as required. However, s is not correct in τ. To prove this, notice first that the values computed by s, starting with the empty sequences, are unlike the values computed by any serial schedule involving each transaction once, because, if they were the same, s would be serializable by Theorem 2.7. They are also different from the values computed by schedules involving certain transactions more than once or not at all, since such schedules compute sequences in which transactions appear a number of times different from one, whereas the values produced by s contain each transaction exactly once. It follows that, under these semantics, s will lead the database from the consistent empty state to an inconsistent state, and therefore s is incorrect. $\Box$

This last example suggests that serializability is the most concurrency one can achieve with syntactic information alone (and, as was argued in Chapter 2, syntactic information is the most common kind of information acquired in practice). This observation is an *ex post facto* justification of the importance of serializability and its variants as correctness criteria.

Dynamic Information

The notion of information defined earlier in this section corresponds to the *static* mode of information acquisition. The operator Φ remains the same as the schedule progresses. We shall next examine *dynamic information*.

Definition 5.4: A *dynamic information operator* is a mapping Ψ assigning to each transaction system τ and prefix p of a schedule of the transactions in τ a string $\Psi(p, \tau) \in \{0, 1\}^*$, such that if τ and τ' are transaction systems and p is a prefix of q, then $\Psi(q, \tau) = \Psi(q, \tau')$ implies $\Psi(p, \tau) = \Psi(p, \tau')$. $\Box$

The first argument of Ψ in the above definition denotes the part of the schedule that has arrived so far. The condition on Ψ guarantees that the scheduler "does not forget," that is, as new steps of the schedule arrive, Ψ extracts more and more information about the transaction system being handled.

When can a scheduler safely output a schedule s in such an environment of information acquisition? As with static information, the final schedule s must be in the intersection of all $C(\tau')$'s, for all τ''s such that $\Psi(s, \tau') = \Psi(s, \tau)$. What about a prefix p of s? It must also be correct, *with respect to the information available at the time the last step of p was output*. At that time, the transaction system could be any τ' such that $\Psi(p', \tau) = \Psi(p', \tau')$, where p' is the part of the schedule that had arrived at the time the last step of p was output. (If $p \neq p'$, then the steps in p' but not in p are in the queue, and there can be at most one such step per transaction.) If for one such τ' there is no possible completion of p in $C(\tau')$, then p must be considered incorrect: If T' had turned out to be the transaction system actually being handled, then the scheduler would not be able to complete p to a correct schedule.

Definition 5.5: We say that a scheduler S, operating with dynamic information Ψ is *correct* if, whenever prefix p is output while prefix p' has arrived,

$$p \in \text{PREFIX} \left[\bigcap_{\Psi(p',\tau')=\Psi(p',\tau)} C(\tau') \right]. \quad \Box$$

As a consequence of the definition, any prefix p of a schedule in the concurrency $C(S)$ of a correct scheduler S must satisfy

$$p \in \text{PREFIX} \left[\bigcap_{\Psi(p,\tau')=\Psi(p,\tau)} C(\tau') \right], \qquad (5.1)$$

since for such prefixes the scheduler outputs the last step on its arrival. Thus, the set of all schedules the prefixes of which satisfy (5.1), is an upper bound on the concurrency of any correct scheduler operating with the dynamic information operator Ψ. Schedulers that achieve this bound are called *optimal*.

Example 5.6: Consider the important case of *dynamic syntactic information*. In this information environment the scheduler knows only the syntax of the steps that have arrived so far; if a transaction has already terminated, it is reasonable to assume that this information is also available. That is, $\Psi(p, \tau) = \Psi(p, \tau')$ if and only if τ and τ' act on precisely the same entity in each step of p, and the set of transactions that have terminated in p coincides in the two transaction systems.

What schedules can be output without delays under dynamic syntactic information? The answer is, all schedules in which no step conflicts with a previous step of a currently active transaction. Interestingly, these are precisely the schedules output by the dynamic two-phase locking scheduler of Section 3.2.

To show this, first suppose that s is such a schedule, and p a prefix of s. We shall show that in all transaction systems compatible with the syntax of the steps in p, there is a continuation of p which is correct. Consider such a transaction system. Define a directed graph $G(p)$ with nodes the transactions (including those that perhaps do not appear in p), and an arc from A to B if a step of A conflicts with a step of B, and either the step of A is in p and that of B is not, or both are in p, with the step of A occurring first. Notice that $G(p)$ is acyclic, since its arcs go from transactions that terminated earlier to transactions that either terminated later, or have not yet terminated at the end of p. Thus, we can topologically sort the transactions in $G(p)$, to obtain a total order $T_1, T_2, \ldots, T_n$ on the transactions. Now define the following completion s' of p: s' consists of p, followed by the remaining steps (if any) of T_1, followed by the remaining steps of T_2, and so on. We claim that s' is serializable. In proof, notice that the graph $G(s')$ (Theorem 2.8) consists of arcs compatible with the total order above, and is therefore acyclic. We have shown that, for all extensions of the syntax of p, there is a serializable continuation of p, that is, a continuation which is correct for all interpretations, domains, and integrity constraints. It follows that all schedules with the property that no step conflicts with a previous step of an active transaction can be output with no delays when dynamic syntactic information is available.

Conversely, let s be any schedule in which a step does conflict with a previous step of an active transaction. That is, for some $A(x)$ steps of transactions B and C, $C : A(x)$ comes second, and B has not terminated at the $C : A(x)$ step. Let p be the prefix of s up to the $C : A(x)$ step. Consider now a transaction system in which the syntax of transactions up to p is the given one, the domains are the integers, the semantics of $B : A(x)$ is $x := x + 1$, that of $C : A(x)$ is $x := 2 * x$, and there is another $B : A(x)$ step in the continuation with semantics $x := x - 1$[1]. The integrity constraints are "$x = 0$", and all other steps are "no-ops" (e.g., $y := y$). It is immediate that p has no correct continuation in this transaction system, which completes the proof.

We conclude that the dynamic two-phase locking scheduler is optimal in an environment of dynamic syntactic information. There is a catch, however. For some prefixes of schedules in this class there are indeed always correct extensions; however, it is possible that these extensions cannot be realized by dynamic two-phase locking. This fact reflects the *deadlock* situations inherent in dynamic two-phase locking. □

5.3 MULTIVERSION SCHEDULERS

The same issues of performance and efficiency are important in the study of multiversion schedulers. Once more, the concurrency of such a scheduler S can be measured as the set $\mathcal{C}(S)$ of schedules that are not delayed by it. In the case in which this set coincides with the set of schedules output by S, $\mathcal{O}(S)$, we can say as before that S *realizes* this set (in the case of multiversion schedulers, these sets may contain schedules that are not view serializable). As with ordinary schedulers, we call a multiversion scheduler efficient if (a) its *state* data structure does not grow more than polynomially in its initial size and the number of steps, and (b) the algorithms *test* and *assign-version* (recall Figure 4.8) are both polynomial time bounded. There are, however, a number of important differences in applying these ideas to the multiversion case. As a result, we must develop a new set of concepts and results.

Schedulability

The proof of Theorem 5.1 suggests that any set $\mathcal{C}$ of view serializable schedules

---

[1] If we insist that each transaction acts on an entity only once, as is the case in the read-write model, then the optimal scheduler is a little more relaxed.

can in principle be realized by a scheduler (of course, the complexity of this scheduler may be tremendous, as determined by the complexity of $\text{PREFIX}(\mathcal{C})$). Can we say the same of any set of multiversion serializable schedules? Is it true that, for any such set, there is a safe multiversion scheduler that outputs it?

Example 5.7: Consider these two schedules:

$$s = \begin{array}{l} A : R(x)W(x) \qquad\quad R(y)W(y) \\ B : \qquad\qquad\quad R(x) \qquad\qquad R(y)W(y) \end{array}$$

$$s' = \begin{array}{l} A : R(x)W(x) \qquad\qquad\qquad\quad R(y)W(y) \\ B : \qquad\qquad R(x)R(y)W(y) \end{array}$$

Both s and s' are multiversion serializable. s is equivalent to the serial schedule AB if transaction B reads x from A, and this is the only version function that makes s equivalent to a serial schedule. Also, s' can be made equivalent to BA if B reads x from A_0 (the initial transaction), this again being the only way to serialize s'. Suppose now that $\mathcal{M}$ is a set of multiversion serializable schedules, containing both s and s'. Is there a safe multiversion scheduler S such that $\mathcal{M} = \mathcal{O}(S)$? The answer here must be "no." The reason is, intuitively, that s and s', although both multiversion serializable, are *incompatible* in terms of the version functions that they need to become correct full schedules. What would S do when, at the third step of both schedules, transaction B requests to read a version of x? So far, the steps seen could be a prefix of either s or s', so the request cannot be turned down (remember, S is supposed to realize all of $\mathcal{M}$). S has thus two choices: presenting the version written by A, or the initial version. In either case, S's action excludes the possibility that one of s, s' will be output, and so S does not realize $\mathcal{M}$. $\square$

Any set of multiversion serializable schedules that contains the two schedules of Example 5.6 cannot be realized by a safe mutiversion scheduler; we may say that such a set "is not schedulable." To formalize this concept, call a set $\mathcal{M}$ of multiversion serializable schedules *schedulable* if, for any prefix p of a schedule in $\mathcal{M}$, there is a version function V defined on p such that, for each schedule pq in $\mathcal{M}$, there is a view serializable full schedule (pq, V'), such that the version function V' agrees with V on the steps of p. In other words, $\mathcal{M}$ contains no incompatible continuations of the same prefix.

If a set is not schedulable, then no superset can be. As a result, any set containing s and s' is not schedulable; this includes the set of all multiversion serializable schedules, and even the set of conflict multiversion serializable schedules—it can be easily checked that both s and s' are conflict multiversion serializable.

The following result justifies our definition of schedulable sets:

Proposition 5.2: *Let $\mathcal{M}$ be a set of multiversion serializable schedules. There is a multiversion scheduler S such that $\mathcal{C}(S) = \mathcal{O}(S) = \mathcal{M}$ if and only if $\mathcal{M}$ is schedulable.*

Proof: If $\mathcal{M}$ is not schedulable, then we can use the argument in Example 5.6 to show that no safe scheduler can output all schedules in $\mathcal{M}$. In particular, there must be a prefix p of a schedule in $\mathcal{M}$ such that there are two extensions pq and pq' with the property that any two version functions V and V' such that (pq, V) and (pq', V') are view serializable must disagree on steps of p. Suppose that a safe scheduler S exists that realizes $\mathcal{M}$. How would S respond if presented with p? Since S realizes $\mathcal{M}$, it must output all of p, and present a version to each read step. However, no matter what versions are presented, not both pq and pq' can now be output, a contradiction.

Conversely, if $\mathcal{M}$ is schedulable, then we can design a multiversion scheduler that realizes it. The test of the scheduler simply makes sure that the step under consideration, when added to the prefix output so far, makes up a prefix p of some schedule in $\mathcal{M}$. As for the "assign-version" part of the scheduler (recall Fig. 4.8), we have from the definition of schedulable sets that there is a version function V for p which has extensions compatible with all $pq \in \mathcal{M}$; we assign to the last read step of p the version assigned to it by V. $\square$

If $\mathcal{M}$ is schedulable, then it can be realized by an *efficient* multiversion scheduler if and only if there are polynomial-time algorithms for determining whether $p \in \text{PREFIX}(\mathcal{M})$, and for computing, given a prefix p, the appropriate version function. The proof (Problem 5.3) is analogous to that of Theorem 5.1. Another algorithmic problem naturally arising in this context is the following: Given a set of schedules, how can we test whether they are schedulable? Unfortunately, this problem is NP-complete (see Problem 5.4).

Maximal Schedulable Sets

In designing single version schedulers, our goal was clear: We wanted it to realize as large a set of schedules as possible, ideally the set of all view serializable schedules. In designing (and evaluating) multiversion schedulers, the goal is not clear any longer. We cannot hope to realize all of multiversion serializable schedules, not even the conflict multiversion serializable ones, as these sets are not schedulable. Among all schedulable sets of multiversion serializable schedules, however, particularly attractive are those that are *maximal*, that is, no multiversion serializable schedule can be added to them if the result is to remain schedulable. It can be shown that there are *infinitely* many maximal schedulable sets of multiversion serializable schedules (Problem 5.5), but they are all reasonable as goals of our design of a performing multiversion scheduler. Unfortunately, we shall show that *none of them* is practically attainable.

Let S be a multiversion scheduler which realizes a maximal schedulable set of multiversion serializable set of schedules $\mathcal{M} = \mathcal{C}(S) = \mathcal{O}(S)$. When a schedule $s \in \mathcal{M}$ is presented to S as an input, S accepts each step, and assigns to each read step of s one of the previously written versions of the entity read (for simplicity, we assume that all versions are kept). Under what circumstances would a step be the first in its schedule to be rejected by S?

Lemma 5.1: *Suppose that S accepts all steps in p but rejects step a of schedule paq. Then there is no view serializable full schedule (paq', V) such that V agrees with the versions assigned to the read steps in p by S.*

Proof: For the sake of contradiction assume that such a schedule paq' exists. Since a was rejected by S, $paq' \notin \mathcal{M}$. Since $\mathcal{M}$ is maximal, it follows that $\mathcal{M} \cup \{paq'\}$ is not schedulable. By the definition of schedulable sets, there is a prefix p' such that, for all version functions V defined on the read steps of p', there exists an extension $p'r \in \mathcal{M} \cup \{paq'\}$ of p' such that there is no version function V' agreeing with V for which the full schedule $(p'r, V')$ is view serializable. Since $\mathcal{M}$ is schedulable, p' must be a prefix of paq'. If p' is a prefix of p, then by our hypothesis there is a version function defined on the steps of p' (namely, the one defined by S) which can be extended to appropriate version functions to all completions of p', including paq'. Thus, we must conclude that p' is not a prefix of p, or equivalently that pa is a prefix of p'. But in this case, for each extension of p' in $\mathcal{M} \cup \{paq'\}$ (of which there is only one, namely paq') there is, by our hypothesis, a version function making it view serializable, a contradiction. $\square$

Corollary: *If a multiversion serializable schedule s has the property that, for any prefix p of s, there is exactly one version function V for the read steps of p such that p and V can be extended to a view serializable full schedule (pq, V'), then s is contained in all maximal schedulable sets of multiversion serializable schedules.*

Proof: Problem 5.7. $\square$

Theorem 5.2: *Let $\mathcal{M}$ be any maximal schedulable set of multiversion serializable schedules. Then it is NP-hard[2] to tell whether a schedule is in $\mathcal{M}$.*

Proof: We shall reduce the problem of testing a polygraph for acyclicity to the membership problem of any such $\mathcal{M}$. Let $P = (V, A, C)$ be a polygraph. We shall construct a schedule $s(P)$ which has the following property: If P is acyclic, then $s(P)$ belongs to *all* maximal schedulable sets of multiversion serializable schedules. On the other hand, if P is not acyclic, then $s(P)$ belongs to no such set of schedules. The theorem then will follow.

As in Theorem 3.2, we assume that for each arc $(A_1, A_2) \in A$ there is a choice (A_1, A_2, A_3) in C. The schedule $s(P)$ has a transaction for each vertex in V, and for each choice c in C it has three entities c, c', and c''. For each

---

[2] A problem is called NP-hard if all problems in NP reduce to it, just as they do to an NP-complete problem, but we do not know whether it is *itself* in NP. NP-hard problems are every bit as hard as NP-complete problems, but perhaps even harder. How hard can a maximal set be? See Problem 5.6.

choice $c = (A_1, A_2, A_3)$ in C, $s(P)$ contains the following segment of a schedule:

$$
\begin{array}{llll}
A_1 : & \dots \quad W(c) \quad R(c') & & R(c'') \dots \\
A_2 : & \dots & W(c')W(c'') & \dots \\
A_3 : & \dots R(c) \quad W(c') & & W(c'') \quad \dots
\end{array}
$$

All segments are concatenated, and this completes the construction of $s(P)$.

We shall now argue that, if P is acyclic, then $s(P)$ is in $\mathcal{M}$, the arbitrary maximal schedulable set of multiversion schedules in our theorem. We shall accomplish this by showing that for each prefix of $s(P)$ there is a unique version function defined on the read steps of the prefix such that the prefix and the version function can be extended to a view serializable full schedule. In particular, consider the acyclic directed graph which is compatible with P, and the serial schedule s' which arranges the transactions in the order of some topological sort of the directed graph. Let V be version function which agrees with $V_{s'}$, the standard version function of this schedule, on all read steps, and maps all write steps to ν. We shall show that for each prefix p of $s(P)$ the version function V restricted to the steps of p is the only version function which can be extended to form a view serializable full schedule, namely $(s(P), V)$.

We show this by induction on the length of the prefix p. Suppose that the last step of p is a read step in the segment corresponding to choice $c = (A_1, A_2, A_3)$. If it is the first read step $A_3 : R(c)$, then there is no write step on c preceding this step, and our only choice is to map it to $A_0 : W(c)$; this agrees with V. If the last step of p is $A_1 : R(c')$, then we can can map it either to $A_0 : W(c')$ or to $A_3 : W(c')$. The first option, however, implies that A_1 comes before A_3, contradicting the fact that A_3 read c from A_0, and thus A_3 comes first. So, we must take the second option, which again agrees with V. Since A_2 also writes c', it follows that in any serial schedule view equivalent to an extension of p, A_2 comes either before A_3 or after A_1; notice that this agrees with V, by the definition of polygraph acyclicity. Finally, if the last step of p is $A_1 : R(c'')$, then again it cannot read from A_0, and by the previous remark it cannot read from A_2 either; so it is mapped to $A_1 : W(c'')$, as is in V. We conclude that there is exactly one version function compatible with any prefix of $s(P)$. Therefore, $s(P)$ is by the corollary in all maximal schedulable sets of multiversion serializable schedules, and thus in $\mathcal{M}$.

Conversely, suppose that $s(P) \in \mathcal{M}$. Let V be a version function and s' a serial schedule such that $(s(P), V)$ is view equivalent to $(s', V_{s'})$. As was argued above, V is uniquely determined on read steps, and $V_{s'}$ agrees with it. Therefore, for each choice $c = (A_1, A_2, A_3)$ in C, A_3 must come in s' before A_1, and A_2 either before A_3 or after A_1. It follows that the total order defined by the serial schedule s' is compatible with the polygraph P, and so P is acyclic. $\square$

Corollary: *Unless P=NP, there is no efficient multiversion scheduler which realizes a maximal schedulable set of multiversion serializable schedules.*

Proof: See Problem 5.8. □

By similar techniques we can show that all maximal schedulable sets of *conflict* multiversion serializable schedules cannot be realized by efficient multiversion schedulers (Problem 5.9).

PROBLEMS

5.1 Show that it is NP-complete to decide whether a given prefix p can be extended to a view serializable schedule.

5.2 Show that, if we allow transactions with only one step, there are schedules which are not serial, and still are correct, for any combination of syntax and semantics of the transactions and integrity constraints. Give a characterization of correct schedules in this case.

5.3 Suppose that $\mathcal{M}$ is a schedulable set of multiversion serializable schedules. Show that $\mathcal{M}$ can be realized by an efficient multiversion scheduler if and only if there are polynomial-time algorithms for deciding whether a prefix p can be extended to a schedule $s \in \mathcal{M}$, and for computing a version function on the read steps of p which can be extended to a version function for any such s.

5.4 Show that it is NP-complete to tell whether two schedules form a schedulable set.

5.5 Show that there are infinitely many maximal schedulable sets of multiversion serializable schedules, and of conflict multiversion serializable schedules.

**5.6 Show that there is a maximal schedulable set of multiversion serializable schedules which is undecidable.

5.7 Prove the corollary to Lemma 5.1.

5.8 Prove the corollary to Theorem 5.2.

5.9 Suppose that $\mathcal{M}$ is a maximal schedulable set of *conflict* multiversion serializable schedules. Show that, unless P=NP, there is no efficient scheduler which outputs $\mathcal{M}$.

5.10 Give an example of a schedule which is not view serializable, and still is the prefix of a view serializable schedule. Now give an example of a schedule which is not view serializable, but becomes view serializable if it is concatenated with another schedule (involving new transactions). In view of these examples, what is the largest subset of view serializable schedules that can be realized by a scheduler with declaration information? Repeat for dynamic information.

NOTES AND REFERENCES

The qualitative framework for the study of the performance of schedulers introduced in Sections 5.1 and 5.2 is from [Papadimitriou 1979] and [Kung and Papadimitriou 1984]. A result analogous to that of Example 5.5 was also shown in [Rosenkrantz et al. 1982]. There is an extensive literature on evaluating quantitatively the performance of schedulers; see for example [Chesnais et al. 1983], [Irani and Lin 1979], [Papadimitriou and Tsitsiklis 1986], [Potier and Leblanc 1980], [Sevcik 1983], [Shum and Spirakis 1981], [Tay, Suri, and Goodman 1984], [Thomasian and Ryu 1983]. Most of the work in this direction is confined to the simplest locking schedulers, and is based on rough assumptions; still the analytical problems encountered are formidable, and there are still no breakthroughs and definitive results in this area. The material of Section 5.3 on the performance of multiversion schedulers is from [Hadzilacos and Papadimitriou 1985], where the solutions of Problems 5.4 and 5.9 can be found.

6

THE THEORY OF LOCKING

Locking—that is, inserting locks and unlocks among the steps of transactions—has been historically the first method used to control the concurrent execution of database transactions. In fact, in the first years of the development of this area, locking was almost synonymous to concurrency control. Although we have seen that several other ideas and structures besides locking are important for concurrency control, it is also beyond doubt that locking is always by far the single most common and important concurrency control mechanism. Besides, it turns out that the study of locking has resulted in some of the most deep and important theoretical results in concurrency control. In the present chapter we develop this theory of locking, with an eye towards discovering the power and limitations of the locking approach. In the process, we point out some new and interesting possibilities for more powerful and general schedulers based on locking.

Our study of locking proceeds along models of increasing "structure." In the beginning, the transactions are completely uninterpreted, and the locks are simply binary semaphores, unrelated to the steps of the transactions; in this context locking is shown to be surprisingly powerful. We then proceed to take into account the syntax of the transactions, and the relation of the locks to the database entities; an interesting geometric method is very helpful in pointing out the power of locking in this model. Finally, we explore the general principles involved in the design of correct locking protocols which exploit the structure of the underlying transactions.

6.1 UNINTERPRETED LOCKING

In this first section we shall study locking simply as a synchronization primitive, more or less independently of the database context. Let us consider a transaction $A = a_1a_2 \ldots a_m$. (Notice that, since we shall postpone for a later section the subject of the connection between the lock steps and the entities acted upon by the transaction, we are in the *fully uninterpreted* model of transactions, in which steps are just distinct symbols.) We let the symbols $\ell_i, u_i, i = 1, 2, \ldots$ be new steps, intended to represent the several kinds of lock and unlock steps that we may wish to insert among the steps of A. A *locking* of A is any element of $A * \ell_1u_1 * \ell_2u_2 * \cdots * \ell_ku_k$, for some $k > 1$. In other words, a locking is a way of inserting lock steps, and matching unlock steps, among the steps of A, with each unlock step always following the corresponding lock step. For example, if $A = a_1a_2a_3a_4$, then $\bar{A} = \ell_1\ell_2a_1u_2\ell_3a_2a_3u_3a_4u_1$ is a locking of A. The indices $1, 2, \ldots, k$ of the lock and unlock steps are called the *locks*. If τ is a transaction system, then a *locking* of τ is a set λ of lockings, containing one locking of each transaction in τ. If s is a schedule involving locked transactions, the *reduction* of s, denoted $\rho(s)$, is defined to be s with all lock-unlock steps deleted.

We are now ready to define what it means for an ordinary schedule s (without lock and unlock steps) involving transactions $\tau = \{A_1, \ldots, A_n\}$ to be *legal* with respect to the locking $\lambda = \{\bar{A}_1, \ldots, \bar{A}_n\}$ of the same transactions. Intuitively, s is legal if it is a possible execution order, when the locks are respected. Formally, consider a schedule $\bar{s} \in \bar{A}_1 * \cdots * \bar{A}_n$ of the locking. We say that $\bar{s}$ is *legal* if between any two consecutive occurrences of a lock step ℓ_j, there is an occurrence of the corresponding unlock step u_j[1] (informally, this means that no transaction locks a lock which is locked by another transaction and is not yet unlocked). A schedule $s \in A_1 * \cdots * A_n$ is legal if there is a legal schedule $\bar{s} \in \bar{A}_1 * \cdots * \bar{A}_n$ such that $s = \rho(\bar{s})$. Thus, a schedule s is legal with respect to a locking if there is a legal way of executing the steps of the locking, attaching to "lock" and "unlock" their intuitive meaning, so that s is a subsequence of the resulting schedule. For example, in the locking $\bar{A} = \ell_1a_1\ell_2u_1a_2u_2a_3$, $\bar{B} = b_1\ell_1b_2\ell_2u_2b_3u_1$, the schedule $a_1b_1b_2a_2a_3b_3$ is legal, as it is a subsequence of the legal schedule $\ell_1a_1\ell_2u_1b_1\ell_1b_2a_2u_2a_3\ell_2u_2b_3u_1$. In contrast, the schedule $b_1b_2a_1a_2a_3b_3$ is not legal, because intuitively lock 1 is locked before step b_2 and unlocked after step b_3, and hence there is no way for step a_1, during which lock 1 is locked, to execute in between. In fact, given a schedule of n transactions, and a locking for these, it is easy to tell efficiently

---

[1] Notice that in our linear notation for a schedule of locked transactions, there may be an ambiguity concerning the transaction from which a particular lock or unlock step originates (consider, e.g., the first ℓ_1 step in the schedule $a_1\ell_1c_1\ell_1b_1a_2u_1c_2\ell_1u_1u_1b_2$ of the transactions $a_1\ell_1a_2u_1$, $\ell_1b_1u_1b_2$, and $c_1c_2\ell_1u_1$). This ambiguity could be avoided by displaying uninterpreted schedules in the "multi-level" notation we have used for the read-write model. Fortunately, this ambiguity is completely harmless to our arguments; for example, the several possible interpretations of the schedule above are essentially the same schedule. Furthermore, in *legal* schedules, the only ones of interest, there is essentially no ambiguity of this sort. Therefore, no change in our notation is necessary.

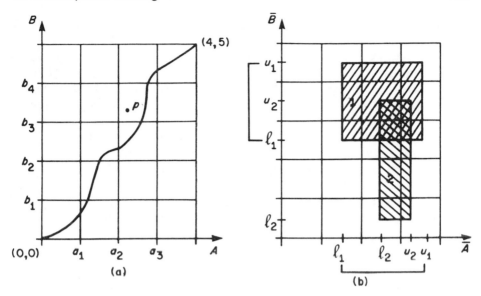

Figure 6.1. Geometric Interpretation of Locking.

whether the schedule is legal (Problem 6.1).

When only two transactions are involved, locking has an interesting geometric interpretation, introduced next. We can think of the steps of the transactions $A = a_1 \ldots a_m$ and $B = b_1 \ldots b_n$ as being the first few integer points on the two axes of the Euclidean plane (see Figure 6.1(a) for an illustration). Any point on the $m \times n$ square represents a certain degree of progress towards completing the two transactions. For example, point p in Figure 6.1 stands for a state in which we have executed the two first steps of A and the three first steps of B. (More formally, the open squares defined by the grid lines are *equivalence classes* with respect to this notion of "progress.") We call points with integer coordinates *grid points*; the horizontal and vertical lines with integer coordinates are *grid lines*. Schedules can be depicted as *curves* from point $(0, 0)$ of the plane to point $(m + 1, n + 1)$, such that the only grid points on the curve are its two endpoints, and both coordinates are strictly increasing on the curve. We call such curves *monotone*. For example, curve c in Figure 6.1(a) represents the schedule $a_1 b_1 b_2 a_2 b_3 b_4 a_3$; to find the schedule represented by a given monotone curve, we first determine the sequence of grid lines crossed by the curve, in the order they are crossed, and then replace each such line by the corresponding transaction step.

Lock and unlock steps inserted among the transactions A and B can be thought of as points on the two axes with fractional coordinates (Figure 6.1(b)). Furthermore, locking adds to the picture certain "inaccessible regions," as follows. Consider for example the locking $\lambda = (\bar{A}, \bar{B})$ of transactions A and B, where $\bar{A} = a_1 \ell_1 a_2 \ell_2 a_3 u_2 u_1$ and $\bar{B} = \ell_2 b_1 b_2 \ell_1 b_3 u_2 b_4 u_1$. Each of the two locks defines an interval on each axis, extending from the lock step to the unlock step for that transaction. For example, lock 1 defines the two intervals shown in Figure 6.1(b). The two intervals corresponding to a lock define a *rectangle*, namely their Cartesian product (these are the two rectangles shaded and labeled with the corresponding locks in Figure 6.1(b)). Any point within such a rectangle represents a state of the joint execution in which both transactions hold the same lock (and is therefore "forbidden"). To say it in a different way, crossing the boundary of such a rectangle corresponds to a transaction locking a lock that another transaction has locked and not yet unlocked. Consequently, *legal schedules*, as defined above, correspond to *monotone curves that avoid all forbidden rectangles*. This insight will be particularly useful in most of this chapter.

The Power of Locking

Each locking of a transaction system defines a set of legal schedules. Can all sets of schedules be realized by locking? If so, locking would prove to be a remarkably powerful concurrency control primitive, able in principle to realize any concurrency control algorithm imaginable. And if not, *what exactly is the power of locking?* That is, which are those sets $\mathcal{C}$ of schedules of a fixed set of transactions, for which there is a locking of the transactions, such that $\mathcal{C}$ is precisely the set of legal schedules under the locking? We are interested in this question, because the richness of the sets of schedules realized by locking is a measure of the "power" or "versatility" of locking as a primitive, its ability to "approximate" concurrency control principles by realizing a satisfactorily large subset of the desired set of schedules. To pose the problem more formally, let us fix a set of transactions $\tau = \{A_1, \ldots, A_n\}$, and consider a set of schedules $\mathcal{C} \subseteq A_1 * \cdots * A_n$. We call $\mathcal{C}$ *realizable* if there is a locking $\lambda = \{\bar{A}_1, \ldots, \bar{A}_n\}$ of τ such that the set of reductions of all legal schedules of λ is precisely $\mathcal{C}$. We would like to characterize the realizable subsets of $A_1 * \cdots * A_n$.

We shall first look at the case of two transactions $A = a_1 \ldots a_m$ and $B = b_1 \ldots b_n$; in this case we can use the geometric methodology introduced above to show an elegant characterization of all realizable sets of schedules. This characterization states that, in order for a class of schedules to be realizable, it suffices that two intuitive properties are satisfied. The first property is the obvious requirement that both serial schedules AB and BA be in the class, as no locking can exclude these. The second is a certain intuitive *closure* property. The precise statement of the result is the following (in what follows a, a', etc. stand for steps of A, and b, b', etc. for steps of B; s, t, s', etc. are subsequences of schedules involving the transactions A and B):

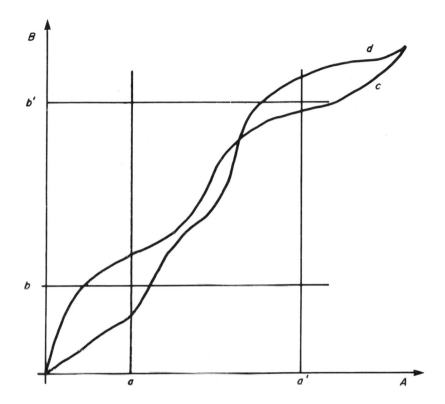

Figure 6.2. The Proof of the *only if* Direction.

Theorem 6.1: C *is realizable if and only if the following two conditions hold:* (a) $AB, BA \in C$, *and* (b) *for each pair of schedules* $sara's'$, $tbrb't' \in C$ *with* STEPS(sa) = STEPS(tb), *the schedules* $sarb'l'$, $tbra's'$ *are also in* C.

Proof: For the *only if* part, it is clear that all realizable sets must contain both serial schedules AB and BA, as these schedules are always legal (the reason is that schedules $\bar{A}\bar{B}$ and $\bar{B}\bar{A}$, for any locking $\bar{A}, B$, are trivially legal). To show property (b), we shall use the geometric approach. Consider two monotone curves c and d corresponding to the schedules $sara's'$ and $tbrb't'$ (Figure 6.2), and in particular the two segments of the curves between the steps a-a', and b-b', respectively (highlighted in Figure 6.2). If we consider now the rectangle defined by these four steps (also highlighted in Figure 6.2), we notice that the two curve segments join two pairs of points on the perimeter of the rectangle. However, these two pairs are such that the two points of each are nonconsecutive on the perimeter of the rectangle. As a result, the two curves must cross at some point in the rectangle, call it p. But then it is clear that the curve which

coincides with c up to p and with d after this, and the one that does exactly
the opposite, are legal monotone curves, also corresponding to legal schedules.
These two schedules, however, are exactly $sarb't'$ and $tbra's'$, and the *only if*
part is complete.

The other direction is the more interesting and nontrivial part. Suppose
that we are given a set $\mathcal{C}$ of schedules obeying conditions (a) and (b) of the
theorem. We shall give an explicit contruction of a locking $\bar{A}, \bar{B}$ of $A, B,$ such
that the set of schedules that are legal under this locking is exactly $\mathcal{C}$. Again,
we use the geometric approach. Our construction proceeds by visiting one
by one the $(m + 1)(n + 1)$ squares formed by the grid lines, and adding to
the locking certain lock and unlock steps that will create a certain pattern of
forbidden rectangles in the square. We shall show that the resulting overall
locking realizes $\mathcal{C}$.

Consider the square enclosed by the lines a_i, a_{i+1}, b_j, b_{j+1}, for some $0 \leq$
$i \leq m$, $0 \leq j \leq n$. We call this the ijth square. With each such square we can
associate a set P_{ij} of prefixes of schedules in $\mathcal{C}$, and a set S_{ij} of suffixes, namely
$P_{ij} = \{s : st \in \mathcal{C}, \text{ and } \text{STEPS}(s) = \{a_1, \ldots, a_i, b_1, \ldots, b_j\}\}$, and $S_{ij} = \{s : ts \in$
$\mathcal{C}, \text{ and } \text{STEPS}(t) = \{a_1, \ldots, a_i, b_1, \ldots, b_j\}\}$. In other words, P_{ij} (respectively,
S_{ij}) is the set of prefixes (respectively, suffixes) of all schedules in $\mathcal{C}$, such
that the corresponding monotone curve passes through the ijth square, up to
(respectively, starting at) the ijth square. We can furthermore define a natural
total order on these sets. For $s, s' \in S_{ij}$, we write that $s \prec s'$ if s and s' can
be written as $s = s_1 a s_2$ and $s' = s_1 b s'_2$; that is, in the first place in which they
differ s has a step of A and s' a step of B. (This is the natural *lexicographic
order* on S_{ij}, if we assume that all steps of A come before all steps of B in our
"alphabet.") We can also define the lexicographic order *on the reverses* of the
prefixes in P_{ij}: (also denoted $\prec$): $p \prec p'$ if $p = p_1 a p_2$ and $p' = p'_1 b p_2$. Much of
the argument that follows relies on an interesting structure of the sets P_{ij} and
S_{ij}, captured in the following lemma:

Lemma 6.1: If for some $p, p', p'' \in P_{ij}$ and $s, s' \in S_{ij}$ we have $p \prec p' \prec p''$ and
$ps, p''s \in \mathcal{C}$, then $p's \in \mathcal{C}$, and one of $ps', p''s' \in \mathcal{C}$.

Proof: Since $p \prec p' \prec p''$, one of the two following two possibilities holds:
Either $p = p_1 a p_2 a p_3$, $p' = p'_1 b p_2 a p_3$, and $p'' = p'_2 b p_3$, or the symmetric possibility, namely $p = p_2 a p_3$, $p' = p_1 a p'_2 b p_3$, and $p'' = p'_1 b p'_2 b p_3$ (here we use a
and b to stand for arbitrary steps of A and B, respectively). We shall examine the first case (the second case is completely symmetric). If $s \prec s'$, then
$s = s_1 a s_2$, $s' = s_1 b s'_2$ (this part of the proof is diagrammed in Figure 6.3). Now
notice that $ps = p_1 a p_2 a p_3 s_1 a s_2 \in \mathcal{C}$, and $p's' = p'_1 b p_2 a p_3 s_1 b s'_2 \in \mathcal{C}$. These two
schedules, however, satisfy the hypothesis for condition (b) of the theorem, with
$r = p_2 a p_3 s_1$, and thus $p's, ps' \in \mathcal{C}$. Similarly, if $s' \prec s$, we have that $s = s_1 b s_2$
and $s' = s_1 a s'_2$; therefore, $p''s = p'_2 b p_3 s_1 b s_2 \in \mathcal{C}$, and $p's' = p'_1 b p_2 a p_3 s_1 a s'_2 \in \mathcal{C}$,

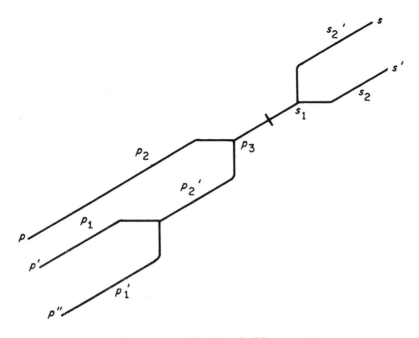

Figure 6.3. The Proof of Lemma 6.1.

which again satisfies the hypothesis of condition (b) with $r = p_3 s_1$, and thus $p'' s', p' s \in C$. $\square$

For each prefix $s \in P_{ij}$ define $\text{SUFFIX}(p)$ to be the set of all suffixes s such that $ps \in C$; we consider two prefixes $p, p' \in P_{ij}$ to be *equivalent*, denoted $p \equiv p'$, if $\text{SUFFIX}(p) = \text{SUFFIX}(p')$. It is an immediate consequence of Lemma 6.1 that, if $p \prec p' \prec p''$ and $p \equiv p''$, then $p \equiv p'$; in other words, the equivalence classes of P_{ij} under $\equiv$ are *intervals* of the total order $\prec$ (that is, sets of the form $\{p : p_1 \preceq p \preceq p_2\}$ for some appropriate boundary points p_1 and p_2). Our construction will guarantee that these equivalence classes also correspond to (literally) intervals of line ADC of the ijth square (see Figure 6.5), in the following sense: This line will be partitioned into a set of intervals, one for each equivalence class, and in increasing order, with respect to $\prec$, from A to C, such that the following is true: *The set of all possible monotone curves from the origin to a point of the kth such interval contains precisely the prefixes in the kth equivalence class under $\equiv$ in P_{ij}.* We shall prove this assertion by double induction on i and j.

Notice that the assertion is vacuously true when either i and j is zero, because in this case there is only one class (the one containing the prefix $a_1 a_2 \ldots a_i$ or $b_1 b_2 \ldots b_j$, depending on which one of i, j is zero, since $AB, BA \in C$), which

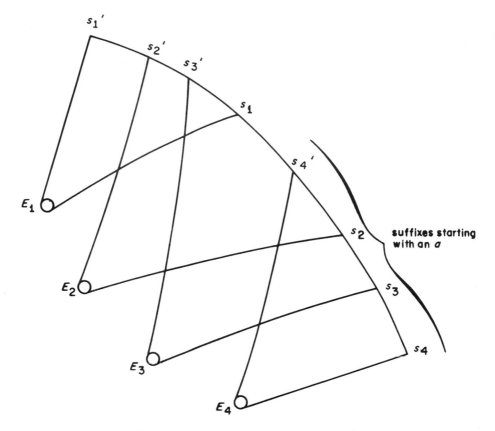

Figure 6.4. Example of a suffix Function.

is indeed the one described by any curve through the S and W^2 boundary of the square. In what follows, we shall outline a construction which inductively guarantees that the condition holds for all squares.

Consider the ijth square. We shall argue that the equivalence classes under $\equiv$ in the $(i+1,j)$th and $(i,j+1)$th square are derived in a simple way from classes in the ijth square. Naturally, if P_{ij} is empty there is nothing to prove. Suppose that there are $k > 0$ equivalence classes under $\equiv$ in P_{ij}, call them $E_1, \ldots, E_k$, ordered in increasing $\prec$. It is quite easy to see that the corresponding suffix sets are also intervals of S_{ij}, although they may not be disjoint; call them $[s_1, s_1'], \ldots, [s_k, s_k']$. It is easy to see that, by Lemma 6.1, $s_1 \succeq s_2 \succeq \ldots \succeq s_k$, and similarly $s_1' \succeq s_2' \succeq \ldots \succeq s_k'$ (see Figure 6.4 for an illustration). Also, let

---

^{2} To navigate through the geometric arguments of this section, we use the symbols N, S, E, and W, to stand for the upwards, downwards, right, and left direction, respectively.

q be the smallest index such that s'_q starts with an a. (see Figure 6.4); thus, the SUFFIX sets of classes $E_1, \ldots, E_{q-1}$ contain suffixes that start with b_{j+1} (in Figure 6.4, $q = 4$). Define, for $r = 1, \ldots, q - 1$, F_r to be the set of prefixes $F_r = \{pb : p \in E_r\}$. Evidently, these prefixes in $P_{i,j+1}$ have the same SUFFIX set, namely $\text{SUFFIX}(F_r) = \{s : bs \in \text{SUFFIX}(E_r)\}$. We can similarly define the corresponding equivalence classes $G_{r'}$ of $P_{i+1,j}$.

The construction for the ijth square is the following (illustrated for the classes of Figure 6.4 in Figure 6.5): By the induction hypothesis, curves corresponding to all prefixes in E_r cross the ADC line of the ijth square at the rth of k intervals into which the line is partitioned (possibly some other prefixes with a SUFFIX set that covers that of E_r also cross the ADC line at the same interval). We define $2k - 2$ points on line ABC corresponding to the boundaries s_r and s'_r of the SUFFIX intervals, in the same order from A to C as these suffixes, and such that B corresponds exactly to the change from suffixes starting with an a to suffixes starting with a b (see Figures 6.4 and 6.5). The points corresponding to the two extreme boundaries s'_1 and s_k coincide with A and C, respectively. We then connect the N or W end of the rth interval on ADC with the point on ABC corresponding to s_r, and the other end with s'_r (see Figure 6.5). These connections are made by monotone curves; since lengths are meaningless in these geometric constructions and arguments, and the construction can always be re-scaled as needed, we can assume that the $k - 1$ points are such that connection by monotone curves is possible.

Intuitively, these curves are "walls," and will ultimately be realized by locks forming appropriately long forbidden rectangles; it is quite clear that such realization will be possible (see Figure 6.7), although the formal details would be rather tedious. The purpose of these walls is to "channel" the prefixes in $E_1, \ldots, E_k$ to the line ABC, thus creating curves that correspond to the classes F_r of $P_{i,j+1}$, and the classes G_r of $P_{i+1,j}$. Thus, since the inductive hypothesis for the W side of square $i + 1, j$ and the S side of square $i, j + 1$ is therefore met, it would appear that the construction is completed.

There is a last difficulty, however. As we see in Figure 6.5, some of these walls "block" certain corridors created by others. There is an interesting way around this problem: For each point at which two walls intersect (there are five such points in Figure 6.5), we create small openings on both walls to the N and E of the point (see Figure 6.6). It turns out that, by using small "trapdoors," as in Figure 6.6, we can achieve flow of monotone curves *in only one direction* through the openings. In particular, horizontal trapdoors (e.g., h in Figure 6.6) allow only curves from W to E, while vertical trapdoors (e.g., v) allow curves from S to N. Realizing all this by locks between the steps a_i and b_j is tedious, but clearly possible.

Next we argue that our construction is correct. We have clearly achieved that for each schedule in F_r there is an equivalent curve crossing the corre-

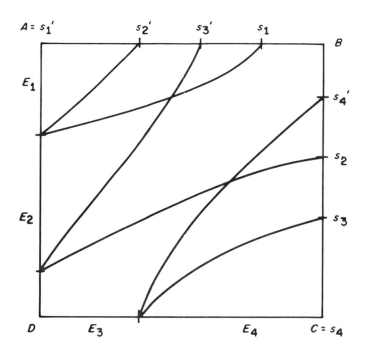

Figure 6.5. Channeling the Prefixes.

sponding interval of AB. The F_r's are not necessarily all equivalence classes of the $(i, j+1)$st square, but are definitely a refinement, and this suffices for the inductive assertion. Also, the same is true of the G_r sets. Therefore, we can show the assertion for square ij from the inductive hypothesis and the construction for squares $(i-1, j)$ and $(i, j-1)$.

If we apply the inductive assertion to the mnth square, we notice that there is only one equivalence class in P_{mn}, namely C. Thus, the only curves crossing the S and W side of the mnth square correspond to schedules of C, which proves the theorem. $\square$

The construction used in the sufficiency part of the proof is admittedly complicated and wasteful in its use of locks. By a more elaborate analysis, reasonable bounds on the number of locks required can be derived (see Problem 6.2). Another important open question is to find a necessary and sufficient condition on realizability for more than two transactions. Unfortunately, little is known here. The following, however, is a simple necessary condition:

Proposition 6.1: *If* $C \subseteq A_1 * A_2 * \ldots * A_n$ *is realizable, then the projection of* C *on any pair of transactions must also be realizable.* $\square$

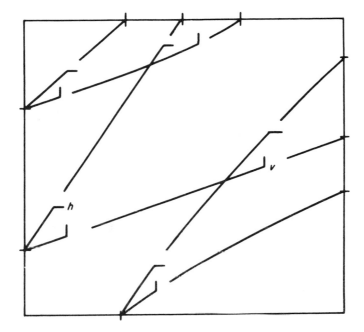

Figure 6.6. Openings and Trapdoors.

For a proof, see Problem 6.4. Unfortunately, this condition fails to be sufficient (see Problem 6.5).

Locking and Conflict Serializability

In practice, we are not interested in realizing by locking just any set of schedules, but only view serializable ones. Which sets of view serializable schedules, then, are realizable by locking? (We are now in the read-write model of transactions, although our locks are still uninterpreted, in no way connected with the entities accessed.) To answer, we must recall the following interesting result from Chapter 2:

Theorem 2.10: *A schedule s is conflict serializable if and only if, for all subsets τ' of the transactions in s, $s_{\tau'}$ is view serializable.* $\square$

Recall that $s_{\tau'}$ stands for the projection of schedule s to the set of transactions τ', in other words, s with all steps of transactions not in τ' removed. We need the following two facts:

Lemma 6.2: *Suppose that, for some subset τ' of the set τ of transactions appearing in s, $s_{\tau'}$ is not view serializable. Then $ts_{\tau'}$ is not view serializable either, where t is a serial schedule of the transactions in $\tau - \tau'$.*

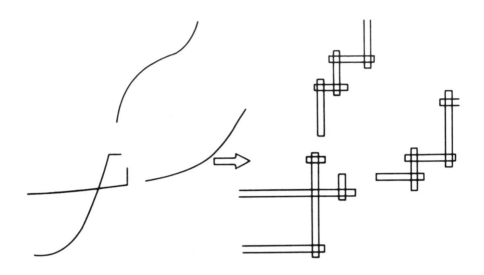

Figure 6.7. Realizing the Construction by Locks.

Proof: If $s_{\tau'}$ is not view serializable, this means that there is an interpretation and initial state that makes it behave differently from any serial schedule. However, this interpretation can be extended to an interpretation of $ts_{\tau'}$, simply by having the write steps of t write the initial state. This interpretation is obviously different from all serial schedules. □

Lemma 6.3: *Suppose that the class $\mathcal{C}$ of schedules involving transactions in τ is realizable by locking, and $s \in \mathcal{C}$. Then $ts_{\tau'} \in \mathcal{C}$, where $\tau' \subseteq \tau$, and t is a serial schedule involving the transactions in $\tau - \tau'$.*

Proof: Consider the locking λ of τ which realizes $\mathcal{C}$, and a schedule s' of λ such that $\rho(s') = s$. Let λ' be λ restricted to the transactions in τ', and t' be the serial schedule of the locked transactions in $\lambda - \lambda'$ in which transactions are ordered in the same way as the corresponding unlocked transactions are ordered in t. Consider now any lock step in the schedule $t's'_{\lambda'}$. Whether the lock step belongs to a transaction in λ' or not, it is clear that the same or fewer locks are held when this lock step is requested in $t's'_{\lambda'}$ than in the corresponding point in s'. Thus, since s' is by hypothesis a legal schedule, the same is true of $t's'_{\lambda'}$, and thus for $\rho(t's'_{\lambda'}) = ts_{\tau'}$. $\square$

Theorem 6.2: *Suppose that a set C of view serializable schedules involving transactions in a set τ is realizable by locking. Then C contains only conflict serializable schedules.*

Proof: Suppose for the sake of contradiction that $s \in C$ is not conflict serializable. By Theorem 2.10, there is a set $\tau' \subseteq \tau$ of transactions such that $s_{\tau'}$ is not view serializable. Let t be any serial schedule involving the transactions in $\tau - \tau'$. By Lemma 6.3, $ts_{\tau'} \in C$, and by Lemma 6.2 $ts_{\tau'}$ is not view serializable, a contradiction. $\square$

Theorem 6.2 is an additional reason why conflict serializability is a popular and practically important concurrency control principle: By locking we can only realize sets of conflict serializable schedules. The additional concurrency of view serializability cannot be captured in practice, not only because of the complexity reasons pointed out in Chapters 2 and 5, but also because realizing supersets of conflict serializability, at least by locking, is not possible even *in principle*.

Locking Modes

So far we have considered the simplest kind of locks, in which a lock step of a transaction can proceed precisely in the case that no other transaction is holding the same lock; we call such locks *ordinary locks*. In concurrency control practice, however, more complex kinds of locks are sometimes used. For example, we have seen in Section 4.2 that a read lock on an entity may coexist with another read lock on the same entity, but not with a write lock. Similarly for intention locks. What is a general framework for studying such extensions of locking? And do such extensions enhance the power of locking as a concurrency control primitive?

To describe a general locking situation let us first fix a countably infinite set $T = \{1, 2, \ldots\}$ of locks, so an adequate supply is available to lock any set of transactions, no matter how large the set and long the transactions. Each lock $i \in T$ has a lock and an unlock step ℓ_i, u_i associated with it, and these steps can be inserted to transactions in pairs, the lock step first. A *mode of locking* is a monotone function $\mathcal{M} : 2^T \to 2^T$ assigning to each set $S \subseteq T$ of locks another set $\mathcal{M}(S) \subseteq T$ of locks. $\mathcal{M}$ is *monotonic* in that, if $S \subset S'$, then $\mathcal{M}(S) \subset \mathcal{M}(S')$. Intuitively, $i \in \mathcal{M}(S)$ means that the ℓ_i step of a transaction cannot proceed if all locks in S are held by transactions. Monotonicity means that locking yet another lock cannot enable a lock that was previously forbidden.

Having fixed a mode $\mathcal{M}$ of locking, we can define what it means for a schedule of a set of locked transactions with locks from the given set of locks to be *legal*. At each step a of the schedule, define $L(a) \subseteq T$ to be the set of locks held at a, that is, the set of $i \in T$ such that for at least one transaction step ℓ_i is before a in the schedule and the corresponding u_i is not. A schedule of transactions locked by locks in T is said to be *legal under locking mode* $\mathcal{M}$ if, whenever a is an instance of a lock step ℓ_i, $i \notin \mathcal{M}(L(a))$. This is a straightforward generalization of the notion of legal schedules introduced earlier in this section. A set $\mathcal{C}$ of schedules of the transactions $A_1, \ldots, A_k$ is called *realizable* by locking mode $\mathcal{M}$ defined on the set of locks T if there is a way of inserting lock and unlock steps of the locks in T to the transactions to produce the locked transactions $\bar{A}_1, \ldots, \bar{A}_k$, so that $\mathcal{C}$ is precisely the set of legal schedules of these locked transactions under locking mode $\mathcal{M}$, after the deletion of lock and unlock steps.

For example, the ordinary locks that we have studied so far constitute the simplest locking mode denoted $\mathcal{M}_0$, and defined by $\mathcal{M}_0(S) = S$ for all $S \subseteq T$. In the *shared mode*, denoted $\mathcal{M}_s$, of which read locks and intention locks are examples, the set of locks is partitioned into pairs $T = \{i, i' : i = 1, 2, \ldots\}$; unprimed locks are exclusive locks, primed ones are shared locks. For each $S \subseteq T$, $\mathcal{M}_s(S) = \{i : i \in S \text{ or } i' \in S\} \cup \{i' : i \in S\}$. There can be more involved modes of locking, such as the version locks used in Section 4.6. A somewhat far-fetched mode of locking, which can be called M_3, is defined as follows: T is partitioned into triples of locks, denoted $T_i, i = 1, 2, \ldots$. Then $\mathcal{M}_3(S)$ is defined as $\{j : j \in T_i, \text{ and } |T_i \cap S| \geq 2\}$. In other words, a lock can proceed unless two or more locks in its triple are being held.

How can we measure the *power* or *expressiveness* of a mode $\mathcal{M}$? We propose *the set of all realizable sets of schedules* as such a measure. The larger this set, the more expressive the mode, as more concurrency control principles can be implemented using this mode of locking. We denote the class of all sets of schedules that are realizable by mode $\mathcal{M}$ as $\mathbf{R}(\mathcal{M})$. Thus, Theorem 6.1 is an attempt at characterizing $\mathbf{R}(\mathcal{M}_0)$—in fact, its intersection with all sets of schedules of two transactions. We can now formalize our original question, of whether the various modes of locking enhance the expressive power of ordinary locking as a concurrency control primitive as follows: How do the sets $\mathbf{R}(\mathcal{M})$ for various locking modes $\mathcal{M}$ compare to $\mathbf{R}(\mathcal{M}_0)$?

It may seem that even unsophisticated modes of locking, such as shared locks, are more expressive than ordinary locks. This is not the case. Given any set of transactions locked using shared locks, there is a way of inserting ordinary locks to the same transactions so that the set of legal schedules of the first set of locked transactions under $\mathcal{M}_s$, after the removal of locks, is precisely the corresponding set for the second set of locked transactions under $\mathcal{M}_0$. The idea is to replace the jth *appearence* of a locking step on a shared lock i' by a locking step on a new ordinary lock i_j, and each locking step on an exclusive lock i by a sequence of locking steps on *all* ordinary locks used to replace i'. It follows that $\mathbf{R}(\mathcal{M}_s) = \mathbf{R}(\mathcal{M}_0)$ (the formal proof is the object of Problem 6.6). In view of this rather unexpected power of ordinary locks, the question arises: Are there modes that are more expressive than $\mathcal{M}_0$?

Recall that we have required, quite sensibly, that modes should be monotone functions from sets of locks to sets of locks. This implies that $\mathcal{M}(S) \supseteq \cup_{i \in S} \mathcal{M}(\{i\})$. We call a mode *elementary* if the opposite inclusion also holds, and $\mathcal{M}(S) = \cup_{i \in S} \mathcal{M}(\{i\})$. That is, a mode is elementary if, whenever $i \in \mathcal{M}(S)$ and thus lock i cannot be locked, there is a *single* lock in S that causes this. Elementary modes can be represented by a "conflict table", such as the one in Figure 4.10. It should be clear that $\mathcal{M}_0$, $\mathcal{M}_s$, and the other locking modes we have encountered in locking protocols are all elementary; $\mathcal{M}_3$ is not.

Theorem 6.3: *If $\mathcal{M}$ is an elementary mode of locking, then $\mathbf{R}(\mathcal{M}) \subseteq \mathbf{R}(\mathcal{M}_0)$.*

Proof: Suppose that $\mathcal{M}$ is elementary, and let $\mathcal{C}$ be a set of schedules in $\mathbf{R}(\mathcal{M})$; we shall show that $\mathcal{C} \in \mathbf{R}(\mathcal{M}_0)$. Consider the transactions $A_1, \ldots, A_k$ involved in $\mathcal{C}$, and the lock and unlock steps inserted among the steps of these transactions, resulting in a set of locked transactions $\{\bar{A}_1, \ldots, \bar{A}_k\}$, which realize $\mathcal{C}$ under mode $\mathcal{M}$. We shall show how to insert lock and unlock steps of ordinary locks to $A_1, \ldots, A_k$ to form locked transactions $\bar{A}_1', \ldots, \bar{A}_k'$ such that the set of legal schedules of these transactions under $\mathcal{M}_0$, after the removal of the lock and unlock steps, is $\mathcal{C}$. The construction is the following: We replace the jth instance of a ℓ_i step in the transactions by a lock step ℓ_{i_j} on a *new lock* i_j (from the infinite supply T). We also replace the corresponding instance of u_i by u_{i_j}. We then do the following: At each ℓ_{i_j} step that has replaced ℓ_i, and for each lock m such that $i \in \mathcal{M}(\{m\})$, we insert the steps $\ell_{m_1} \ldots \ell_{m_n}$ immediately before the ℓ_j step, and $u_{m_1}, \ldots, u_{m_n}$ immediately after it, where $m_1, \ldots, m_n$ are all locks used to replace m at the previous step. This completes the construction of the $\bar{A}_i'$'s.

We now have to show that the set of legal schedules of the $\bar{A}_i'$'s under $\mathcal{M}_0$ after the deletion of the lock and unlock steps coincides with the corresponding set of the $\bar{A}_i$'s under $\mathcal{M}$. First notice that for each legal schedule $\bar{s}$ of the $\bar{A}_i$'s there is a legal schedule $\bar{s}'$ of the $\bar{A}_i'$'s in which each ℓ_i step is replaced by the corresponding ℓ_{i_j}, preceded by a string of ℓ_{m_p}'s and followed by a string of u_{m_p}'s, one for each occurrence in another transaction of each lock m such that $i \in \mathcal{M}(\{m\})$. Notice that no m_p lock can be held at this point by another transaction, since this would mean that an m lock is held at the corresponding point of the $\bar{s}$ schedule, impossible since $i \in \mathcal{M}(\{m\})$ and $\bar{s}$ is legal under $\mathcal{M}$. Also, neither is the i_j lock held, since the only other instance of this lock in $\bar{s}'$ can be in strings of lock steps on locks such as the m_p's above, and such strings in $\bar{s}'$ are immediately followed by the corresponding unlock steps. Since $\bar{s}'$ with all lock and unlock steps deleted (which we denote by $\rho(\bar{s}')$) coincides with $\rho(\bar{s})$

we have shown that the set of reductions of legal schedules, under $\mathcal{M}_0$, of the $\bar{A}'_i$'s is a superset of $\mathcal{C}$.

To show that it is a subset of $\mathcal{C}$, consider any legal (under $\mathcal{M}_0$) schedule of the $\bar{A}'_i$'s. It is easy to see that this schedule can be transformed into another legal, under $\mathcal{M}_0$, schedule $\bar{s}'$ such that all lock and unlock steps that are consecutive in the transactions $\bar{A}'_i$ are also consecutive in $\bar{s}'$, without changing the relative position of the steps of the A_i's. In $\bar{s}'$ each run of a ℓ_j step (corresponding to an instance of ℓ_i, say) preceded and followed by lock and unlock steps respectively on the m_p's can be replaced by a single ℓ_i step, and similarly u_j by u_i. The resulting schedule $\bar{s}$ of the $\bar{A}_i$'s is legal, since at this point there is no lock m held by another transaction such that $i \in \mathcal{M}(\{m\})$, and hence (here we use the fact that $\mathcal{M}$ is elementary) $i \notin \mathcal{M}(L)$, where L is the set of all locks held at this point. Now $\bar{s}$ with lock and unlock steps removed is the same as the original schedule of the $\bar{A}'_i$'s with lock and unlock steps removed. It follows that $\mathcal{C} \in \mathbf{R}(\mathcal{M}_0)$. $\square$

The class of elementary locking modes is very broad, and contains all variants of locking that have been proposed in the concurrency control literature, so Theorem 6.3 suggests that ordinary locking is quite powerful indeed.

6.2 ENTITY LOCKS

In the most interesting applications of locking, the locks are identified with the entities of the database, and the lock-unlock steps inserted in each transaction depend on the pattern whereby this transaction accesses the corresponding entities. In this and the next section we explore this connection between locks and entities, which brings about the most interesting results in the theory of locking.

In studying the relationship between transaction structure and locking, it is quite simplifying to use the *action model* of transactions (Section 2.7), in which each step $A(x)$ is an indivisible, simultaneous read and write operation on entity x. Therefore, a transaction is a finite sequence of $A(x)$ steps, $x \in E$. Now, a *locked transaction* in this model is a sequence of steps of the forms $A(x)$, $L(x)$, and $U(x)$—the latter two read "lock x" and "unlock x." We shall assume that locked transactions have the following two properties:

1. If there is one or more occurrences of an $A(x)$ step in a transaction, then there is a single occurrence of $L(x)$ before the first occurrence of $A(x)$, and a single occurrence of $U(x)$ following the last occurrence of $A(x)$ in the transaction.

2. Conversely, if there are no occurrences of $A(x)$, then there are no occurrences of $L(x)$ or $U(x)$ either.

Assumption (1) is a convenient "normal form," observed by all existing locking methods. There are circumstances in which we could safely violate it, but they are so far-fetched (e.g., when x is accessed by no other transaction besides the present one) that they are best disregarded in developing a theory. Assumption (2) rules out methods that use locks on variables other than entities (and there are only artificial examples of such methods). It is an assumption "on the safe side," because it can only make our methods and criteria more restrictive than necessary. Besides, this assumption has the advantage that it allows us to essentially *do away completely with the action steps.* More specifically, let us define the *pattern* of a locked transaction to be the transaction with the action steps deleted. For example, the pattern of $\bar{A} = L(x)A(x)L(y)U(x)L(z)A(z)A(y)U(y)A(z)U(z)$ is $L(x)L(y)U(x)L(z)U(y)U(z)$. As we shall see soon (Proposition 6.2 below), it is the pattern that determines the crucial properties of locked transactions obeying Assumptions (1) and (2).

A *locking* of a set $\tau = \{A_1, \ldots, A_n\}$ of transactions is a set $\lambda = \{\bar{A}_1 \ldots, \bar{A}_n\}$ of locked transactions, such that the subsequence of $\bar{A}_i$ consisting of its $A(x)$ steps coincides with A_i. In other words, a locking inserts lock and unlock steps to each transaction of a transaction system according to Assumptions (1) and (2). As in the previous section, we consider a schedule of locked transactions *legal* if between any two occurrences of a $L(x)$ step there is an occurrence of an $U(x)$ step. A schedule s of τ is legal with respect to a locking λ of τ if it is the reduction of a legal schedule of λ (that is, the resulting schedule once the lock and unlock steps have been removed). Finally, a locking λ of a transaction system τ is *safe* if all legal schedules of τ with respect to λ are serializable (as usual, we use the term "serializable" to encompass all notions of correctness which coincide in the action model). This section is devoted to understanding the structure of safe lockings.

Example 6.1: If $A_1 = A(x)A(y)A(x)A(z)$ and $A_2 = A(z)A(y)A(x)A(y)$, then a possible locking is $\bar{A}_1 = L(x)A(x)L(y)A(y)U(y)L(z)A(x)U(x)A(z)U(z)$ and $\bar{A}_2 = L(z)A(z)L(y)U(z)L(x)A(y)A(x)U(x)A(y)U(y)$. A legal schedule of the original transactions with respect to $\{\bar{A}_1, A_2\}$ is the following:

$$s = \begin{array}{ll} A_1: & A(x)A(y)A(x) \qquad\qquad\qquad A(z) \\ A_2: A(z) & \qquad\qquad A(y)A(x)A(y) \end{array}$$

As it is quite easy to check, s is not serializable, and thus the locking $\lambda = (\bar{A}_1, \bar{A}_2)$ is not safe. In the next subsection we develop a systematic method for determining this. $\square$

Before proceeding to a more detailed discussion of safety, let us first point out that it only depends on the *patterns* occurring in the locking, and not on the particular occurrences of the action steps:

Proposition 6.2: *If two lockings $\lambda = \{\bar{A}_1, \ldots, \bar{A}_n\}$ and $\mu = \{\bar{B}_1, \ldots, \bar{B}_n\}$ are such that $\bar{A}_i$ and $\bar{B}_i$ have the same pattern for $i = 1, \ldots, n$, then λ is unsafe if and only if μ is unsafe.*

Proof: Suppose that λ is unsafe. There is a legal, with respect to λ, schedule s of the unlocked transactions such that the conflict graph $G(s)$ (recall Theorem 2.8) has a cycle. Consider now the corresponding legal schedule $\bar{s}$ of λ, and a schedule $\bar{t}$ of μ that has the same sequence of lock and unlock steps. Since λ and μ have the same patterns, such a $\bar{t}$ exists. We claim that the schedule $t = \rho(\bar{t})$ resulting from $\bar{t}$ by removing lock and unlock steps has a conflict graph $G(t)$ which is a supergraph of $G(s)$, and thus contains a cycle.

In proof, consider any two transactions A_i and A_j of s, with an arc in $G(s)$ from A_i to A_j. Evidently, there is an entity x accessed by both transactions, first by A_i. Thus, by Assumption (1) on locked transactions, in $\bar{s}$ $\bar{A}_i$ locks and unlocks x before $\bar{A}_j$ locks it, and similarly $\bar{B}_i$ locks and unlocks x before $\bar{B}_j$ locks it. However, by Assumption (2), this means that in t transaction B_i accesses x before B_j, and thus there is an arc in $G(t)$ from B_i to B_j. $\square$

An important consequence of this result is that, in studying the safety of lockings, we need only examine the patterns of the locked transactions involved.

Two Transactions

In the case of a locking consisting of only two transactions, the geometric approach introduced earlier in this chapter leads to an elegant characterization of safe lockings. As before, the steps of the unlocked transactions define a grid, the locks add certain forbidden rectangles, and monotone curves representing legal schedules flow around the rectangles. There are two new elements introduced by the syntax of the transactions. First, each of the forbidden rectangles corresponds to an entity, namely the one that is locked at its interior. Second, certain grid points correspond to *conflicts* of the two schedules, that is, steps that access the same entity. This set of *conflict points*, is our geometric way of capturing the syntax of the transactions involved (that is, the names of the entities acted upon at each step). By our basic Assumptions (1) and (2), each conflict point is in the interior of some forbidden rectangle, namely the one that corresponds to the entity that caused the conflict, and conversely, each rectangle contains at least one conflict point.

Example 6.1 (continued): We show in Figure 6.8 the geometric representation of the transactions and locking of Example 6.1. The conflict points are the five solid small circles, each in the corresponding rectangle. We also show the monotone curve corresponding to the (non-serializable) schedule s in the example. $\square$

Let us call two monotone curves *homotopic* if one can be transformed into the other by a continuous transformation, without ever crossing any forbidden rectangle; in other words, two curves are homotopic if they do not enclose a rectangle between them. For example, curves $\bar{s}$ and $\bar{s}'$ in Figure 6.8 are homotopic, whereas curves s and $\bar{s}$ are not. We can show the following interesting

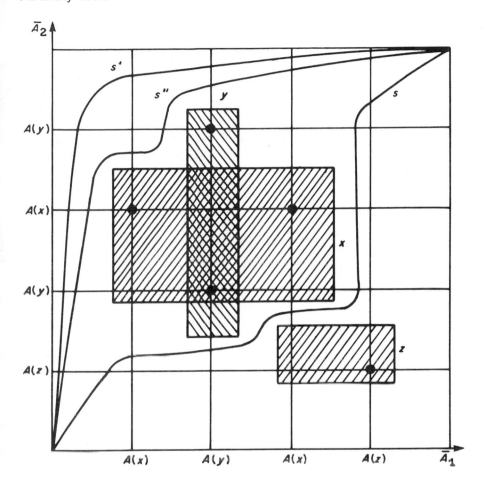

Figure 6.8. Two Locked Transactions.

result:

Lemma 6.4: *Two legal schedules are equivalent if and only if the two corresponding curves are homotopic.*

Proof: It is easy to see that every continuous transformation of a curve that avoids the rectangles can be broken down into a finite number of transformations of the following two sorts: First, transformations like the one in Figure 6.9(a) which preserve the corresponding schedule; and second, transformations such as the one in Figure 6.9(b) which represent a switching of the order of two non-conflicting steps (nonconflicting because we know that if point p of Figure 6.9

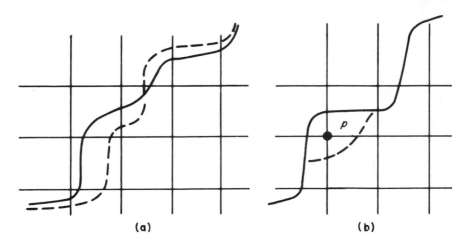

Figure 6.9. Elementary Curve Transformations.

were a conflict point, then it would be surrounded by a forbidden rectangle, and
thus would not correspond to a legal curve transformation). Therefore, if two
curves are homotopic, then the corresponding schedules can be transformed into
one another, by a sequence of switchings of nonconflicting adjacent steps. One
direction follows now from Theorem 2.9, stating that two schedules are conflict
equivalent (and in the action model this is the same as view equivalence) if
and only if one can be transformed to the other by a sequence of switchings of
adjacent nonconflicting steps.

   For the other direction, suppose that two curves are not homotopic; this
means that a forbidden rectangle, and thus a conflict point, is enclosed between
them. Let a and b be the two conflicting steps. In the schedule corresponding
to the curve above the conflict point, b comes before a, whereas in the schedule
represented by the curve below the conflict point, a comes first. Therefore,
the two schedules have a different directed graph D_2 (recall Theorem 2.7), and
therefore are not equivalent. $\square$

   Since the two serial schedules are curves that pass either above all rectangles or below all rectangles, an important characterization of serializability
follows immediately from Lemma 6.4:

Theorem 6.4: *A schedule is serializable if and only if the corresponding curve
does not separate two rectangles.* $\square$

   Thus, a locking is safe if it is such that no monotone curve can pass through
the rectangles, so that it leaves at least one on each side. To further understand
this idea, we need to introduce some new geometric concepts.

   Let us call a region of the plane *rectilinear* if it is the union of a finite

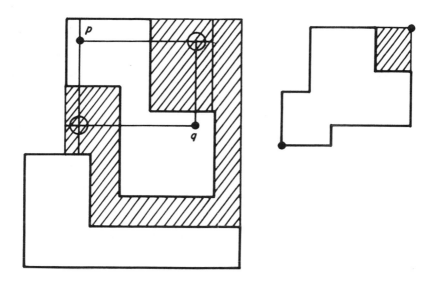

Figure 6.10. A Region (a) and its Closure (b).

number of rectangles with sides parallel to the axes (precisely as the forbidden region in our representation of locking). We shall next introduce a variant of convexity relevant to our geometric model. Call two points (x_1, y_1) and (x_2, y_2) *incomparable* if $(x_1 - x_2) \cdot (y_1 - y_2) < 0$, that is, if neither has both coordinates larger than the other, or, equivalently, one is to the SE of the other (points p and q in Figure 6.10). Two points of a region are said to be *connected* in R if there is a curve joining the two points which lies within R. Let R now be a rectilinear region (possibly disconnected). We say R is *closed*[3] if the following is true: If (x_1, y_1) and (x_2, y_2) are incomparable connected points in R, then the points (x_1, y_2) and (x_2, y_1) are also in R (see Figure 6.10). The *closure* of a region R is the smallest closed region containing R. For example, in Figure 6.10 the shaded areas must be added to the given rectilinear region to form its closure. The closure is shown in Figure 6.10(b).

It is easy to show certain elementary facts about closedness and closure (see Problem 6.11):

1. First, if two regions are closed, then their interesection is closed (although their union may not be). This follows directly from the definition.
2. The closure of a region is well-defined and unique. In proof, suppose not,

---

[3] Possible confusion with the *topological* notion of a closed region is avoided, because regions under consideration in this section are closed in the topological sense (i.e., they contain their boundary). In the one exception (in the proof of Theorem 6.5), we make the necessary distinction.

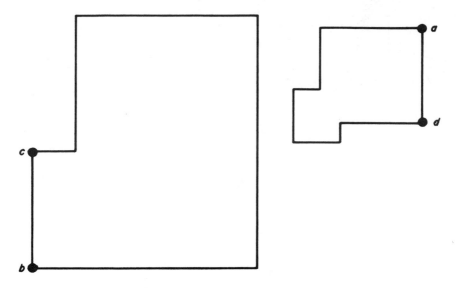

Figure 6.11. Properties of Closure.

and take the intersection of all alleged closures.

3. Define a NW or SE extreme point of a region R to be a point (x, y) of R such that $|x - y|$ attains a local maximum in the intersection of some open neighborhood and R (points c and d in Figure 6.11). The closure of a region has the same NW and SE extreme points as the original region. This follows from the definition of closure, which never allows the addition of such a new extreme point.

4. Any connected component of a closed region is itself closed. Also, it has one NE and one SW extreme point (points where $x + y$ is local maximum and minimum, respectively); unless the component has a dimension lower than two (i.e., is a line or point), these extreme points are the intersection of a horizontal and a vertical boundary line (e.g., the points a and b in Figure 6.11). This is true because multiple NE and SW extreme points, or NE and SW extreme points of any kind other than the one described, would violate the definition of closedness.

5. As a result of Properties (3) and (4) above, the closure of a rectilinear region is always rectilinear, and is the union of connected closed components. The boundary of each of these components consists of two monotone rectilinear lines that intersect only at their endpoints (see Figure 6.10).

We can also show the following fact concerning our particular concurrency control application:

Lemma 6.5: *Given any closed rectilinear subset R of the $m + 1 \times n + 1$ square,*

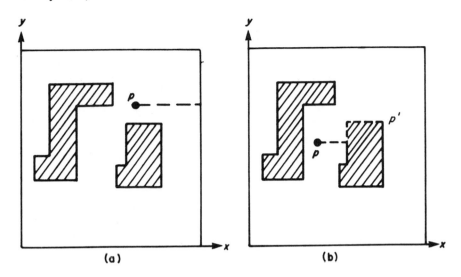

Figure 6.12. The Proof of Lemma 6.5.

and any point p outside R, then there is a monotone curve avoiding R from point $(0,0)$ to p to point $(m+1, n+1)$.

Proof: We shall show that there is a monotone curve from p to $(m+1, n+1)$, the other part being completely symmetric. The construction is the following: Starting from p we go directly to the E (see Figure 6.12). If we hit the vertical line $x = m+1$, we are done, and the monotone curve has been found (Figure 6.12(a)). Otherwise, we have hit one of the components of R (Figure 6.12(b)). We can thus follow the (monotone by property (5) above) boundary of this component, keeping a small enough distance from it so that no other component is encountered (see Figure 6.12(b)). Once the NE extreme point p' has been reached, we repeat our horizontal traversal. Evidently, after a finite number of such attempts, no more components of R will be left, and we are done. □

We can now show our main result of this section:

Theorem 6.5: *A locking of two transactions is safe if and only if the closure of the forbidden region is connected.*

Proof: Suppose that the locking is not safe, and thus, by Theorem 6.4, there is a monotone curve c that separates two forbidden rectangles. Consider the set $\bar{c}$ consisting of the whole $(m+1) \times (n+1)$ square *minus the curve.* This set is closed (in our geometric sense), and contains all forbidden rectangles. Thus, the closure of the forbidden rectangles is a subset of $\bar{c}$. Since both connected components of $\bar{c}$ contain a rectangle, it follows that each contains a non-empty part of this closure. Therefore, the closure has at least two components, and is

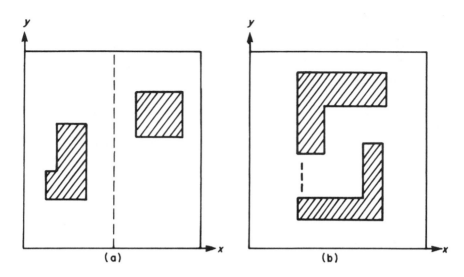

Figure 6.13. The Proof of Theorem 6.5.

thus disconnected.

Conversely, suppose that the closure of the forbidden rectangles is disconnected. We shall exhibit a non-serializable schedule—in fact, the corresponding curve. Order the connected components in terms of their smallest x coordinate, and consider the two first ones. There are two cases: either there is a vertical line that separates the two components (see Figure 6.13(a)), or the projections of the components on the x axis overlap (Figure 6.13(b)). In the first case, the nonserializable monotone curve consists of the separating line, with two horizontal segments before it and after it (one that avoids all grid points can easily be found by perturbing such a curve).

Suppose now that the x projections of the components of the closure overlap. In fact, since each such projection starts with a lock step and ends with an unlock step, it follows that they intersect at more than one point. This, however, means that there is a vertical line segment, outside the closure, which hits the two components (Figure 6.13(b)). Choose the leftmost such segment, and consider its midpoint; by the previous lemma, there is a monotone curve from the origin to the midpoint of the segment, and then to point $(m+1, n+1)$. This curve corresponds to a nonserializable legal schedule, because it separates the two components. $\square$

Based on Theorem 6.5 we can derive a fast algorithm for testing whether a given pair of locked transactions is safe (see Problems 6.11). It turns out that the same methodology is useful for analyzing the problem of *deadlocks* (see Problems 6.12 and 6.13).

More Than Two Transactions

It may seem tempting to generalize the geometric arguments of the previous subsection for understanding the safety of lockings containing more than two locked transactions. In the case of three transactions, for instance, the three-dimensional monotone curves that correspond to legal schedules must avoid certain *cylinders*, having as bases the forbidden regions of the two-transaction subsystems. However, no direct analog of Theorem 6.5 seems to hold. For example, there are unsafe lockings in which these forbidden cylinders are connected (Problem 6.14). Still, we shall see next that the solution for the case of two transactions provides the necessary basis for understanding the general problem as well.

Consider a locking, that is, a set of $d > 2$ locked transactions, $\lambda = \bar{A}_1, \ldots, \bar{A}_d$; we wish to determine conditions under which λ is safe. Naturally, if there are two transactions $\bar{A}_i, \bar{A}_j$ in λ that are not safe considered as a two-transaction system, then λ cannot be safe. So, let us assume that all pairs of transactions in λ are safe; by the results in the previous subsection, this means that the closure of the forbidden rectangles of any pair is connected —or, of course, empty. In fact, it is useful to distinguish between the case of an empty forbidden region (i.e., no common entities), and the case of a nonempty connected closure. To this end, we define the *interaction graph* of λ, $I(\lambda)$, to be a graph with the transactions of λ as nodes, and an undirected edge between A_i and A_j if the two transactions access the same entity (equivalently, lock the same entity; the forbidden region in the corresponding plane is nonempty).

Suppose that λ is unsafe; that is, there is a legal nonserializable schedule s of the corresponding unlocked transactions. By Theorem 2.8, the conflict graph $G(s)$ contains a cycle. Now this cycle cannot have length two, because this would imply that the two corresponding transactions of λ were unsafe, contrary to our assumption that all two-transaction subsystems are safe. Thus, there are three or more transactions that form a cycle in $G(s)$.

There is a relation between the conflict graph $G(s)$ and the interaction graph $I(\lambda)$; namely, $I(\lambda)$ is the undirected graph underlying $G(s)$. In other words, each arc in $G(s)$ is obtained by orienting an edge of $I(\lambda)$, and conversely each edge of $I(\lambda)$ joins two nodes that are joined by a single arc in $G(s)$ (there is only one such arc because we have already excluded cycles of length two in $G(s)$). In fact, there is a geometric interpretation of the process of directing the edges of $I(\lambda)$ to obtain $G(s)$. Each edge of $I(\lambda)$ is a pair of locked transactions, let us say $\bar{A}_i$ and $\bar{A}_j$, such that the closure of the forbidden region in the corresponding plane is nonempty, and of course closed (see Figure 6.14). The schedule s corresponds to a monotone curve in d-dimensional space, starting from the origin and ending at the point $(n_1 + 1, \ldots, n_d + 1)$, where we assume

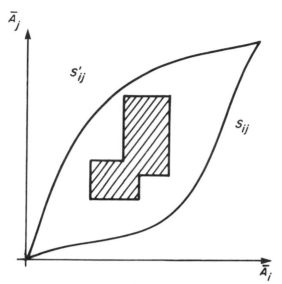

Figure 6.14. Projection of a Schedule.

transaction A_i has n_i steps. This curve is projected on the plane of A_i, A_j to a monotone curve s_{ij} that avoids the closure of the forbidden rectangles in the two-transaction subsystem (see Figure 6.14). Now consider the relative position of s_{ij} and the closure. If s_{ij} is between the closure and the $\bar{A}_i$ axis (Figure 6.14), then it is clear that steps of A_i appear in s *before* conflicting steps of A_j, and thus edge $[A_i, A_j]$ is directed in $G(s)$ from A_i to A_j. If, on the other hand, the projection is between the closure and $\bar{A}_j$ (s'_{ij} in Figure 6.14), then edge $[A_i, A_j]$ is directed from A_j to A_i.

Consider a cycle $(\bar{A}_1, \bar{A}_2, \ldots, \bar{A}_k)$ in $I(\lambda)$ where $k \geq 3$, and fix this direction around the cycle. We therefore have a directed cycle, which is potentially a cycle in the conflict graph of some nonserializable schedule s. The question is, under what conditions is there a schedule s such that the cycle under consideration is indeed a cycle in the conflict graph of s. In the plane of transactions $\bar{A}_i, \bar{A}_{i+1}$ (where addition of transaction indices will henceforth be modulo k), the closure is nonempty (see Figure 6.15 for an example with four transactions, the axes of which are displayed for convenience on the same plane). By Property (5) of closures, the boundary of each closure consists of two monotone rectilinear curves. Now consider, for each pair $(\bar{A}_i, \bar{A}_{i+1})$ of transactions, the monotone curve that is closest $\bar{A}_i$, and the extreme points on this curve. Call the set of these extreme points E_i; E denotes $E_1 \cup \ldots \cup E_k$, all extreme points of the cycle C (these are the points numbered 1 through 7 in Fig. 6.15). Notice that each extreme point p in E_i corresponds naturally to an unlock step of the $\bar{A}_i$ transaction and a lock step of $\bar{A}_{i+1}$, on the same entity. We call this entity the

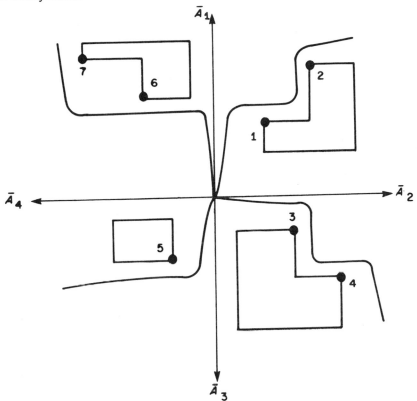

Figure 6.15. A Cycle of Transactions.

entity associated with p, and the corresponding lock and unlock steps *the lock
and unlock steps associated with p.*

　　We next construct for each cycle $C = (\bar{A}_1, \ldots, \bar{A}_k)$ of $I(\lambda)$, directed in
this order, a directed graph $B_C = (E, P)$. The set of nodes of this graph
coincides with the set E of extreme points of C. For two extreme points p and
q, $(p, q) \in P$ if one of the following two holds: Either (1) $p, q \in E_i$ for some i,
and both coordinates of p are less than those of q, or (2) $p \in E_{i-1}$, $q \in E_i$, and
the common $(\bar{A}_i)$ coordinate of p is less than the corresponding one of q. The
construction is illustrated in Figure 6.16 for the example in Figure 6.15. Edge
$(1, 2)$ is due to type(1) above, whereas edges $(1, 4)$ and $(6, 2)$ are of the second
type.

　　The usefulness of the construction of B_C is established next.

Lemma 6.6: *Suppose that a legal schedule s is such that $(A_1, \ldots, A_k)$ is a
cycle in $G(s)$. Furthermore, assume that for two extreme points p, q of the
cycle $(C = \bar{A}_1, \ldots, \bar{A}_k)$, the arc (p, q) is in B_C. Then in the corresponding legal*

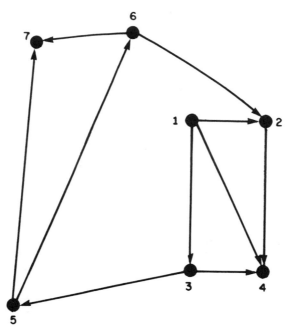

Figure 6.16. The Graph B_C.

schedule $\bar{s}$ of the locked transactions we have that the unlock step associated
with p happened before the unlock step associated with q.

Proof: If the (p, q) arc is of type (1), then the unlock step associated with p
comes before that of q in the same transaction, and thus the result is trivial.
For arcs (p, q) of the second type, recall that the projection of $\bar{s}$ on the $\bar{A}_i, \bar{A}_{i+1}$
plane is between the closure and $\bar{A}_i$. This implies that the projection intersects
first the line parallel to the $\bar{A}_{i+1}$ axis through p (i.e., the unlock step associated
with p occurs), and then the one parallel to the $\bar{A}_i$ axis. However, by the
condition in part (2) of the definition of B_C, the unlock step associated with q
cannot occur until after this second line is crossed. The lemma follows. $\square$

Call a directed cycle (i.e., a cycle with one of the two senses of traversal
fixed) $(\bar{A}_1, \ldots, \bar{A}_k)$ of $I(\lambda)$ *minimal* if for all edges $\bar{A}_i, \bar{A}_j$ of $I(\lambda)$ we have
$j = i + 1$ or $i = j + 1$; in other words, a cycle is minimal if it has no *chords*,
edges joining nodes that are not consecutive on the cycle. Equivalently, a cycle
is minimal if there is no other cycle containing a subset of its nodes. We are now
ready to state our characterization of safety for more than two transactions:

Theorem 6.6: *A locking λ is safe if and only if (a) All its two-transaction
subsets are safe, and (b) For each minimal directed cycle C of $I(\lambda)$, B_C has a
cycle.*

Proof: Suppose that λ is unsafe. That is, there is a legal schedule s such that $G(s)$ has a cycle. If the cycle has length two, then (a) of the theorem is violated, and we are done. So, assume that (a) holds, and the cycle, call it $C = (A_1, \ldots, A_k)$, contains more than two transactions. In fact, among all cycles of $G(s)$ choose C to have the smallest number of transactions. Suppose that C does not correspond to a minimal cycle of $I(\lambda)$; that is, there is an edge between two nonconsecutive transactions A_i, A_j of C. Since this edge stands for a common entity acted upon by the two transactions, one of the arcs (A_i, A_j) or (A_j, A_i) is in $G(s)$. However, this arc, together with the directed path $A_j, A_{j+1}, \ldots, A_i$ or $A_i, A_{i+1}, \ldots, A_j$ form a cycle of $G(s)$ with fewer transactions than C, a contradiction. So, we can assume C is minimal.

Now Lemma 6.6 is applicable, and for each pair of extreme points p, q with (p, q) an arc of B_C, the unlock step associated with p occurs in the legal schedule $\bar{s}$ corresponding to s before that of q. However, this means that the nodes of B_C can be linearly ordered according to the order of the associated unlock steps in $\bar{s}$, in a manner consistent with all arcs of B_C. Thus, B_C has no cycles, and condition (b) of the theorem is violated.

Conversely, suppose that λ is safe. Clearly, condition (a) must be satisfied; we shall prove condition (b). Consider any directed minimal cycle C in $I(\lambda)$, and the corresponding graph $B_C = (E, P)$. For the sake of contradiction, suppose that B_C has no cycles. Therefore, there is a *topological sorting* of the points in E, that is, a linear order $p_1, p_2, \ldots, p_\ell$, consistent with all arcs in P. Based on this order, we shall construct a legal schedule $\bar{s}$ of the transactions appearing in C, such that the corresponding schedule s of the unlocked transactions is not serializable; in fact, our construction will be such that $G(s)$ contains the cycle corresponding to C. For $r = 1, \ldots, \ell$, denote by $\bar{A}_{i_r}, \bar{A}_{i_r+1}$ the pair of transactions, at the plane of which p_r lies. We start the construction of $\bar{s}$ by executing $\bar{A}_{i_1}$ until just after the unlock step associated with p_1, then $\bar{A}_{i_2}$ up to the unlock step associated with p_2, and so on. At the rth such step, we continue the execution of $\bar{A}_{i_r}$ from the point it had progressed up to now until after the unlock step associated with p_r. Finally, after the unlock step associated with the last extreme point p_ℓ, we execute the remaining steps of each transaction, in any order among transactions. (In Fig. 6.15 we illustrate this construction for the four transactions shown, and the linear order $1, 3, 5, 6, 7, 2, 4$ of the extreme points). This concludes the construction of $\bar{s}$. It follows directly from the construction that the conflict graph of the schedule corresponding to $\bar{s}$ (with lock-unlock steps removed) contains the cycle C. We claim that $\bar{s}$ is a legal schedule for λ, which would complete the proof.

Since the last part of $\bar{s}$ (i.e., the serial execution of the remaining parts of the transactions in C) can always be done legally, $\bar{s}$ is not legal only if, at the rth stage of the construction, the part of $\bar{A}_{i_r}$ up to the unlock step associated with p_r locks an entity currently locked by another transaction. Since C is minimal, this other transaction is either $\bar{A}_{i_r+1}$ or $\bar{A}_{i_r-1}$. The former case is impossible, because in the fragment of $\bar{s}$ constructed so far transaction $\bar{A}_{i_r+1}$ obtains locks only after $\bar{A}_{i_r}$ has released them (in other words, on the plane of $\bar{A}_{i_r}$ and $\bar{A}_{i_{r+1}}$ the projection of the schedule is between the closure and the $\bar{A}_{i_r}$ axis). In the case of A_{i_r-1}, the entity locked corresponds to an extreme point p_t in the plane $\bar{A}_{i_r-1}, \bar{A}_{i_r}$, which has smaller $\bar{A}_{i_r}$ coordinate than p_r. It follows that (p_t, p_r) is an arc of B_C, by (2) of the definition of B_C. Hence, we have that $t < r$, and $\bar{A}_{i_r-1}$ has already been advanced beyond the unlock point corresponding to p_t; thus no such lock violation is possible. We conclude that $\bar{s}$ is legal, and the proof is now complete. $\square$

Closely related to Theorem 6.6 is an interesting "normal form" result for nonserializable schedules coming from unsafe lockings. Consider the following schedule.

$$s = \begin{array}{ll} A_1: & A(x_1) \hspace{6cm} A(x_4) \\ A_2: & \quad\quad A(x_1)A(x_2) \\ A_3: & \quad\quad\quad\quad\quad A(x_2)A(x_3) \\ A_4: & \quad\quad\quad\quad\quad\quad\quad\quad A(x_3)A(x_4) \end{array}$$

This schedule is obviously nonserializable, because its conflict graph contains the cycle (A_1, A_2, A_3, A_4). In some sense, this schedule is representative of all schedules that contain this cycle. It consists of a sequence of transactions, each interacting with the next, inserted between the steps of a transaction that interacts with both ends of the sequence. We call such schedules *standard nonserializable schedules*. Formally, a schedule s is called standard nonserializable if it is of the form $s = B_1 \ldots B_k s'$, where (a) for $j = 1, \ldots, k$, the B_j's are prefixes of distinct transactions A_j, such that only transactions adjacent in the sequence (modulo k) act on the same entity; (b) A_1 acts on entities x_1 and x_k, but B_1 contains only its action on x_1, and not that on x_k; (c) and finally, B_j acts on entities x_{j-1} and x_j, for $j = 2, \ldots, k$. The suffix s' in the definition above is called the *tail* of the standard nonserializable schedule.

Corollary 1: *A locking is unsafe if and only if it has a legal standard nonserializable schedule.*

Proof: Clearly, if there is a legal schedule which is standard nonserializable, then the locking is unsafe. For the other direction, suppose that the locking is indeed unsafe. If there are two transactions A_1, A_2 that form an unsafe locking by themselves, then it is easy to check that the legal schedule constructed by a geometric argument in the proof of the *only if* direction of Theorem 6.4 is standard nonserializable. Otherwise, if no two such transactions exist, we must conclude that condition (b) in the statement of Theorem 6.6 is violated. As a consequence, we can construct a legal nonserializable schedule as in the proof of the *only if* direction of Theorem 6.6. A more careful choice of the linear order of E on which the construction is based will yield a standard one.

In particular, recall the notation $B_C = (E, P)$, where E is the set of extreme points of λ, and denote again by E_i the set of extreme points-nodes of B_C that lie on the $\bar{A}_i, \bar{A}_{i+1}$ plane. It is clear that the nodes of E_i are totally ordered by B_C. Consider in each E_i the point, call it e_i, which is minimum with respect to this order (in Figures 6.15 and 6.16, the minima are the points $1, 3, 5$ and 6). Now consider those points in E_i from which there is a path (possibly empty) in B_C to some e_j; denote by E_i' this nonempty subset of E_i, and by E' the union of all E_i''s. The graph $B_C' = (E', P')$, which is B_C restricted to the points in E', is also acyclic, and thus is compatible with a linear order. We shall next argue that, among the possible linear orders, there is one in which all points of E_i' are ordered consecutively, for each i. To show this, suppose that such a linear order is impossible, and extreme point p' cannot be ordered immediately after its predecessor p, $(p, p') \in E_i'$. This means however that there is a path from p to p' in B_C', *other than the direct arc* (otherwise, p and p' could be identified in B_C' and an acyclic graph would result, implying that a way to order them consecutively exists). Since arcs are directed from E_j' to E_{j+1}', such an indirect path must pass through extreme points in all the E_j''s. However, p' is the predecessor of some e_j, and thus of some point on that path. Hence, there is a path from p' to itself, absurd.

We conclude that there is a linear order of the extreme points in E' compatible with B_C' such that for each j all points in E_j' are ordered consecutively. Since no point in E' has an ancestor in $E - E'$, the points in $E - E'$ can be arranged linearly after those in E' to form a linear order of E compatible with B_C. Now, if we perform the construction in the proof of the *only if* part of Theorem 6.6 based on this particular order, we obtain a schedule which starts with some transaction $\bar{A}_1$, executes it until some entity x_1 accessed also by $\bar{A}_2$ is unlocked (and therefore has been acted on), then executes $\bar{A}_2$ until an entity x_2 also accessed by $\bar{A}_3$ is unlocked, and so on, until $\bar{A}_k$ unlocks x_k, also accessed by $\bar{A}_1$. If we remove the lock-unlock steps from this schedule, a standard nonserializable schedule results. $\square$

Using Theorem 6.6 and its Corollary 1, we can now derive very simple proofs of the safety of certain locking protocols that we have already studied in Chapter 4. For example, recall the *two-phase locking* protocol (Theorem 4.5). In this scheme we only require that in each transaction no lock step follows an unlock step. We have:

Corollary 2: *Any locking obeying the two-phase protocol is safe.*

Proof: For two transactions, two-phase locking means that all forbidden rectangles intersect (the coordinates of the intersection points correspond to *lock points*, that is, the times during the execution of the transactions at which all locks have been acquired and none has been released). Thus, the forbidden region is connected, and therefore so is its closure. It follows that condition

(a) of the theorem holds. As for condition (b), notice that two-phase locking requires that we have in B_C arcs from all extreme points at the $\bar{A}_{i-1}, \bar{A}_i$ plane to all extreme points at the $\bar{A}_i, \bar{A}_{i+1}$ plane. This is true, since extreme points on the $\bar{A}_{i-1}, \bar{A}_i$ plane correspond to lock steps of $\bar{A}_i$, whereas extreme points in the $\bar{A}_i, \bar{A}_{i+1}$ plane are unlock steps of the same transaction, and thus must come later. It follows that all B_C graphs have cycles, and the locking is safe.

There is an even easier proof, based on Corollary 1. Just notice that the definition of a standard nonserializable schedule requires that transaction $\bar{A}_1$ locks x_k after it has unlocked x_1; thus $\bar{A}_1$ is not two-phase locked. $\square$

We could also at this point give simple proofs based on Theorem 6.6 that the path protocol and its generalization, the tree protocol, (Theorems 4.8 and 4.9) are safe. However, we shall do something better: We shall show that a further generalization, the *DAG protocol* is also safe. In the DAG protocol, the entities are considered as nodes of a directed acyclic graph $D = (E, A)$ with a *single source* x_0 (i.e., node with no incoming edges). In a transaction, we can lock an entity x if either (0.) x is the first entity locked, or the following two conditions hold:

1. All entities y with $(y, x) \in A$ have been locked (and possibly unlocked), and
2. For at least one entity y with $(y, x) \in A$, y has not yet been unlocked.

Thus, the tree protocol is the special case in which all entities have only one y such that $(y, x) \in A$—in other words, (E, A) is a tree. (A formal treatment of locking protocols in general will have to wait until the next section. For the time being, however, notice that we state protocols in terms of the structure of their lock and unlock steps, since this is enough information in our model. One or more actions on an entity can take place at any time at which the entity is locked.)

Corollary 3: *Any locking obeying the DAG protocol is safe.*

Proof: For a proof based on Corollary 1, see Problem 6.15. A stronger fact is shown in the next section. $\square$

Besides adding to our understanding of the correctness of established locking schemes, Theorem 6.6 suggests an algorithm for testing whether a locking λ is safe:

Corollary 4: *We can test whether a locking λ is safe in time polynomial in the total length of the transactions, and the number of minimal cycles of $I(\lambda)$.* $\square$

For a fixed number of transactions (say, three or four) this corollary suggests a polynomial time algorithm. Unfortunately, the number of minimal cycles in a graph can be *exponential* in the number of nodes (Problem 6.16). The following result suggests that this exponential dependence on the number of transactions is inherent:

Theorem 6.7: *Testing whether a locking is unsafe is NP-complete.*

Proof: Unsafeness is in NP, because, given a locking, in order to prove it unsafe we simply have to exhibit a legal nonserializable schedule (and test in polynomial time that it is both nonserializable and legal). To prove completeness, we shall reduce SATISFIABILITY to this problem. In fact, we shall start from a special case of SATISFIABILITY, which is still NP-complete:

Lemma 6.7: *SATISFIABILITY remains NP-complete even if each clause has two or three literals, and each variable appears twice unnegated and once negated.*

Proof: Given any formula with at most three literals per clause, we shall show how to produce an equivalent one with the restriction of the lemma. Consider a variable x, appearing, say, k times. We replace x in its first occurrence by x_1, its second by x_2, etc. We also add the clauses $(x_1 \vee \bar{x}_2), (x_2 \vee \bar{x}_3), \ldots, (x_k \vee \bar{x}_1)$, which force all x_j's to assume the same truth value. The resulting formula has the required structure, except that there may be a variable with the opposite number of occurrences than required (two negative and one positive). Replacing such formulae with their negation, we are done. $\square$

Starting with any such formula with n variables and m clauses, we shall construct a locking λ such that λ is unsafe if and only if the formula is satisfiable. The locking will involve several entities:

(a) For each clause C_j, $j = 1, \ldots, m$ we have the entities a_j, b_j, c_j, and d_j. There are also two entites a_0 and c_0, and an entity e.

(b) For each variable x, say appearing in clauses C_i and C_j unnegated and in clause C_k negated, we have eight entities, namely x, x', x_i, x_i', x_j, x_j', $\bar{x}_k$, $\bar{x}_k'$.

As for transactions, there are two transactions A_j, A_j' for each clause C_j (for the purposes of this proof all transactions are locked, and a prime does not signify a locked transaction). In particular, suppose that C_j contains the literals x, y, and z (each could be a variable or its negation). Then A_j and A_j' are the following transactions (notice that we only specify the lock-unlock steps, which, by Proposition 6.2, are adequate for determining safety).

$$A_j : L(a_{j-1})L(x_j)L(y_j)L(z_j)L(b_j)U(x_j)U(y_j)U(z_j)$$
$$L(c_{j-1})U(b_j)U(a_{j-1})U(c_{j-1})$$
$$A_j' : L(a_j)L(x_j')L(y_j')L(z_j')L(c_j)U(a_j)L(d_j)U(x_j')U(y_j')U(z_j')U(c_j)U(d_j)$$

The only exception is A_m', the last primed transaction, which is

$$A_m' : L(x_m')L(y_m')L(z_m')L(e)U(e)L(d_m)U(x_m')U(y_m')U(z_m')U(d_m')$$

We also have a transaction $A_0' : L(a_0)L(c_0)U(a_0)L(e)U(e)U(c_0)$. Finally, if a transaction C_j has just two literals x and y, then the steps on z_j and z_j' are simply omitted.

For each variable x, say appearing positively in C_i and C_j, and negatively in C_k, we have the following three transactions:

$B_{xi} : L(x)L(x_i)L(x_i')L(d_i)U(x_i')L(b_i)U(x_i)U(d_i)U(x)U(b_i),$

$B_{xj} : L(x')L(x_j)L(x_j')L(d_j)U(x_j')L(b_j)U(x_j)U(d_j)U(x')U(b_j),$ and

$B_{\bar{x}k} : L(x)L(x')L(\bar{x}_k)L(\bar{x}_k')L(d_k)U(\bar{x}_k')L(b_k)U(\bar{x}_k)U(d_k)U(x)U(x')U(b_k).$

This completes the construction of λ. The claim is that λ is *unsafe* if and only if the formula we started with was satisfiable.

Suppose that λ is not safe. By Corollary 1, there is a legal standard non-serializable schedule involving transactions of λ. Consider the first transaction mentioned in that schedule (we shall call it *the first transaction*). The first transaction is interrupted, and continued later on; the last transaction to appear before this continuation is called the *last transaction*. In this standard nonserializable schedule

$$s = \begin{array}{ll} A_1 : A(x_1) & \hspace{4cm} A(x_4) \\ A_2 : \hspace{1cm} A(x_1)A(x_2) & \\ A_3 : \hspace{2.5cm} A(x_2)A(x_3) & \\ A_4 : \hspace{4.5cm} A(x_3)A(x_4) & \end{array}$$

for example, the first transaction is A_1 and the last is A_4. The first and last transactions of λ are the corresponding locked transactions. The question is, which of the transactions in the locking that we have constructed in this NP-completeness proof is first, and which is last?

Let us suppose that the first transaction is A_j, for some j. Then the transaction must be interrupted after some entity is unlocked, and before all entities are locked, that is, after the $U(x_j)$ and before the $L(c_{j-1})$ step. Thus, the last transaction must access the entity c_{j-1}; hence the last transaction must be A_{j-1}', the only other transaction accessing c_{j-1}, and its step $L(c_{j-1})$ must be executed before the corresponding step of A_j. However, this is impossible, because this would require that A_{j-1} obtain a lock on a_{j-1}, an entity safely locked by A_{j-1} until its end.

Next, suppose that the first transaction is B_{wj} for some literal w occurring in clause C_j. Then, for the same reasons as in the previous case, the last transaction must lock b_j before the first. Hence, the last transaction must be either A_j (impossible since that transaction locks w_j before b_j), or B_{uj} for some other literal u of C_j (again impossible, since d_j must be locked).

Thus, the first transaction must be an A_j'. If, however, $j \geq 1$, then the last transaction must lock d_j, and thus it must be B_{wj}; this is impossible, since w_j, already locked in the first transaction, must be locked in the last transaction before the first resumes. We must conclude that the first transaction is A_0', interrupted between the $U(a_0)$ step and the $L(e)$ step. Next in the standard nonserializable schedule must come a transaction that accesses a_0, namely A_1. At which point is A_1 interrupted? Certainly before the $L(c_0)$ step, at which point only the three entities corresponding to the three occurrences of literals in C_1 have been unlocked. As a consequence, the next transaction is of the form

$B_{w(1)1}$, where $w(1)$ is some literal occurring in C_1, and must proceed at most until the $L(b_i)$ step, at which point only $w(1)'_1$ has been unlocked. The next transaction must be A'_1, interrupted before the $L(d_1)$ step, when the only entity unlocked is a_1. Hence, the next transaction is A_2, then $B_{w(2)2}$ for some literal $w(2)$ occurring in C_2, then A'_2, then A_3, and so on, until A'_m. The remaining parts of the transactions, and the remaining transactions, are somehow executed after this point.

We claim that by setting the literals w_j chosen by this schedule to **true** we obtain a truth assignment satisfying all clauses. That it is a truth assignment follows from the fact that no two transactions B_{xj} and $B_{\bar{x}k}$ can appear in this sequence, because the first transaction starts by locking one of x and $\bar{x}$, whereas the second starts by locking both entities. That the truth assignment satisfies all clauses comes from the fact that each clause C_j is assigned a literal w_j occurring in it. We conclude that the original formula was satisfiable.

Conversely, if the formula is satisfiable by a truth assignment, we can find a nonserializable safe schedule as in the proof of the other direction, that is, by executing A'_0 up to $L(c)$, then A_1 up to $L(c_0)$, then the transaction B_{w1} for some *true* literal w of C_1, up to $L(b_j)$, then A'_1 up to $L(d_1)$, and so on, until we execute A'_m up to $L(d_m)$. That the remaining steps can be completed is trivial, since all entities that remain to be locked in the transactions that have already started have been unlocked by all other transactions. Finally, the transactions corresponding to the remaining occurrences of the literals are executed serially after all this. $\square$

Notice that the locking constructed in the proof of the theorem has a special structure, in that any two transactions access at most two common entities. Hence, testing for safety is apparently difficult even for such lockings. It is interesting to note that this result is in some sense the best possible: Lockings in which any two transactions share at most one entity can be tested for safety in polynomial time (see Problem 6.17).

6.3 LOCKING PROTOCOLS

Theorem 6.7 suggests that determining whether a locking is safe is a quite complex task. Fortunately, in practice we are not interested in certifying the safety of just any locking. Usually, the locking of interest is the result of inserting lock and unlock steps in a set of transactions according to the rules of some *locking protocol*, such as the two-phase locking protocol (Section 4.2), the path protocol, or its generalization, the tree protocol (Section 4.3). In this section we turn to the problem of determining *when a locking protocol is safe*, in the hope that this will turn out to be a more tractable problem.

But what is a locking protocol? If we define a protocol to be any set of rules specifying the conditions under which a locked transaction satisfies the protocol, then any locking can in principle define a locking protocol. Locking protocols that are encountered in practice, however, have a certain structure. Let us recall the locking protocols that we have seen so far. The two-phase locking protocol says that the next step of a locked transaction can be a $L(x)$ step only if there has been no unlock step in the transaction so far (it goes without saying that our basic Assumptions (1) and (2) on locking must also be observed). The path protocol states that a $L(x)$ step is allowed if either it is the first step, or in the transaction so far there is a $L(y)$ step and no $U(y)$ step, where y is the entity immediately preceding x on the path. The tree protocol can be stated in the same manner, where y is now the parent of x in the tree. Finally, the DAG protocol introduced in the previous section is the following: $L(x)$ can be the next step if either it is the first step of the transaction, or there is a $L(y)$ step in the schedule so far for each y such that (x, y) is an arc in the underlying directed acyclic graph, and not all corresponding $U(y)$ steps have appeared. We observe that all these protocols are stated as conditions on the prefix of a transaction under which a $L(x)$ step can be the next step of the transaction (in our discussion of locking protocols we ignore action steps, as we are enabled to do by Proposition 6.2).

What locking protocol would deviate from this style? We could impose restrictions on the next step being an $U(x)$ step; or, we could impose restrictions based on subsequent steps. Both circumstances, however, are in some sense "unnatural," as they seem to have some element of "anticipation" of future steps. In fact, all of the great variety of locking protocols proposed so far in the literature on concurrency control are "causal" in this sense. Motivated by this, let us define a locking protocol to be a mapping π assigning to each prefix $\bar{B}$ of a locked transaction a subset of the set E of entities; if $x \in \pi(\bar{B})$, this means that $L(x)$ could be the next step in this transaction. For example, two-phase locking maps all prefixes containing an $U(x)$ step to the empty set, and all prefixes containing only lock steps (including the empty prefix) to E. The path protocol maps the empty prefix to E, and all other prefixes $\bar{B}$ to the set containing all entities that are not locked in $\bar{B}$, but have an immediate predecessor in the path that is locked and not unlocked. And so on.

Any locking protocol π can be thought of as a locking, namely, the set of all locked transactions such that for each transaction $\bar{A}$ in the set, and each $L(x)$ step in $\bar{A}$, the prefix $\bar{B}$ of $\bar{A}$ up to $L(x)$ satisfies $x \in \pi(\bar{B})$.[4] Evidently, not all lockings can be viewed as locking protocols. The next proposition characterizes those which can; to state it we need the concept of the *truncation* of a locked transaction. Consider a locked transaction $\bar{A}$, and a prefix $\bar{B}$ of $\bar{A}$. The *truncation of $\bar{A}$ at $\bar{B}$* is the subsequence of $\bar{A}$ that results if we concatenate to

---

[4] Notice that a locking protocol, considered as a set of locked transactions, can be infinite. This however poses no difficulty, since schedules are always finite, and the results of the previous section apply trivially to infinite sets of locked transactions.

$\bar{B}$ all $U(x)$ steps[5] such that $L(x)$ is a step of $\bar{B}$ but $U(x)$ step is not. We say that a locking λ is closed under truncation if for each $\bar{A} \in \lambda$ and prefix $\bar{B}$ of $\bar{A}$, the truncation of $\bar{A}$ at $\bar{B}$ is also in λ.

Proposition 6.3: *A locking is the set of all locked transactions that obey some locking protocol if and only if it is closed under truncation.*

Proof: Suppose that a locked transaction $\bar{A}$ obeys some protocol π. This means that each $L(x)$ step of $\bar{A}$ is in the π image of the prefix up to the step. However, the same is true for any truncation of $\bar{A}$. Hence, any protocol, considered as a locking, must be closed under truncation.

Conversely, suppose that λ is closed under truncation. Consider the function π mapping any prefix $\bar{B}$ of a transaction of λ to the set of all entities x such that $\bar{B}L(x)$ is also a prefix of a transaction of λ; π maps all other prefixes to the empty set. Consider any transaction $\bar{A} \in \lambda$. Clearly, for any step $L(x)$ of $\bar{A}$, x is in the π image of the prefix up to this step. Conversely, suppose that $\bar{A}$ has the property that for any $L(x)$ step in it, the π image of the prefix up to this step contains x. This means that up to the last $L(x)$ step, $\bar{A}$ is a prefix of a transaction in λ, and hence $\bar{A}$ is the truncation of a transaction in λ. We conclude that $\bar{A}$ is itself in λ. $\square$

Closure under truncation is the key property that makes the safety of locking protocols a much more tractable affair than the safety of lockings in general. Recall the definition of a standard nonserializable schedule and its tail (preceding Corollary 1 to Theorem 6.6). A schedule is standard nonserializable with empty tail if it is nonserializable and of the form $B_1 A_2 \ldots A_k C_1$, where $A_1 = B_1 C_1, A_2, \ldots, A_k$ are transactions. Corollary 1 said that all unsafe lockings have a standard nonserializable schedule, but possibly one with a nonempty tail. We next show that, if a locking is closed under truncation, then a standard nonserializable legal schedule *with empty tail* exists. This will turn out to be the key technical fact underlying the tractability of safety in a locking closed under truncation. The reason is that the requirement that the tail be empty cuts down the possibilities for such a schedule enough, so that a search for such a schedule is now a feasible test for nonsafety.

Lemma 6.8: *If a locking λ is closed under truncation and unsafe, then it has a standard nonserializable legal schedule with empty tail.*

Proof: Just truncate each transaction A_j $j = 2, \ldots, k$ in the standard nonserializable schedule constructed in the proof of Corollary 1 to Theorem 6.6 after the unlock step on x_j. $\square$

Lemma 6.8 immediately suggests a method for testing whether a locking closed under truncation is unsafe: Check all possible legal standard nonserial-

---

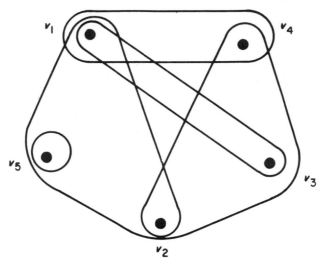

Figure 6.17. A Hypergraph.

izable schedules with empty tail. Naturally, we could have done such a search
based on Corollary 1. However, it turns out that the property of empty tail
is crucial in cutting down the number of possibilities enough, so that a graph-
theoretic technique can be employed to perform the task in polynomial time.

The combinatorics of this situation are best captured in terms of a generalization of a graph called a *hypergraph*. A hypergraph $H = (V, F)$ is a set V
of vertices, and a set F of *hyperedges*, that is, finite subsets of V. A path from
vertex u to vertex v in a hypergraph H is a sequence $h_1, \ldots, h_n$ of hyperedges
such that $u \in h_1$, $v \in h_n$, and $h_{i-1} \cap h_i \neq \emptyset$ for $i = 1, \ldots, n$. We say that
a set S of vertices *separates* u from v if there is no path from u to v in the
hypergraph obtained by deleting all hyperedges containing vertices in S. For
example, in the hypergraph shown in Figure 6.17, with five nodes and five hyperedges, $\{v_1, v_2\}$ separates v_4 from v_5. A *directed hypergraph* is a hypergraph
with one vertex of each hyperedge distinguished as a *head* of the hyperedge. In
directed hypergraphs, paths and separation are defined by ignoring the heads.
It is easy to see that, given a hypergraph with n vertices and m hyperedges,
and two vertices u and v, it can be determined in $O(mn)$ time whether there
is a path from u to v.

With each locking λ (in fact, with any set of transactions λ, locked or not)
we can naturally associate a particular hypergraph $H(\lambda) = (E, F)$ as follows[6]:
The vertices of $H(\lambda)$ are all entities and the hyperedges are all those sets h of

---

[6] This is an infinite set, but we allow our hypergraphs to be infinite. If λ is finite, then
the *relevant part* of $H(\lambda)$, that is, all hyperedges and all vertices incident upon some
hyperedge, is finite.

entities such that there is a transaction in λ which accesses precisely the entities in h. We can now restate Lemma 6.8 as follows:

Corollary 1: *A locking λ closed under truncation is safe if and only if for each prefix $\bar{B}_1$ of a transaction $\bar{A}_1$ in λ the set of all entities locked (and not yet unlocked) at the end of $\bar{B}_1$ separates in $H(\lambda)$ each entity unlocked in $\bar{B}_1$ from each entity locked in $\bar{A}_1$ after $\bar{B}_1$.*

Proof: This is a necessary and sufficient condition for the existence of a legal standard nonserializable schedule which is obtained from a schedule of λ with a single interruption of a transaction. However, the schedule produced in the proof of Lemma 6.8 has this property. $\square$

Corollary 2: *We can test whether a finite locking λ closed under truncation is safe in time $O(n^3)$, where n is the total length of all transactions in λ.*

Proof: We try all n prefixes $\bar{B}_1$ of transactions in λ, and for each we determine whether the set of entities locked at the end separates all entities unlocked in $\bar{B}_1$ from all entities locked later on in $\bar{A}_1$. This can be done in $O(n^2)$ time in the size of the relevant part of the corresponding hypergraph. $\square$

Suppose that we are given a set τ of transactions, closed under truncation, and wish to determine a safe locking policy for τ. Naturally, we want to find the "most liberal" such policy, that is, the one in which lock steps come immediately before the first access on the corresponding entity, and unlock steps come as early as possible. This protocol, denoted π_τ, can be stated as follows:

> "A previously accessed entity x can be unlocked if the set of other entities that are locked separates x in $H(\tau)$ from any entity which is locked later on in the transaction."

Despite the fact that this rule is deceptively stated in terms of unlocking steps, it is indeed a locking protocol (see Problem 6.18). Finally, Lemma 6.8 yields a surprisingly powerful characterization of safe locking protocols. After the path, tree, and the DAG protocol, let us define their ultimate generalization, the *hypergraph* protocol. This protocol is based on a directed hypergraph $H = (E, F)$ defined on the entities (pretty much as the path protocol was based on a path, the tree protocol on a tree, and the DAG protocol on a directed acyclic graph). The protocol (i.e., the function π telling when a lock is allowed) is defined in terms of the following rules:

1. The first lock is always allowed.
   Subsequently, a lock on entity x is allowed if:
2. There is a directed hyperedge h with x its head, so that all other entities in h have already been locked (and possibly unlocked) in the transaction, and
3. For each y currently unlocked, the set of entities currently locked separate x from y in H.

Corollary 3: *The hypergraph protocol is safe.*

Proof: Follows from Corollary 1. $\square$

We shall now show formally that the hypergraph protocol is indeed the ultimate generalization of the tree protocol, the DAG protocol, *and in fact of all safe protocols*:

Corollary 4: *A locking protocol* π *is safe if and only if there is a hypergraph protocol* π_H *such that for any prefix* $\bar{B}$ *of a locked transaction* $\pi(\bar{B}) \subset \pi_H(\bar{B})$.

Proof: The *if* direction is immediate by Corollary 3. For the other direction, let π be a safe protocol, and consider the set λ of all transactions which are legal under π. Define now the hypergraph $H = (E, F)$ where we add a directed hyperedge h with head x to F whenever there is a transaction in λ which accesses precisely the entities in h, and locks x last. Since π is safe, every locked transaction of π is also in π_H. $\square$

This is a surprisingly powerful characterization of safe locking protocols, since it states that they are all versions and guises of the hypergraph protocol, each for some appropriate hypergraph. For example, two-phase locking can be thought of as the hypergraph policy with the *complete directed graph* as H. That is, the hyperedges of H are all possible ordered pairs of entities. The path protocol and the tree protocol are the hypergraph protocol when the underlying hypergraph is a path or a tree, respectively. The DAG protocol is only slightly harder to reformulate in these terms: For each node x in the directed acyclic graph D, we can define its *dominator* to be the lowest ancestor y of x such that any path from the unique source x_0 to x must pass through y. Define now a hypergraph $H(D)$ that has a hyperedge with head x for each entity x; this hyperedge contains all entities that lie in D on some path from the dominator of x to x. It turns out that $\pi_H(D)$ is precisely the DAG protocol for D (Problem 6.19).

PROBLEMS

6.1 Give an efficient algorithm which, when presented with a set of locked transactions and a schedule of the *reductions* of these transactions, decides whether the schedule is legal.

*6.2 Show that any set of schedules of two transactions which is realizable by locking can be realized by $O(n^3)$ locks, where n is the total number of steps.

6.3 Show that there is a set of two transactions (in the action model) such that the set of all conflict-serializable schedules of these two transactions is not realizable by locking.

6.4 Prove Proposition 6.1.

*6.5 Give an example of a set of schedules of three transactions such that the projection of the set on any pair of transactions is realizable by locking, whereas the set is not.

6.6 Show that the shared mode of locking can be simulated by ordinary locks.

*6.7 Show that the converse of Theorem 6.3 is false. That is, there are non-elementary modes of locking which can be simulated by locking.

**6.8 Is $R(\mathcal{M}_3) \subset R(\mathcal{M}_0)$? That is, can the mode $\mathcal{M}_3$ be simulated by ordinary locks?

*6.9 Show that any set of schedules of three transactions, such that the projection of the set on any pair is realizable by locking, can be realized by $\mathcal{M}_3$.

6.10 Show properties (1) through (5) of the closure preceding Lemma 6.5.

6.11 Give a $O(n \log n)$ algorithm for determining whether a pair of locked transactions is safe.

6.12 Consider a set λ of locked transactions. We say that λ is *deadlock-free* if any legal prefix of schedule of λ can be continued to a legal schedule.
    (a) Show that the transactions $\bar{A} = \ell_1 a_1 \ell_2 u_1 a_2 u_2 a_3$ and $\bar{B} = b_1 \ell_1 b_2 \ell_2 u_2 b_3 u_1$ are deadlock-free.
    (b) Show that the transactions $\bar{A} = \ell_1 a_1 \ell_2 u_1 a_2 u_2 a_3$ and $\bar{C} = c_1 \ell_2 c_2 \ell_1 u_2 c_3 u_1$ are not deadlock-free

6.13 Define the *SW boundary* of a rectilinear region to be the set of points (x,y) of the region for which for all sufficiently small $\epsilon > 0$ either $(x - \epsilon, y)$ or $(x, y - \epsilon)$ is not in the region.
    (a) Show that a set of two transactions is not deadlock-free if and only if the SW boundary of the closure of the forbidden region is a subset of the SW boundary of the forbidden region.
    (b) Based on (a), give an $O(n \log n)$ algorithm for determining whether a pair of locked transactions is deadlock-free.
    (c) Show that it can be decided in $O(n^k)$ time whether a set of k transactions is deadlock-free, where n is the total number of steps.
    (d) Show that it is NP-complete to tell whether a set of transactions is deadlock-free.
    (e) Repeat (d) when the given set of transactions obeys conditions (1) and (2) of two-phase locking.

6.14 Give an example of an unsafe set of three locked transactions (in the action model) for which the forbidden region is connected.

6.15 Prove Corollary 3 to Theorem 6.6.

*6.16 Exhibit a sequence $\{G_j : j = 1, \ldots\}$ of graphs such that G_j has at most cj nodes and at least $2^{c'j}$ minimal cycles, where j and c' are positive constants.

*6.17 Suppose that a set of locked transactions is such that any two transactions have at most one entity in common. Show that the set is safe if and only if all biconnected components of the intersection graph obey two-phase locking.

6.18 Recall the protocol π_τ defined for any set of transactions τ closed under truncation. Define explicitly its values for each possible prefix of transactions in τ.

6.19 Show that, for any directed acyclic graph D, the DAG protocol for D is identical to the hypergraph protocol for $H(D)$, defined at the end of Section 6.3.

NOTES AND REFERENCES

Theorem 6.1 is from [Papadimitriou 1982] and Theorem 6.2 from [Yannakakis 1984]. The material in Section 6.2 is from [Papadimitriou 1983] and [Yannakakis 1982a], first presented in [Yannakakis et al. 1979]. Section 6.3 is from [Yannakakis 1982a]. Problems 6.2, 6.5, and 6.9 are due to Peter Rathmann, and Problem 6.3 to Mihalis Yannakakis. Problem 6.11 is from [Soisalon-Soininen and Wood 1984]; see also [Lipski and Papadimitriou]. A solution to Problem 6.14 can be found in the latter paper. Problem 6.13 is from [Papadimitriou 1983] and [Yannakakis 1982b].

7

DISTRIBUTED CONCURRENCY CONTROL

In the beginning of this book we described a database as a collection of data stored in a computer system. A *distributed database* is a collection of data stored in a *computer network*. As with all databases, the information stored in a distributed database should comprise a cohesive representation of a "part of the world," and should be organized and managed following certain uniform principles.

There are many reasons why we may wish to distribute a database on a computer network. First, the part of the world represented by the database may consist of smaller parts that are geographically dispersed. As a result, the most natural and convenient way to store the representation is by distributing the data in a manner reflecting the distribution of the objects represented. This way, most frequently needed "local" data will be available locally, thus enhancing the speed and reliability of the system. Besides, in many cases a distributed database is simply the merger of smaller databases, located in various sites, or the "spilling over" of a single database, reflecting the growth of the represented enterprise. In the case of data stored in a *local* network, the database may be distributed simply because a single computer could not satisfy the storage and processing needs of the system. Finally, another argument in favor of distributed databases is *reliability*. By storing information in a redundant way over a computer network we decrease the probability that urgently needed data is unavailable because of a computer failure or other adverse circumstance.

Distributed databases are only one among the many facets of *distributed computation*, an area which has come to prominence in the past decade as the result of growing needs and opportunities. Unfortunately, new unresolved and challenging problems, particular to distributed computation, have also been encountered. The basic difficulty inherent in distributed computation is that a global goal must be achieved by actions taken locally at each site. Because of communication delays, costs, and failures, each site has a different incomplete view of the progress of the computation, the status of the network, even of time. Having all sites agree on everything before performing each step is not practical, or even possible. Much of the work on distributed systems and databases deals with such important and extremely complex general issues as distributed agreement, reliability, and synchronization. A comprehensive treatment of distributed concurrency control would require us to discuss these issues as well, something that is well outside our scope. Instead, we shall examine the problem of distributed concurrency control in a somewhat artificial isolation from these other important aspects of distributed computation.

Indeed, we shall see that concurrency control becomes considerably harder in a distributed environment. First, transactions are no longer linearly ordered sequences of actions on data. Since data are distributed, the actions take place in various sites, and thus it is not always possible to establish a temporal order among actions. Consequently, transactions are *partial orders* of steps. To make matters worse, the scheduler is itself a distributed program. At each site the local module of the scheduler receives a stream of requests for the execution of steps, and must make decisions about granting or delaying them based only on locally available information. Non-local information can of course be obtained, but at a serious *communication cost;* part of this cost is the uncertainty inherent in any communication over unreliable links. As a result of all this, the computational problems associated with distributed concurrency control are considerably more difficult than the corresponding centralized ones. Our main goal in this chapter is to capture formally this increase in complexity.

7.1 THE MODEL

A distributed database differs from a centalized one in that it resides in a non-empty set S of *sites*, whose elements are referred to as Site 1, Site 2, etc., and each entity is stored at exactly one site. There is a function δ, called the *distribution function*, which maps the set E of entities to S; $\delta(x)$ is the site at which entity x is stored. As usual, we denote entities as x, y, etc. If the site must be emphasized, we use the notation x^1 to mean "entity x stored at Site 1."

Distributed Transactions

A *distributed transaction A* is a set $\{a_1, \ldots, a_m\}$ of steps, together with a partial order on them. If there is a path from step a to step b of the partial order (or if $a = b$), we write $a \prec_A b$. Each step a is an indivisible read and write operation (an action, that is) on an entity $\text{ENTITY}(a) \in E$. If, for two steps a and b of a transaction, $\delta(\text{ENTITY}(a)) = \delta(\text{ENTITY}(b))$, then either $a \prec_A b$ or $b \prec_A a$.

We now define the *interpretation* of a distributed transaction. For each step a of a distributed transaction A, let us define the set $B(a)$ of entities that *were acted upon before* step a; that is,

$$B(a) = \{x \in E : \text{For some } b \prec_A a \; \text{ENTITY}(b) = x\}.$$

An *interpretation* of A is a pair $I = (\mathbf{D}, \mathbf{F})$, where $\mathbf{D} = \{D_x, D_y, \ldots\}$ is a set of *domains*, one for each entity in E, and $\mathbf{F} = \{f_a : a \text{ a step of } A\}$ is a set of *functions*. For each step a, f_a is a mapping

$$f_a : \prod_{x \in B(a)} D_x \rightarrow D_{\text{ENTITY}(a)}.$$

Distributed transactions are executions of distributed programs that act on the entities of the database. Since the context of distributed databases is already the source of considerable complexity, we limit ourselves from the beginning to the simpler action model of transactions. In distributed transactions, steps are not totally ordered, as in the centralized case. If two steps act on entities stored at different sites, there may be no way (or reason) for determining which happened first. However, two steps acting on entities at the same site must be ordered one way or the other. Also, if the value written by step a depends on the value read by step b, then again $b \prec_A a$, even though a and b may take place at different sites. Integrity constraints in a distributed database present no difficulty: They are an arbitrary predicate on the values of the entities. The clauses of the integrity constraints may involve entities stored at different sites. In fact, the presence of such "inter-site" integrity constraints is expected in a distributed database which is not just a set of independent centralized databases.

Example 7.1: In a database distributed on two sites we may wish to store two copies of each of the data items x and y. To describe such a situation in our model, we have in our set E four entities x_1, x_2, y_1, y_2, with $\delta(x_1) = \delta(y_1) =$ Site 1, and $\delta(x_2) = \delta(y_2) -$ Site 2. The fact that x_1 and x_2 are copies of the same data item is reflected in the integrity constraint "$x_1 = x_2$"; similarly, "$y_1 = y_2$."

Consider the centralized transaction "$x := x + 1; y := y - 1$" accessing and acting on x and y; in the action model, this transaction is abstracted as $A(x)A(y)$. In the distributed environment, this transaction would be translated into one of the distributed transactions shown in Figure 7.1, among other possibilities. In transaction A shown in Figure 7.1(a) the value of x is read and updated at site 1, that of y at site 2, and the copies at the other sites are also updated at the end. The semantics of the various steps are: $f_1(x_1) = x_1 + 1$, $f_2(y_2, y_1, x_1) = y_2 - 1$, $f_3(y_2) = y_2 - 1$, $f_4(x_1, y_2, x_2) = x_1 + 1$. In transaction B of Figure 7.1(b) the

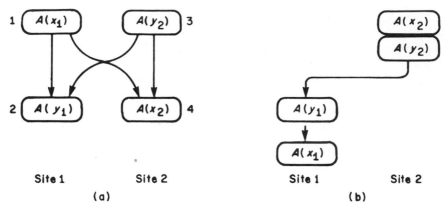

Figure 7.1. Two Distributed Transactions.

values of x and y are first updated in site 2, and then the updates are also copied in site 1, but (for no particular reason) in the opposite order. $\square$

In the rest of this chapter we shall consider only distributed transactions in the action model, with the interpretations hidden. The integrity constraints are also hidden. This means that we shall not take into account, among other things, the *redundancy* of the database, that is, the fact that certain entities are copies of the same data item. This will spare our exposition some of the most involved problems in distributed databases, which stem precisely from this issue of redundancy. For example, as is evident from the above example, the translation from a centralized transaction to a distributed transaction can be done in a number of different ways (recall Figures 7.1(a) and 7.1(b)). This translation process is one important aspect of distributed concurrency control that we shall not examine: We shall assume that the distributed transactions to be handled by our schedulers are given and fixed.

Schedules and Correctness

A *distributed schedule* $s = (\tau, \prec_s)$ is a finite set τ of transactions (in the action model), together with a partial order on all steps of the transactions; if there is a path from step a to step b in the partial order, we write $a \prec_s b$. A schedule must have the following properties: (a) If two steps a and b act on entities at the same site, that is, $\delta(\text{ENTITY}(a)) = \delta(\text{ENTITY}(b))$, then either $a \prec_s b$ or $b \prec_s a$; and (b) if for two steps a and b of s and some transaction $A \in \tau$ we have $a \prec_A b$, then $a \prec_s b$. For example, we show in Figure 7.2 a schedule s of the transactions A and B shown in Figure 7.1. Notice that s has more arcs than those required by the definition of a schedule. We shall represent schedules as in Figure 7.2, with steps at the same site arranged in columns, and

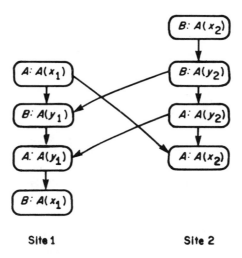

Figure 7.2. A Distributed Schedule.

time progressing downwards.

Is the schedule in Figure 7.2 correct? The criteria are the same as in centralized databases. A schedule s is *serial* if there exists a total order $\prec$ on the transactions such that, whenever a step a of transaction A and step b of B satisfy $a \prec_s b$, then $A \prec B$. For example, the schedule of Figure 7.2 is not serial, since $B : A(y_1) \prec_s A : A(y_1) \prec_s B : A(x_1)$, and thus the definition is satisfied by neither of the two possible orders on $\{A, B\}$. Finally, a schedule is considered correct if it is *serializable*. A schedule s is called serializable if there is a serial schedule s' with the same transactions such that s has precisely the same effect on the values of the entities as s', regardless of the interpretations of the transactions and the initial values of the entities.

As always in the action model, serializability can be tested by considering the conflicts among the transactions. Given a schedule $s = (\tau, \prec_s)$, we can create its *conflict graph* $G(s)$. The nodes of $G(s)$ are the transactions in τ. There is an arc from transaction A to transaction B if there is a step a of A and a step b of B such that $\text{ENTITY}(a) = \text{ENTITY}(b)$ and $a \prec_s b$. This completes the definition of $G(s)$.

Theorem 7.1: *A distributed schedule s is serializable if and only if $G(s)$ is acyclic.*

Proof: The proof is based on familiar ideas, very similar to those in Theorems 2.2, 2.8, and 2.12 (see Problem 7.1). $\square$

The distributed schedule in Figure 7.2 is not serializable, as can be checked by inspecting its conflict graph (Figure 7.3).

Figure 7.3. The Conflict Graph of the Schedule in Figure 7.2.

Notice that in all of our examples we have used only transactions on two sites only. This is no accident. It turns out that most of the novelty and complexity of distributed concurrency control is already brought out when the data is distributed in two sites (although exceptions do exist, see Section 7.4).

7.2 DISTRIBUTED SCHEDULERS

A scheduler in a distributed database must consider, and rearrange if necessary, the stream of steps arriving at each site. Consequently, the scheduler must be a distributed program, with a subprogram, called a *module*, executing at each site. The computation of a module is a sequence of steps of the following three kinds:

1. Local computation like that performed by ordinary schedulers (recall Figure 4.1). This includes receiving a database step and granting the execution of one.
2. Sending a message to another site.
3. Receiving a message.

A message is either a *transaction message* or a *scheduler message*. A transaction message is the implementation of an arc between two steps in the transaction (in Figure 7.1(a), after the action on x_1, the module at Site 1 sends a message to Site 2, reflecting the arc between the two steps accessing x_1 and x_2). Such arcs denote both temporal precedence and information transfer between the steps, and the transaction message serves both purposes. A scheduler message is sent by a module in order to request from another module information needed to reach a scheduling decision, or in order to let another module know of some worthwhile information it has. The latter action could be either spontaneous, or in response to a request from the other module.

Our working hypothesis in this chapter is that messages are extremely costly. One aspect of the cost of messages is the fact that they subject the modules to *arbitrary delays*: We shall assume that, once a message is sent, the time it takes to arrive at another site can in principle be any nonnegative integer. Later in this section we shall introduce a formal framework for describing distributed schedulers and for analyzing their performance. But first, we give some examples of distributed schedulers, which are simply distributed implementations of familiar schedulers examined in Chapter 4.

Distributed Two-Phase Locking

Let us design a distributed scheduler based on the dynamic two-phase locking scheduler (Section 4.2). Recall the test of this scheduler:

> "*A step can always proceed, unless it conflicts with a previous step of an active transaction (other than its own).*"

In the distributed implementation the test is precisely the same. To carry out the test, the module checks whether the entity accessed by the step in question has been accessed by an active transaction. Since the entity is stored at the site of the module, the step sought is also a local one. The nontrivial part is determining whether or not a transaction is active. A transaction may have many *sinks* (steps with no arcs leaving them; see the transaction in Figure 7.1(a)), and a transaction has terminated if all sinks have been executed. Unfortunately, a site does not know whether a sink has been executed at another site, unless it is told so explicitly via scheduler messages. Thus, once a module executes a step which is the last step of a transaction on the module, and it has no outgoing arcs, it sends to all other sites a scheduler message called a *termination message* announcing that the step-sink has executed.

A new difficulty arises: How does a module know that it has received termination messages from all sites at which the transaction has executed a sink step? Although easy remedies exist, it is simplifying to assume throughout this chapter that *the scheduler knows the syntax (steps, partial order, etc.) of all transactions* beforehand. Thus, once termination messages have been received from all sites at which the transaction has sink messages (and has also terminated at the local site), the transaction is *declared to have terminated* for the purposes of the test.

Theorem 7.2: *All schedules output by the distributed two-phase locking scheduler are serializable.*

Proof: First notice that, if A and B are distributed transactions in the input schedule which conflict, then all modules at sites at which entities accessed by both A and B are stored will declare them terminated in the same order (if at all). This is because, in accordance with the test, the action of the second transaction will not be granted until after the first transaction has been declared terminated. Thus, it is impossible for another site to have declared the second transaction terminated, since it has yet to execute a step.

Based on the above observation, it is easy to show that the schedule output by the distributed two-phase locking scheduler is equivalent to any serial schedule compatible with the partial order on transactions in which a transaction precedes another if it has been declared terminated first at a site at which they conflict. $\Box$

As in the centralized version, this scheduler can be implemented using locking. Before the first access of an entity by a transaction, the transaction acquires a lock on the entity. The lock is released at the instant that the transaction is declared terminated. Needless to say, deadlocks are likely to occur in the distributed version as well. Detecting deadlocks in a distributed environment is an extremely hard problem, which we shall not examine. For a taste of the issues involved in monitoring a distributed deadlock graph see the discussion of the distributed conflict graph scheduler in the next section.

Distributed Timestamps

The timestamp scheduler (Section 4.4) is perhaps the easiest to transplant in a distributed environment. In the action model of transactions each entity has a single timestamp, namely the timestamp of the youngest transaction that has accessed it. The test is:

> *"A step can proceed if the timestamp of its transaction is larger than the timestamp of the entity accessed. If the step proceeds, the timestamp of the entity accessed is updated to become the timestamp of the transaction."*

The only question is, how do we define the timestamp of each transaction, so that it is known to all sites? In the centralized timestamp scheduler we had defined the timestamp of a transaction to be the time at which the first step of the transaction was received (and output). In the centralized environment, time can be defined in an unambiguous way—say, as the rank of the step in the output schedule. In a distributed environment, however, there may be no way of ordering two events occurring at two remote sites. Naturally, all events (arrivals and grantings of steps and messages, steps of local computation, etc.) happening at a particular site are ordered. Also ordered are the acts of sending and receiving a message—the first precedes the latter. But these are the only possible temporal precedences. Time has itself become a partial order!

How do we then assign a timestamp to each transaction? Consider an event, such as the arrival of a new step, taking place at some site. As we said before, there are several events at this and other sites which precede the present event in the temporal partial order. We can define the "relative time" of that event to be *the total number of grantings of steps which precede it* (notice that this is a direct generalization of the centralized case). This measure has the desirable property that, at the moment that a site receives a message from another, its relative time becomes at least as great as the relative time at the other site, at the moment the message was sent.

Now each transaction has at least one *source* step, that is, a step with no incoming arcs. The site of one such source step is designated to be the *residence* of the transaction. We now define the *arrival time* of the transaction to be the relative time at which the first step of the transaction arrived at the residence of the transaction; suppose the arrival time is t. Finally, suppose that there are

k sites, of which the residence of the transaction is the ith. *The timestamp of the transaction is defined to be $t * k + i$.*

This definition is not as arbitrary as it may look at first. It essentially says that the timestamp of a transaction is the reading of a local clock at the moment of its arrival, juxtaposed with certain low-order bits which are particular to the site, to ensure uniqueness. For example, suppose that Site 1 is the residence of transaction A in Figure 7.2, and Site 2 of B. The arrival time of A is 0, and that of B is also 0. The timestamp of A is thus $0 * 2 + 1 = 1$, and the timestamp of B is $0 * 2 + 2 = 2$. Timestamps defined this way have two crucial properties: First each timestamp is unique (as we shall see, the first step of a transaction is never delayed at its residence). Second, a transaction whose arrival precedes that of another is guaranteed to have a smaller timestamp than the other transaction.

Once the timestamp of a transaction has been defined, it must be broadcasted to all other sites at which source steps of the same transaction will be processed (for steps that are not sources, the timestamp is known from their predecessors). Each module then simply submits each step to the test (naturally, it delays any step whose timestamp it does not know).

Theorem 7.3: *All schedules output by the distributed timestamp scheduler are serializable.*

Proof: The schedule output is clearly equivalent to the serial schedule which orders the transactions in increasing timestamps. $\square$

Distributed Conflict Graph Scheduler

Generalizing the conflict graph scheduler (Section 4.5) to the distributed case is far more difficult than it was for the two schedulers examined previously. The intuitive reason is that the conflict graph is a "global" test of consistency, and global computational tasks are the most demanding ones in a distributed environment. In the next section we shall give a formal proof of the difficulty of implementing the distributed conflict graph scheduler. In this subsection we shall start getting acquainted with the subtle issues involved.

As before, we assume that the scheduler has at the beginning of its operation a complete knowledge of the syntax of the transactions to occur in the input schedule. As in the subsection on static information schedulers of Section 4.5, this knowledge can be captured by the *conflict multigraph* of the transactions, in which there is an edge for each conflict between two transactions. For example, in Figure 7.4 we show three distributed transactions and their conflict multigraph. We have drawn the edges of the conflict multigraph either solid or dashed, depending on whether the conflict takes place at Site 2 or Site 1, respectively. We shall call solid edges *red* and dashed edges *green*.

Each edge of the conflict multigraph represents a conflict. As the operation of the scheduler proceeds and steps are output, these conflicts are resolved one

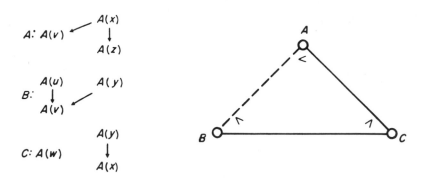

Figure 7.4. Three Transactions and Their Conflict Multigraph.

by one. For example, if in Figure 7.4 we output the $A(v)$ step of transaction A at Site 1 before the $A(v)$ step of B, then it has been decided that B follows A in any equivalent serial schedule. We say that the conflict between A and B on v has *been resolved*, and the corresponding edge of the conflict multigraph has been directed from A to B. Thus, we can view the operation of the conflict graph scheduler (centralized or distributed) as a sequence of resolution of conflicts, which leave the graph acyclic. Not all sequences of conflict resolutions can occur, however. For example, since the $A(x)$ step of A precedes the $A(v)$ step, the conflict between A and C on x must have been resolved before the conflict between A and B on v can be resolved from A to B. Thus, there is a partial order $\succ_A$ among the edges of the conflict multigraph which are incident upon transaction A, such that an edge e cannot be directed away from A until all edges e' such that $e' \succ_A e$ have been somehow directed. This partial order is also shown in Figure 7.4.

We next sketch a simple way for implementing a distributed version of the conflict graph scheduler: Each module maintains a copy of the conflict multigraph, with some edges directed. Once a step arrives, the module broadcasts a request to all other sites for information concerning the state of the multigraph. When such a request is received, the receiving module transmits its current multigraph, and refrains from any activity until the outcome of the attempt to schedule is received (if two modules receive one another's request we may assume that the site with smallest index, say, prevails). When the original module receives the local states of the multigraph from all other sites, it directs any edge which is directed at some site, and then sees whether the proposed step would create a cycle. If not, it outputs the step; otherwise it rejects it. In both cases it sends messages to all other sites notifying them that they can now proceed with scheduling their own steps. Although this algorithm is efficient in the conventional sense of requiring only polynomially many steps, it should

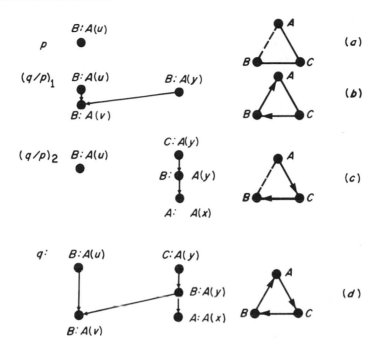

Figure 7.5. A Bad Extension for Serializability.

be clear that it is *extremely costly in communication*, that is, in the number of messages sent.

Still, some form of communication is inevitable in implementing the conflict graph scheduler, because local information can be insufficient and misleading. In Figure 7.5(a-d) we show a situation in which each site has directed certain edges corresponding to local conflicts in a manner that looks perfectly acyclic at both sites, but if the directed edges are combined a cycle is formed (the underlying transactions are those of Figure 7.4). Naturally, the scheduler could decide to reject steps which, although they do not form a local cycle, are suspected of helping to create an overall cycle. However, such a policy will necessarily delay the steps of certain serializable schedules, and thus the scheduler could not be claimed to realize the set of all serializable schedules.

Apparently a compromise is needed between these two extremes of no communication and full broadcasting. As we shall see in the next section, the right compromise is an extremely complex policy.

The Performance of Distributed Schedulers

There are three performance measures for distributed schedulers: The *time complexity*, the *concurrency* supported, and the *communication requirements*; in the centralized case we only had the first two. As we shall see, the issues and trade-offs regarding performance are far more complex in distributed concurrency control.

We measure the time complexity of a distributed scheduler pretty much in the same way as with centralized schedulers, that is, by the total count of the operations performed by all modules of the scheduler, as a function of the initial state and the number of steps in the input schedule. We shall also briefly discuss the *space complexity* of a distributed scheduler, which is the total number of memory locations the scheduler uses up in its computation.

We next define our measure of concurrency. It turns out that it is best to approach this notion within the domain of *total orders of steps*, instead of partial orders. Each partial order s can be considered as a *set of total orders*, namely, all those total orders which are compatible with s. The fewer arcs s has, the larger it is when considered as a set of total orders. The interpretation of distributed schedules as sets of ordinary schedules is a useful device for avoiding some of the complexities of partial orders without departing from the distributed environment. For example, it is easy to show that a distributed schedule s is serializable if and only if, when considered as a set of ordinary schedules, is a subset of the serializable schedules (Problem 7.2). In the sequel we shall represent by s both the schedule and the set of total orders on the steps involved. If $\mathcal{C}$ is a set of schedules, we shall denote by $\hat{\mathcal{C}}$ the set of all total orders compatible with some schedule in $\mathcal{C}$, that is, $\hat{\mathcal{C}} = \cup_{s \in \mathcal{C}} s$.

Our measure of concurrency for a scheduler S is the set $\hat{\mathcal{C}}$ of total orders, where $\mathcal{C}$ is the set of schedules *realized* by S. We are therefore interested in defining what it means for a distributed scheduler to *realize* a set $\mathcal{C}$ of schedules. The notion is only meaningful when $\mathcal{C}$ consists of schedules which include no other precedences among actions on different sites besides those inherited by the transactions. Only such schedules can be the input of a scheduler. A set $\mathcal{C}$ of schedules with no extra precedences is called a *concurrency control principle*.

We must first formalize the computation of distributed schedulers, at least in terms of their input-output behavior. Let S be a distributed scheduler. We think of the input to S not as a schedule but as a *total order*; that is, we assume that the temporal order in which these steps arrived at the differnt sites is known. Once we have totally ordered the arrivals of the steps of the input, we can postulate that, as with centralized schedulers, the jth step arrives at time j. That is, we pretend that absolute time exists, and its "tics" are precisely the arrivals of the steps of the input. This again is not a departure from our premise that schedules, schedulers, and time are distributed, but a simplifying mathematical device. We also assume that local computation introduces no delays (a reasonable assumption, since message delays are usually orders of magnitude larger than the time requirements for local computation). Under these assumptions it is clear that the behavior of scheduler S on the input $\hat{s}$ is completely determined, *except for the unpredictable message delays*. We shall use the term *indeterminism* for unpredictability of this kind[1].

We next formalize the fact that the behavior of S on input $\hat{s}$ is completely determined by the message delays. Let $\mathbf{d} = d_1, d_2, \ldots$ be a sequence of non-negative real numbers, the *message delays*. That is, if t_1 is the earliest time at which any module of S sends a message, then the receiver will get the message at time $t_1 + d_1$. The second message, sent at time t_2, will arrive at time $t_2 + d_2$, and so on. If two modules must send a message at the same time, the one with smallest index, say, goes first. Notice that each t_j is completely determined by algorithm S, the arrival times 1, 2, etc. of the steps of $\hat{s}$, and the previous delays d_i, $i < j$ (under our assumption of negligible local computation time and the tie-breaking rule). Notice also that not all delay sequences are meaningful. What may go wrong is that $\mathbf{d}$ may dictate a long delay, so that a step of the input is processed after the arrival of a successor of the step[2]. Such delay sequences are called *infeasible*. For all schedulers and inputs feasible sequences exist. For example, the *zero* delay sequence $\mathbf{0} = 0, 0, \ldots$ is always feasible.

Thus, scheduler S, with the given delays $\mathbf{d}$, is a completely specified algorithm, which we may call $S_{\mathbf{d}}$. The *output* of $S_{\mathbf{d}}$ on input $\hat{s}$, $S_{\mathbf{d}}(\hat{s})$, is a pair $(\hat{p}, \mathbf{t})$, where $\hat{p}$ is a total order on the steps of $\hat{s}$, and $\mathbf{t}$ is a function mapping each step a of $\hat{p}$ to the delay between the time of arrival of a and the time it was output. Naturally, if a and b are the ith and jth steps of $\hat{s}$, and a comes before b in $S_{\mathbf{d}}(\hat{s})$, then $i + \mathbf{t}(a) \leq j + \mathbf{t}(b)$, and, in case of equality, a's site has a smaller index than b's. The identically zero function is also denoted $\mathbf{0}$.

We have at last defined the input-output behavior of a distributed scheduler. We shall now define when a scheduler *realizes* a concurrency control principle. Let $\mathcal{C}$ be a concurrency control principle and S a distributed scheduler which is supposed to realize $\mathcal{C}$. When a total order $\hat{s} \in \hat{\mathcal{C}}$ is input to S, the scheduler will strive to output it without delays, if possible. As we have seen in the last subsection, however, some communication between modules may be necessary, and thus delays resulting from communication are inevitable. In order for S to realize $\mathcal{C}$, we insist that:

(a) For all $\hat{s} \in \hat{\mathcal{C}}$, $S_{\mathbf{0}}(\hat{s}) = (\hat{s}, \mathbf{0})$, and

(b) For all $\hat{s}$ and any delay sequence $\mathbf{d}$, if $S_{\mathbf{d}}(\hat{s}) = (\hat{p}, \mathbf{t})$, then $\hat{p} \in \hat{\mathcal{C}}$.

---

[1] *Nondeterminism* would be an inappropriate term here, since a nondeterministic program is correct if *any* of its possible computations is correct. In our case, the scheduler must be correct in the face of *all* possible delays.

[2] We could make the reasonable assumption that, if two messages were sent from Site 1 to Site 2, then they were received by Site 2 in the same order that they were sent. That is, the link between the two sites acts as a queue (actual communication networks may not behave this way). This would then be another reason why a delay sequence may be infeasible.

Condition (b) says that, for all inputs, the schedule output by S must always be safely in $\hat{\mathcal{C}}$. Furthermore, condition (a) requires that, if the input schedule is in $\hat{\mathcal{C}}$, then it can only be delayed because of necessary communication; if the communication delays are zero, then it should not be delayed at all. Notice that for inputs outside $\hat{\mathcal{C}}$ the scheduler has complete freedom of response—it can even output a precalculated schedule, as long as it is in $\hat{\mathcal{C}}$.

Proposition 7.1: *If $\mathcal{C}$ is a concurrency control principle such that the set of all prefixes of $\hat{\mathcal{C}}$ is in P, then there is a polynomial-time scheduler which realizes $\mathcal{C}$.* $\square$

The proof is a generalization of the scheduler described in the previous section, which realizes serializability by broadcasting all arriving requests and waiting for all answers before proceeding. This solution is, of course, not an acceptable one, because of the excessive communication costs; this is our next subject.

Communication Costs

Let S be a scheduler, which handles transactions in the set τ (which we shall henceforth consider fixed, according to our assumption of static information), and which realizes concurrency control principle $\mathcal{C}$. The *communication cost* of S is the maximum number of scheduler messages that are exchanged by $S_{\mathbf{d}}$ on input $\hat{s}$ for all delay sequences $\mathbf{d}$ and schedules $\hat{s}$. The *communication inherent in $\mathcal{C}$* is the smallest communication cost over all possible schedulers S that realize $\mathcal{C}$. Notice that we charge a unit of communication cost for any scheduler message, however long. As a result, we can assume that each message (transaction message or scheduler message) carries with it the total state of the sending module.

In this section we shall show that the communication inherent in some concurrency control principle $\mathcal{C}$, denoted $b^*(\mathcal{C})$, can be calculated by a surprisingly simple recursive formula (however, in the next section we show that evaluating this formula is PSPACE-complete). In this and the next section, we assume that *there are only two sites* in our distributed database. Since we shall prove mostly negative results, our main results are applicable to any database. The occasional positive results can also be generalized to more than two sites, but this is left to the Problems.

If s is a schedule, that is, a partial order on certain steps, a *prefix* of p is a partial order on a subset of the steps of s such that, if a is a step in p and $b \prec_s a$, then also b is in p, and $b \prec_p a$. If p is a prefix of a schedule involving the transactions in τ (which we shall assume fixed), then the steps in p define an orientation on certain edges of the multigraph associated with τ. The corresponding *ordered mixed multigraph* (i.e, a graph containing both directed and undirected edges, and a partial order for the edges incident upon each vertex) is denoted $G(\tau, p)$.

If q is a prefix of s, and p a prefix of q, then we can define the *projection of q on site i given p* to be the smallest prefix of q which contains all steps in p plus all steps in q that are at site i. The projection of q on site i given p is denoted $(q/p)_i$. For example, in Figure 7.5(a-d) we show four prefixes of a schedule. The prefix p in Figure 7.5(a) is a prefix of q (7.5(d)); in Figures 7.5(b) and (c) we show $(q/p)_1$ and $(q/p)_2$. Intuitively, $(q/p)_i$ is the information that site i has if prefix q has arrived and the last exchange of messages was when prefix p had arrived.

In fact, Figure 7.5 shows something more interesting: q is such that its projections on both sites have an acyclic mixed multigraph which has no directed cycle, and $G(\tau, q)$ does contain a cycle. This was described earlier in this section as a situation which forces the scheduler to communicate. To formalize this notion in the case of a general concurrency control principle C (and not in the case of serializability, in which the multigraph is relevant), consider a prefix p of a schedule in C. An extension q of p is said to be *bad for C* if q is not a prefix of a schedule in C whereas $(q/p)_1$ and $(q/p)_2$ are prefixes of schedules in C.

We are now almost ready to state our result concerning the recursive formula for the communication inherent in a concurrency control principle C, $b^*(C)$. To write the formula, we have to generalize the concept a bit: We define $b^*(C, p)$ to be the number of messages that a scheduler S would have to expend on some schedule s which is an extension of p under some delay sequence $\mathbf{d}$ *when S is started at an instant at which p has already arrived and is known to both sites*, maximized, as always, over all $\mathbf{d}$ and s, and minimized over all S. Thus, the communication inherent in C is simply $b^*(C, e)$, where e is the empty prefix.

Theorem 7.4: $b^*(C, p) = \max_q [2 + \min_{i=1,2} b^*(C, (q/p)_i)]$, where the maximum is taken over all bad (for C) extensions q of p, and is zero if no such extension exists or if p is not a prefix of a schedule in C.

Proof: . To show that $b^*(C, p)$ is at least equal to $2 + \min_{i=1,2} b^*(C, (q/p)_i)$ for any bad extension q of p, consider such an extension. What should the module at Site 1 of a scheduler which realizes C do if the steps in $(q/p)_1$ arrive? Since the scheduler is supposed to realize C, it should certainly have a way of granting them, perhaps after some communication delays. First, suppose that Site 1 grants these steps with no communication. Then Site 2, when presented with the steps in $(q/p)_2$, cannot grant them without asking Site 1 about the steps that have been granted there, because then a prefix not in C would be output. Thus, the worst-case communication for p is at least two plus the worst-case communication for $(q/p)_2$ (which may, for all we know, be the prefix that has arrived when this message was received by Site 1). For the other case, suppose that Site 1 waits for some information from Site 2 before it grants some step of q. It cannot wait for a message triggered by an event at Site 2, since such an event may be delayed (for example, if a total order in $(p/q)_1$ is a prefix of the total order input to the scheduler), in which case the scheduler would end up not realizing C. So, Site 1 must solicit a message from Site 2, and thus $b^*(C, p) \geq 2 + b^*(C, (q/p)_1)$.

To show now that $b^*(C, p)$ is at most equal to the right-hand side, we shall outline a scheduler S which achieves this cost. We shall describe the operation of S when started at a prefix p, known to both sites. First, if p is not a prefix of C, then both modules of S output, without communication, some precomputed schedule in $\hat{C}$. Also, if there is no bad extension of p, then both modules of S discover this, and grant all steps received. The Theorem holds in this case, since the right-hand side also reduces to zero. So, assume that p is indeed a prefix of a schedule in C, and a bad extension exists.

Each module of S operates by maintaining a prefix r, initially p, which is its record of all the steps which have been granted at this and the other site. If a step is granted at this site, r is updated. If a scheduler message or a transaction message arrives, r is again updated according to the information received. If the module of S at Site 1 receives a step a such that, if granted and juxtaposed to r, would create $(q/p)_1$ for some bad extension q of p and $b^*(C, (q/p)_1)$ is smaller than $b^*(C, (q/p)_2)$ then Site 1 initiates a communication with Site 2 and updates its prefix before granting a. If $b^*(C, (q/p)_1)$ is larger, then Site 1 knows that Site 2 would have initiated a communication had the bad prefix arrived. If the two costs $b^*(C, (q/p)_1)$ and $b^*(C, (q/p)_2)$ are equal, then let us break the tie by saying that Site 1 initiates a communication. Finally, if at any point it becomes apparent that the input is not a prefix of a schedule in C, then both modules switch to a mode of outputting a precomputed schedule in $\hat{C}$. The theorem follows. $\square$

Notice that the only nontrivial local computation performed by either module of the scheduler described in the proof is computing $b^*(C, p)$ for various prefixes p. Unfortunately, we shall see in the next chapter that this is a very hard task, even when C is fixed to be serializability, a concurrency control principle of obvious practical importance. Let us, however, point out the following:

Corollary: *If C is a concurrency control principle such that the set of all prefixes of C can be recognized in polynomial space, then there is a scheduler which implements C and uses only polynomial space.*

Proof: The computation of b^* from the recursive formula in Theorem 7.4 and the search for bad prefixes can be carried out in polynomial space. $\square$

7.3 THE COMPLEXITY OF MINIMIZING COMMUNICATION

In this section we show that implementing the conflict graph scheduler for a given set of transactions on two sites so as to minimize communication is

PSPACE-complete. As we shall argue later on in this section, this is tangible evidence of the difficulty of distributed concurrency control in general.

The CONFLICT Game

As we have seen in the previous section, the operation of a scheduler realizing serializability for a given set of transactions τ can be considered as a process of *resolving* conflicts among transactions. Resolving conflicts can be in turn considered as orienting the edges of an object called an *ordered mixed multigraph* $G(\tau, p)$ depending on the set τ of transactions and the prefix p seen so far (in Figure 7.5(a-d) we show the ordered mixed multigraphs for the set of three transactions of Figure 7.4, and each of the four prefixes shown there). This object is a multigraph, in that it may have more than one edge or arc connecting two vertices, corresponding to conflicts on different entities. It is *mixed*, because undirected edges, corresponding to unresolved conflicts, may coexist with directed arcs, that is conflicts which have been resolved in p. Recall that a conflict between two steps of two transactions is considered to be resolved in p if at least one of the steps is in p. Finally, it is an *ordered* mixed multigraph, because at each vertex A there is a partial order $\succ_A$ among the edges incident upon it, such that edge $[A, B]$ cannot be oriented from A to B until all other edges preceding it in $\succ_A$ have been somehow oriented.

Recall that we assume that the entities are stored over two sites. Consequently, the edges of $G(\tau, p)$ can be divided into two categories, those which are due to conflicts at Site 1, called *green edges* (dashed in the figures), and those which are due to conflicts at Site 2 (these are the *red edges*, represented as solid lines). Directed arcs are always solid. Formally, $G(\tau, p) = (\tau, R, G, A, \succ)$, where R is the set of red edges, G is the set of green edges, A is the set of directed arcs, and $\succ$ is a set of partial orders, one for each transaction in τ.

We can define a *game*, which we call CONFLICT, on such a multigraph. There are two players, called SHORT and LONG, and the board is an ordered mixed multigraph $G = (\tau, R, G, A, P)$. We next describe a typical round of moves in CONFLICT.

First LONG moves. A move by LONG consists of a choice of two sets of edges X_R and X_G, where $X_R - X_G \subseteq R$ and $X_G - X_R \subseteq G$, and proposed orientations of the edges in X_R, forming the set of arcs A_R, and similarly A_G for X_G. Any edges in $X_R \cap X_G$ are oriented the same way in A_R and A_G. The orientation must be such that $A \cup A_R$ and $A \cup A_G$ are acyclic, whereas $A \cup A_R \cup A_G$ contains a cycle (this implies that both X_R and X_G are nonempty). Finally, the move (X_R, X_G, A_R, A_G) must be such that whenever $[A, C] \succ_A [A, B]$ and $(A, C) \in A_R \cup A_G$, then also $[A, B] \in X_R \cup X_G$. Such sets of edges and proposed orientations are termed *closed*. The reason for requiring that the sets chosen be closed is the following: $[A, B] \succ_A [A, C]$ means that the conflict between A and C cannot be resolved in the order (A, C) until the conflict between A and B

has somehow been resolved (presumably because in the transaction modeled by A the action on the common entity with B precedes the action on the common entity with C).

For example, Figure 7.5(b-c) can be seen as a move by LONG, starting at the multigraph shown in Figure 7.5(a) (red edges are shown solid, and green ones broken). In this move, $A_R = \{(C, B), (B, A)\}$ (Figure 7.5(b)), and $A_G = \{(A, B), (B, C)\}$ (Figure 7.5(c)). As required, both $A \cup A_R$ and $A \cup A_G$ are acyclic (Figures 7.5(b) and (c)), and $A \cup A_R \cup A_G$ has a cycle (Figure 7.5(d)). Notice that the move is closed.

Once LONG has moved, SHORT moves. SHORT's move entails choosing one of the two sets of arcs A_R and A_G proposed by LONG, *and fixing their orientation*. That is, if "red" is chosen, then R becomes $R - E_R$, A becomes $A \cup A_R$, and edges in E_R are deleted from $\succ$. For example, in Figure 7.5 SHORT might choose to keep A_R, in which case the multigraph would become as shown in Figure 7.5(b).

After finitely many rounds the game must end, since LONG will have no moves left (for example, there is no move for LONG from the position in Figure 7.5(b), because there are no green edges). What is the outcome? Well, *LONG wants to maximize the number of rounds played, while SHORT tries to minimize it.* There is no winner or loser otherwise. The *value of a game of CONFLICT* (where by "game" we mean a given ordered mixed multigraph, which is the initial position) is the largest number k such that LONG can guarantee k rounds starting from this multigraph, no matter how SHORT plays. We next formalize the connection between distributed concurrency control and this game.

Theorem 7.5: *The communication inherent in realizing serializability for a set τ of transactions starting at some prefix p equals twice the value of CONFLICT starting at the ordered mixed multigraph $G(\tau, p)$.*

Proof (Sketch): The correspondence is the following: SHORT is the scheduler which tries to realize serializability with the smallest possible number of messages, whereas LONG is an adversary who tries to force the scheduler to communicate by inputting bad extensions of the current prefix. Each move A_R and A_G by LONG represents such an extension. A_R contains the conflicts resolved at Site 1 (and implicitly the steps executed) plus all those steps at Site 2 that are necessary for the local steps to occur (these are the green edges added to X_G for closedness). Similarly for A_G and Site 2. Finally, the move by SHORT corresponds to a decision by the scheduler as to which site will initiate communication in the face of the present bad prefix. Once it is established that this correspondence is a faithful one, the result follows from Theorem 7.4. $\square$

The Complexity of CONFLICT

In this subsection we prove the following result:

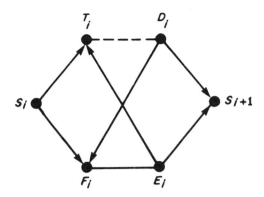

Figure 7.6. A Universal Variable.

Theorem 7.6: *It is PSPACE-complete to determine whether the value of CONFLICT on a particular ordered mixed multigraph is at least equal to a given number k.*

First notice that the value of CONFLICT is indeed computable using only a polynomial amount of space: We can try all strategies for both LONG and SHORT in order to determine the optimum outcome, reusing space after each play, and keeping notes about the strategies tried so far and the results obtained, in polynomial space.

To show completeness, we shall reduce the PSPACE-complete problem QSAT to the problem of determining the value of CONFLICT. Suppose that we are given the following quantified formula:

$$F = \exists x_1 \forall x_2 \ldots \forall x_{2n} \, [C_1 \wedge C_2 \wedge \ldots \wedge C_m]$$

with $2n$ variables and m clauses, each consisting of three literals. Recall from Section 3.3 that we can think of F as a game played between two players, UNIVERSAL and EXISTENTIAL. They take turns setting the variables $x_1, x_2, \ldots,$ in this order, to **true** or **false**, with EXISTENTIAL trying to make the formula **true**, while UNIVERSAL tries to make it **false**. We say F is true if EXISTENTIAL has a winning strategy. Starting from F, we shall construct an ordered mixed multigraph G such that the value of CONFLICT starting from G is at least $2n + 1$ if and only if F is true. We shall describe the construction of G informally, by examining its parts separately, and then describing the connections between the parts. G consists of $2n + m$ smaller ordered mixed multigraphs (graphs for short) connected in series, one for each existential quantifier, one for each universal quantifier, and one for each clause. The long path formed by the series connection of all these graphs is closed by an edge, called the *last edge*. The last edge is red.

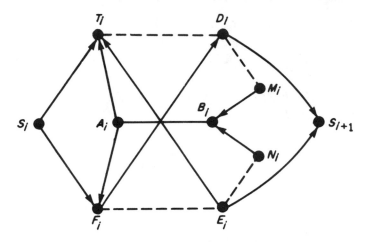

Figure 7.7. An Existential Variable.

The graph corresponding to a universally quantified variable x_i (i even) is shown in Figure 7.6. It consists of six arcs, one red edge, and one green edge. The endpoints, by which it is attached to the other graphs, are marked S_i and S_{i+1}. Notice this: If CONFLICT were played on this graph, LONG would have no choice but to propose the two edges oriented, away from T_i and F_i, respectively, as the two sets of arcs; SHORT would then choose one of them. If the one away from T_i is chosen, then we think of this as meaning that x_i is **true**; otherwise, x_i is **false**. That is, in the graph of Figure 7.6 we can say that SHORT picks the truth assignment. Notice that the edge whose direction is rejected by SHORT is in effect directed in the opposite direction than that proposed by LONG; this is true whenever both A_R and A_G are singletons.

For each existentially quantified variable (x_i odd) we have the graph shown in Figure 7.7. If CONFLICT were started on this graph alone, A_R must consist of (B_i, A_i). However, LONG does have a choice for A_G between the two possibilities $\{(T_i, D_i), (D_i, M_i)\}$ and $\{(F_i, E_i), (E_i, N_i)\}$. We shall next show that SHORT's best response is to pick A_G; thus it can be thought that LONG sets the truth assignment of existential variables by deciding which of T_i and F_i is connected by a path to S_{i+1}. The reason SHORT must play "green" is the following: If "red" is picked, then the direction of the edges $[T_i, D_i]$ and $[F_i, E_i]$ is not fixed as in the previous case, because A_G is not a singleton in this case. This means that, in effect, the direction of the two edges is undecided, and thus LONG can use them to his advantage again later in the game (this would be tantamount to allowing EXISTENTIAL to satisfy the occurrences of both x_i and $\bar{x}_i$ in F).

We connect all these graphs in series in the order of the x_i's in the formula,

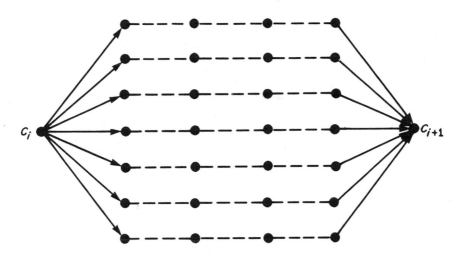

Figure 7.8. A Clause.

identifying the S_i nodes as suggested (remember that in QSAT the order of the quantified variables is very important). After these graphs come the graphs for the clauses. For each clause C_j of F, we have the graph in Figure 7.8. This graph consists of *seven* parallel paths of three green edges each. Why seven? The reason is that there are seven ways to satisfy a clause, as only one out of the $2^3 = 8$ truth assignments to the variables of the clause falsifies it. Each path corresponds to a satisfying truth assignment, and in fact each green edge in the path corresponds to a truth value to a variable. For example, if $C_j = (x_1 \vee x_2 \vee \bar{x}_3)$ then the fifth path may correspond to $x_1 = $ **true**, $x_2 = $ **false**, $x_3 = $ **false**, and the second edge of the path would then correspond to $x_2 = $ **false**. We connect all the graphs corresponding to clauses in series, with $C_1 \equiv S_{2n+1}$, and we add the red last edge $[C_m, S_1]$ to close the cycle.

It remains to put the structure of the clauses of F into our construction (so far our construction depends only on m and n). Remember that each green edge of the clause graph corresponds to a truth value for a variable. If an edge of clause C_j corresponds to $x_i = $ **true**, then we draw an arc from the right-hand (closest to C_{j+1}) endpoint of this edge to F_i (the point of the graph for x_i which corresponds to the value **true**). If it corresponds to $x_i = $ **false**, then the connection is back to T_i.

Our claim is that the value of the CONFLICT game started on this ordered mixed multigraph G (that is, the maximum number of moves that can be forced by LONG) is $2n + 1$ if and only if the formula F is true. Since there are $2n + 1$ red edges in G, it is clear that the value is at most that much (SHORT could always pick "red," and so LONG would run out of red edges after at most $2n+1$

moves). So, suppose that $2n + 1$ is achievable. We show by induction that each move by LONG involves just one red edge. First, if in some move SHORT chooses "red," then this edge is directed and cannot be used again. If SHORT chooses "green," then A_G is added to A, and A_R cannot be used again in this case either, as it now would create a cycle by itself. It is also easy to check that each red edge in G can be used by LONG in only one direction. Thus, each move of LONG can be identified with the red edge used in it.

The main idea is the following: LONG can always guarantee $2n$ moves by playing arbitrarily in the gadgets of the variables (and fixing the values of the variables in the process). The problem is the $(2n + 1)$st move. This move must involve the last edge, and thus it must be based on a path from S_1 to C_m consisting of arcs and green edges (in the clause graphs) oriented in the forward direction, *so that no cycle is formed by this orientation of green edges*. However, such a path must pass through all clause gadgets, and thus must involve for each clause one of the seven paths. Now, this path must be consistent with the truth assignment chosen by the play on the variable gadgets, because, otherwise, a cycle would be formed from the green edge corresponding to the false literal, say x_i, to the node F_i following the back arc, to E_i following the (F_i, E_i) arc (which exists since x_i is false) back to the edge corresponding to x_i via the path. Hence, a last move for LONG exists if and only if the truth assignment chosen by the moves of LONG and SHORT in the variable gadgets satisfies all clauses.

It would appear that the proof is complete! However, there is a major issue which we have not yet faced, namely *the order of the variables*. Nothing in our construction so far prevents, for example, LONG from starting with a move on variable x_3, continuing at x_2, and so on. To force the correct order, we must add certain elements to our construction, and use the partial orders among the edges incident upon each node (which had been empty so far). For each universally quantified gadget we add certain edges and paths between itself and the following two gadgets. In particular, we add a green edge $[A_i, F_{i+1}]$ and a directed path $(A_i, P_i), (P_i, F_{i+1})$, where P_i is a new node. We also add the green edge $[A_i, B_{i+2}]$ and the path $(A_i, Q_i), (Q_i, B_{i+2})$, where again Q_i is new. We then order the edges adjacent to each node A_i, B_i, and F_i according to the indices involved; that is,

at A_i: $[A_i, B_i] \succ_{A_i} [A_i, F_{i+1}] \succ_{A_i} [A_i, B_{i+2}]$

at F_i: $[F_i, A_{i-1}] \succ_{F_i} [F_i, E_i]$

at B_i: $[B_i, A_{i-2}] \succ_{B_i} [B_i, A_i]$.

It can now be shown that, because of the added edges, paths, and precedences among edges, the game on the variable gadgets will be played in the right order (see Problem 7.4). Hence, by the preceding discussion it is clear that there is a one-to-one correspondence between strategies of LONG for achieving $2n + 1$ rounds of the game started at G and strategies of EXISTENTIAL for satisfying

F. The theorem has been proved. $\Box$

Consequences

Theorem 7.6 has some important consequences for distributed concurrency control.

Corollary 1: *It is a PSPACE-complete problem to determine the value of the game CONFLICT, even when the initial graph is undirected.*

Proof: We have to show how to get rid of the directed arcs used in the construction in the proof of Theorem 7.6. Take any such arc (u, v). We shall replace it by a device such that, in any optimal play of the CONFLICT game, a directed arc from u to v will appear before any moves involving u or v. The device is shown in Figure 7.9, where w is a new node. Edge $[v, w]$ is red, the other two edges are green, and the partial order of the new edges at their endpoints are as indicated. We also order all newly added edges to precede all adjacent edges of the original graph G.

We shall show that the added triangle behaves in effect as an arc (u, v). The argument that LONG can guarantee a number of moves equal to the new number of red edges if all its moves use only one red edge is still valid. Suppose that LONG involves the green edge $[u, v]$ in a move involving a red edge other than $[v, w]$. If it is directed from u to v in the proposed move, then everything is as before the substitution. If however it is used from v to u, then SHORT could reply "green," in effect neutralizing, besides the other red edge in the move, $[v, w]$. We next claim that a move of LONG involving the red edge $[v, w]$ must direct it from v to w, and create the cycle (u, v, w). If LONG directs the $[v, w]$ edge from w to v, then there must be a path from v to w in $A \cup A_G$; however, because of the orders, this means that both edges $[v, u]$ and $[u, w]$ have been or are being now directed from v to u to w. In both cases, $A \cup A_G$ contains a cycle. So, consider a move directing $[v, w]$ from v to w. Then both $A_G \cup A$ and $A_R \cup A$ contain (u, v), and so this edge will be fixed immediately after that. Finally, the move on $[v, w]$ must happen before the moves on adjacent edges of the original graph. It follows that the replacement of the arc by the triangle increases the value of the game by the number of triangles added, and the result follows. $\Box$

The following result is now a direct consequence of Corollary 1 and Theorem 7.5:

Corollary 2: *Determining the communication cost inherent in realizing conflict serializability for a given set of transactions is PSPACE-complete.* $\Box$

In fact, it can be shown that Corollary 2 is true even when the transactions to be handled are not too complex (see Problem 7.5).

In conclusion, distributed concurrency control algorithms exhibit the fol-

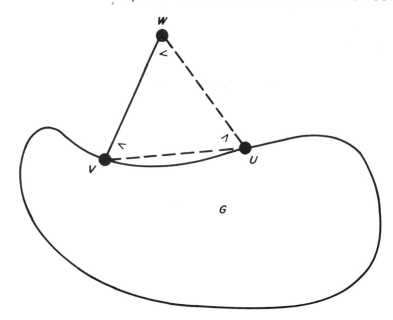

Figure 7.9. The Triangle.

lowing very intricate behavior with respect to performance: At an excessive communication cost, we can always reduce the distributed concurrency control problem to the centralized one, and thus realize by a time-efficient scheduler any concurrency control principle which has polynomially recognizable prefixes (this is Proposition 7.1). If communication costs are a matter of concern, then we can realize any concurrency control principle using the absolutely minimum number of messages possible in polynomial *space* (provided the prefixes can also be recognized in polynomial space, this follows from the corollary to Theorem 7.4). Can we realize such a concurrency control principle at the minimum communication cost in polynomial *time?* The next result says that the answer is negative even for simple and practically useful concurrency control principles as serializability, *unless NP=PSPACE.* Recall that NP is a subset of PSPACE, and in all evidence a proper one. NP=PSPACE is an event that is considered almost as unlikely as P=NP, although largely independent of it.

Corollary 3: *Unless NP=PSPACE, there is no distributed scheduler which realizes serializability, operates in polynomial time, and uses the minimum possible number of messages.*

Proof: If such a scheduler S existed, it could be used to determine whether the value of any given position of the PSPACE-complete problem CONFLICT is k or more in *nondeterministic polynomial time* (see the notes and references)

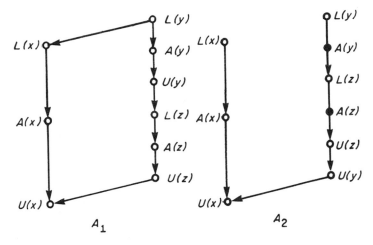

Figure 7.10. Two Locked Distributed Transactions.

as follows: We first create a set of transactions with the given multigraph, and guess a schedule $\hat{s}$ and delays **d** so that S spends k or more messages for $\hat{s}$ when the delays are **d**. $\square$

7.4 DISTRIBUTED LOCKING

In a distributed database system, locking can be used in order to control concurrency. As we shall see in this section, the distributed environment makes concurrency control by locking quite a bit more complex than in centralized databases. But what is a locked distributed transaction? There are lock and unlock steps $L(x)$ and $U(x)$ for each entity x accessed; the site at which these steps take place is the site of x. We generalize rules (1) and (2) for locked transactions (recall Section 6.2) as follows:

1. If there is one or more occurrences of an $A(x)$ step in a distributed locked transaction, then there is a single occurrence of $L(x)$ which precedes (in the partial order of the transaction) the first occurrence of $A(x)$, and a single occurrence of $U(x)$ following the last occurrence of $A(x)$ in the transaction (recall that in distributed transactions the steps at each site are totally ordered).

2. Conversely, if there are no occurrences of $A(x)$, then there are no occurrences of $L(x)$ or $U(x)$ either.

For example, Figure 7.10 shows a pair of locked transactions. Next we must define a legal distributed schedule, and thus a safe set of locked transactions. The simplest way of doing this is by resorting once more to *total orders*. Let $\hat{s}$ be a total order of all the steps in a set of distributed locked transactions, consistent with all precedences in the transactions. It is *legal* if between any

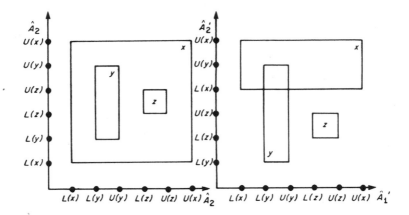

Figure 7.11. Safe and Unsafe Total Orders.

two $L(x)$ steps there is an $U(x)$ step. A set of locked distributed transactions is *safe* if the reduction of all legal total orders is serializable (in the centralized sense). A first consequence of this definition is that, as with the centralized case, the $A(x)$ steps can be omitted, since it is the locks and unlock steps that determine safety (the proof is similar to that of Proposition 6.2). However, the following stronger fact is true:

Proposition 7.2: *A set $\{A_1, \ldots, A_n\}$ of locked distributed transactions is unsafe if and only if there is a total order $\hat{A}_i$ for each transaction A_i, $i = 1, \ldots, n$, such that the set $\{\hat{A}_1, \ldots, \hat{A}_n\}$ of centralized transactions is unsafe.*

Proof: If the set of transactions is unsafe, then there is a legal total order which is not serializable. The restrictions of this order to the transactions form a non-serializable set of centralized transactions. Conversely, if an unsafe set of centralized transactions exists, then any legal non-serializable schedule is a legal non-serializable total order for the set of distributed locked transactions. $\square$

Thus, a set of two distributed locked transactions is unsafe if and only if there is a set of two total orders, one for each transaction, so that in the corresponding geometric representation the closure of the forbidden rectangles is connected. Notice that this implies a search through a potentially exponential set of total orders. In fact, Figure 7.11 shows that some searching is necessary: For the two transactions of Figure 7.10 we show two pairs of total orders, one safe and one unsafe (as indicated by the two closures of the forbidden regions). The following result suggests that an *exponential* search is necessary.

Theorem 7.7: *Telling whether two locked distributed transactions are unsafe is NP-complete.*

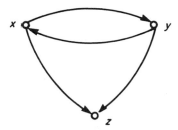

Figure 7.12. The Graph $D(A_1, A_2)$.

Proof: Problem 7.7. □

Thus, testing a pair of transactions for safety, a problem which can be solved in $O(n \log n)$ time in the centralized case, is intractable for distributed transactions. Despite this negative result, there is an interesting *sufficient* condition for safety of pairs of transactions; this condition can be checked in polynomial time. The condition is based on an interesting graph-theoretic construction. Given any two locked distributed transactions A_1 and A_2, we define a directed graph $D(A_1, A_2) = (V, F)$ as follows: V is the set of all entities locked by both transactions. Also, (x, y) is an arc of F if and only if $L(x) \prec_{A_1} U(y)$ and $L(y) \prec_{A_2} U(x)$. For example, for the transactions in Figure 7.10, the directed graph $D(A_1, A_2)$ is shown in Figure 7.12.

We can best understand the intuition of this definition if we recall the geometric interpretation of two centralized transactions. Each entity in V corresponds to a forbidden rectangle on the plane, and a pair of transactions is safe if and only if there is no monotone curve which avoids all forbidden rectangles and separates two of them. Accordingly, a pair of distributed transactions is safe if and only if no such curve exists in any of the possible geometric representations of pairs of total orders compatible with the two transactions. Now, an arc (x, y) of $D(A_1, A_2)$ means that, in all possible geometric representations, the NW corner of the forbidden rectangle corresponding to entity x (x-rectangle for short) will always be to the N and W of the SE corner of the y rectangle (e.g., the entities x and y in Figure 7.11). This turns out to be very useful information for determining safety, as the following result suggests. This theorem is stated in terms of the graph-theoretic concept of *strong connectivity*. A directed graph is strongly connected if for any two nodes x and y there is a path from x to y and from y to x. For example, the directed graph in Figure 7.12 is not strongly connected, since there is no path from z to y.

Theorem 7.8: Let A_1 and A_2 be locked distributed transactions. If $D(A_1, A_2)$ is strongly connected, then the two transactions are safe.

Proof: For the sake of contradiction, suppose that the two transactions are unsafe. Therefore, there are two total orders compatible with the transactions, such that, in the geometric representation, there is a monotone curve s which avoids all rectangles, passes above (that is, to the N and W of) the forbidden rectangle corresponding to some entity x, and below (to the S and E of) the rectangle for another entity y. Since $D(A_1, A_2)$ is strongly connected, there is a path $(x = z_0, z_1, \ldots, z_k = y)$ from x to y. We shall show by induction on j that s passes above all rectangles corresponding to the z_j's. By our hypothesis, this is true for $j = 0$. If it holds for some $j < k$, then the curve s passes above the z_j-rectangle. Since there is an arc from z_j to z_{j+1} in $D(A_1, A_2)$, the NW corner of the z_j-rectangle is above the SE corner of the z_{j+1}-rectangle. It follows that s passes above some point of the z_{j+1}-rectangle, and therefore it passes above all of it. The induction is complete, and we conclude that s passes above the y-rectangle. This contradicts our assumption that it passes below this rectangle. $\square$

The condition of Theorem 7.8 is in general not necessary (Problem 7.8). However, it suggests a very useful test. Since we can test whether a directed graph is strongly connected in time proportional to the number of arcs (see the references), the condition can be tested in $O(n^2)$ time, where n is the number of steps of the two transactions. Finally, it is interesting to note that the condition of Theorem 7.8 is necessary and sufficient *when the number of sites is less than four* (see Problem 7.9).

PROBLEMS

7.1 Prove Theorem 7.1.

7.2 Let s be a distributed schedule. Show that s is serializable if and only if all total orders on its steps which are compatible with $\prec_s$ are serializable, when viewed as ordinary schedules. Does this hold if we replace "serializable" by "a possible output of the distributed two-phase locking scheduler?" The distributed timestamp scheduler?

*7.3 What is the appropriate generalization of Theorem 7.4 when there are three or more sites?

7.4 Show that, after the addition of the edges, paths, and precedences in the end of the proof of Theorem 7.6, it is suboptimal for LONG to make a move involving edges from a variable x_i, unless a move involving each variable $x_j, j < i$ has been made.

7.5 Show that determining the smallest necessary number of messages to realize serializability for a set of distributed transactions remains PSPACE-complete even if the transactions have at most five actions each.

7.6 Suppose that we wish to determine whether LONG has a legal move in a position (that is, order mixed multigraph) of the game CONFLICT. Show that this is NP-complete, but can be done in polynomial time if there are no directed arcs.

7.7 Show that determining whether two transactions are unsafe is NP-complete.

7.8 Give an example of two locked transactions A_1 and A_2 distributed on four sites such that $D(A_1, A_2)$ is strongly connected, but A_1 and A_2 are unsafe.

7.9 Show that for any two safe locked transactions A_1 and A_2 distributed on two sites, $D(A_1, A_2)$ is strongly connected. Repeat for three sites.

**7.10 Show that determining whether two transactions are safe is NP-complete even when there are only four sites.

7.11 We say that two distributed locked transactions are *deadlock-free* if all pairs of total orders compatible with the two transactions are deadlock-free (in the centralized sense; recall Problem 6.13). Prove that it is NP-complete to determine whether two distributed locked transactions are deadlock-free.

NOTES AND REFERENCES

The book by [Ceri and Pelagatti 1984] is an introduction to the general subject of distributed databases, with a nice treatment of the principal methods for concurrency control and reliability. An extensive taxonomy of some of the main methods also appears in [Bernstein and Goodman 1981]. In distributed concurrency control practice, many intricacies are due to the presence of multiple copies of entities in different sites, an issue that we did not need to touch here. The three first sections of this chapter are adapted from [Papadimitriou and Kanellakis 1984]. The material of Section 7.4 is from [Kanellakis and Papadimitriou 1985].

A linear algorithm for determining strong connectivity in a directed graph is explained in [Aho et al. 1974]. It turns out that NP can be alternatively defined in terms of *nondeterministic algorithms*; see [Hopcroft and Ullman 1979] for more on this and also on the relationship between NP and PSPACE.

References

A. V. Aho, J. E. Hopcroft, J. D. Ullman *The Design and Analysis of Computer Algorithms*, Addison-Wesley, Reading Massachusetts, 1974.

R. Bayer, H. Heller, A. Reiser "Parallelism and Recovery in Database Systems," *ACM Trans. on Database Systems, 5*, 2 pp. 139–156, 1980.

R. Bayer and M. Schkolnick "Concurency of Operations on B-Trees," *Acta Informatica, 9* pp. 1–21, 1977.

P.A. Bernstein and N. Goodman "Concurrency Control in Distributed Database Systems," *Computing Surveys 13*, 2, pp. 185–222, 1981.

P. A. Bernstein and N. Goodman "Multiversion Concurrency Control: Theory and Algorithms," *ACM Trans. on Database Systems, 8*, 4 pp. 465–483, 1983.

P. A. Bernstein, N. Goodman, V. Hadzilacos *Concurrency Control and Recovery in Database Systems*, Addison-Wesley, Reading Massachusetts, 1986.

P. A. Bernstein, N. Goodman, J. B. Rothnie, C. H. Papadimitriou "Analysis of Serializability of SDD-1: A System of Distributed Databases," IEEE Trans. on Software Engineering SE-4, pp. 154–168, 1978.

G. Buckley and A. Silberschatz, "A Complete Characterization of a Multiversion Database Model with Effective Schedulers," *Proc. 9th International Conference on Very Large DataBases*, Florence Italy, 1983.

G. Buckley and A. Silberschatz, "Beyond Two-Phase Locking," *J.ACM, 32*, 2, pp. 314-326, 1985

M. A. Casanova *The Concurrency Control Problem of Database Systems*, Lecture Notes in Computer Science Vol. 116, Springer-Verlag, Heidelberg, 1981.

S. Ceri and G. Pelagatti *Distributed Databases: Principles and Systems*, McGraw-Hill, 1984.

A. Chesnais, E. Gelenbe, and I. Mitrani "On the Modelling of Parallel Access to Shared Data," *Communications of the ACM, 26*, 3, pp. 196–202, 1983.

S. A. Cook "The Complexity of Theorem Proving Procedures," *Proceedings of the Third ACM Symposium on the Theory of Computing*, pp. 151-158, ACM, 1971.

C. J. Date *An Introduction to Database Systems*, Third Edition, Addison-Wesley, Reading, Massachusetts, 1981. Volume II, 1983.

S. Even, *Graph Algorithms*, Computer Science Press, Potomac, Maryland, 1979.

K. P. Eswaran, J. N. Gray, R. A. Lorie, I. L. Traiger "The Notions of Consistency and Predicate Locks in a Relational Database System", *Communications of the ACM, 8*, 11, pp. 624-633, 1976.

M. R. Garey, D. S. Johnson *Computers and Intractability: A Guide to the Theory of NP-completeness*, Freeman, San Francisco, 1979.

J. N. Gray "Notes on Database Operating Systems," in *Operating Systems: An Advanced Course*, edited by R. Bayer, R. M. Graham, and G. Seegmüller, Lecture Notes in Computer Science, Vol. 60, Springer Verlag, Heidelberg, 1978.

T. Hadzilacos and C. H. Papadimitriou "Algorithmic Aspects of Multiversion Concurrency Control," *Proceedings of the 4th ACM SIGACT-SIGMOD Symp. on Principles of Database Systems*, Portland, Oregon, pp. 96–104, 1985. Also, to appear in *J. of Computer and System Sciences, 1986*.

T. Hadzilacos and M. Yannakakis "Closing Transactions," to appear in the *Proc. 5th ACM SIGACT-SIGMOD Symp. on Principles of Database Systems*, 1986.

V. Hadzilacos *Issues of Fault Tolerance in Concurrent Computations*, Ph.D. Dissertation, Harvard University, 1984.

V. Hadzilacos "A Theory of Reliability in Database Systems," to appear in *J.ACM*, 1986.

J. E. Hopcroft and J. D. Ullman *Introduction to Automata Theory, Languages, and Computation*, Addison Wesley, Reading, Massachusetts, 1979.

T. Ibaraki and T. Kameda "Multi-Version vs. Single-Version Serializability," Technical Report LCCR 83-1, Simon Fraser University, 1983.

K. B. Irani and H. L. Lin "Queuing Network Models for Concurrent Transaction Processing in a Database System," *Proc. 1979 ACM SIGMOD Conference on the Management of Data*, Boston, pp. 134–142, 1979.

P. C. Kanellakis and C. H. Papadimitriou "Is Distributed Locking Harder?" *J. of Computer and System Sciences, 28*, 1, pp. 103–120, 1984.

P. C. Kanellakis and C. H. Papadimitriou "The Complexity of Distributed Concurrency Control," *SIAM J. on Computing, 14*, 1, pp. 52–74, 1985.

R. M. Karp "Reducibility among Combinatorial Problems," in *Complexity of Computer Computations*, edited by R. E. Miller and J. W. Thatcher, pp. 83–103, Plenum Press, New York, 1972.

Z. Kedem and A. Silberschatz "Controlling Concurrency Using Locking Protocols," *Proc. 20th IEEE Symp. on Foundations of Computer Science*, San Juan, Puerto Rico, pp. 274–285, 1979.

H. T. Kung and C .H. Papadimitriou "An Optimality Theory of Database Concurrency Control," *Acta Informatica, 19*, 1, pp. 1-13, 1984.

H. T. Kung and J. T. Robinson "On Optimistic Methods for Concurrency Control," *ACM Trans. on Database Systems, 6*, 2, pp. 213-226, 1981.

W. Lipski and C. H. Papadimitriou "A Fast Algorithm for Testing for Safety and Dedecting Deadlocks in Locked Transaction Systems," *J. of Algorithms, 2*, pp. 211–226, 1981.

Z. Manna *Introduction to the Mathematical Theory of Computation*, McGraw-Hill, 1974.

C. Mohan, D. Fussel, A. Silberschatz "Compatibility and Commutativity in Non-two-phase Locking Proptocols," *Proceedings of the ACM Symposium in Principles of Database Systems*, Los Angeles, pp. 283–292, 1982.

S. Muro, T. Kameda, and T. Minoura "Multi-version Concurrency Control Scheme for a Database System," *J. of Computer and System Sciences, 29*, pp. 207–224, 1984.

C. H. Papadimitriou "The Serializability of Concurrent Database Updates," *J.ACM, 26*, 4, pp. 631–653, 1979.

C. H. Papadimitriou "A Theorem in Database Concurrency Control," *J.ACM, 29*, 4, pp. 998–1009, 1982. Corrigendum *J.ACM, 32*, 3, p. 750, 1985.

C. H. Papadimitriou "Concurrency Control by Locking," *SIAM J. on Computing, 12*, 2, pp. 215–226, 1983.

C. H. Papadimitriou, P. A. Bernstein, and J. B. Rothnie "Computational Problems Related to Concurrency Control," *Proc. Conf. on Theoretical Computer Science*, University of Waterloo, Canada, 1977.

C. H. Papadimitriou and P. C. Kanellakis "On Concurrency Control by Multiple Versions," *ACM Trans. on Database Systems*, *9*, 1, pp. 89–99, 1984.

C. H. Papadimitriou, K. Steiglitz *Combinatorial Optimization: Algorithms and Complexity*, Prentice-Hall, Englewood Cliffs, 1982.

C. H. Papadimitriou, J. N. Tsitsiklis "The Performance of a Precedence Based Queuing Discipline," to appear in *J.ACM*, 1986.

D. Potier and P. Leblanc "Analysis of Locking Policies in Database Management Systems," *Communications of the ACM*, *23*, 10, pp. 584–593, 1980.

D. Reed "Naming and Synchronization in a Decentralized Computer System," Technical Report 205, M.I.T. Laboratory for Computer Science, 1978.

D. J. Rosenkrantz, R. E. Stearns, and P. M. Lewis II, "Consistency and Serializability in Concurrent Database Systems," Technical Report, Dept. of Computer Science, SUNY at Albany, 1982.

G. Schlageter "Process Synchronization in Database Systems," *ACM Trans. on Database Systems*, *3*, 3, pp. 248–271, 1978.

R. Sethi "A Model of Concurrent Database Transactions," *Proc. 22nd IEEE Symp. on Foundations of Computer Science*, pp. 175–184, IEEE, 1981.

K. C. Sevcik "Comparison of Concurrency Control Methods Using Analytic Models," *Information Processing 83*, edited by R. E. A. Mason, pp. 847-858, North Holland, 1983.

A. Silberschatz and Z. Kedem "Consistency in Hierarchical Database Systems," *J.ACM*, *27*, 1, pp. 72–80, 1979.

A. W. Shum and P. G. Spirakis "Performance Models of Concurrency Control Methods in Database Systems," *Performance 81*, edited by F. J. Kylstra, pp. 1–19, North Holland, 1981.

E. Soisalon-Soininen and D. Wood "Optimal Algorithms to Compute the Closure of a Set of Iso-rectangles," *J. of Algorithms*, *5*, pp. 199–214, 1984.

R. E. Stearns, P. M. Lewis II, D. J. Rosenkrantz "Concurrency Controls for Database Systems," *Proc. 17th IEEE Symp. on Foundations of Computer Science*, pp. 19-32, IEEE, 1976.

R. E. Stearns and D. J. Rosenkrantz "Distributed Database Concurrency Controls Using Before-values," *Proc. 1981 ACM Sigmod Conference on Management of Data*, ACM, New York, pp. 216–223, 1981.

Y. C. Tay, R. Suri, and N. Goodman "A Mean Value Performance Model for Locking in Databases: The Waiting Case," *Proc. 3rd ACM SIGACT-SIGMOD Symp. on Principles of Database Systems*, Waterloo, Canada, 1984. Also, to appear in *J.ACM*.

R. H. Thomas "A Majority Consensus Approach to Concurrency Control for Multiple Copy Systems," *ACM Trans. on Database Systems, 4*, 2, pp. 180–209, 1979.

A. Thomasian and I. K. Ryu "A Decomposition Solution to the Queuing Network Model of a Centralized DBMS with Static Locking," *Proc. ACM SIGMETRICS Conference on Mearuring and Modelling of Computer Systems*, Minneapolis, pp. 82–92, 1983.

J. D. Ullman *Principles of Database Systems*, Second Edition, Computer Science Press, Potomac, Maryland, 1982.

J. S. M. Verhofstad "Recovery Techniques for Database Systems," *ACM Computing Surveys, 10*, 2, pp. 167-195, 1978.

M. Yannakakis "The Various Notions of Correctness in Database Concurrency Control," manuscript, Bell Laboratories, 1980.

M. Yannakakis "A Theory of Safe Locking Policies in Database Systems," *J.ACM, 29*, 3, pp. 718-740, 1982.

M. Yannakakis "Freedom from Deadlock in Safe Locking Policies," *SIAM J. on Computing, 11*, 2, pp. 391–408, 1982.

M. Yannakakis "Serializability by Locking," *J.ACM, 31*, 2, pp. 227–244, 1984.

M. Yannakakis, C. H. Papadimitriou, and H. T. Kung "Locking Policies: Safety and Freedom from Deadlock, *Proc. 20th IEEE Symp. on Foundations of Computer Science*, San Juan, Puerto Rico, pp. 283–287, 1979.

Index

abort 70, 91, 130, 133
access lock 104
action model 51
active transaction 69
acyclic directed graph 12–13, 17
acyclic polygraph 36
adjacency list 13
Aho, A. V. 17, 229
algorithm 13
arc 11
atomic write model 88, 135
audit trail 70
augmented schedule 20

bad prefix 215
Bayer, R. 92, 140, 141
Bernstein, P .A. 17, 56, 92, 140, 141, 229
Boolean formula 15
Boolean variable 15
bridge 119, 140
broad serializability 54
Brzozowski, J. A. 56
Buckley, G. 140, 141

candidate transaction 126
Casanova, M. A. 17
Ceri, S. 229
certificate 15
certifier 137
Chesnais, A. 157
choice 35
chordal graph 109
clause 15, 54
closed region 179
closure 197
commit lock 125
commit step 69
committed transaction 69
communication cost 202, 211
commutativity 26, 46–48, 54–55
complete information 147
complexity 13
concurrency 2, 143, 145, 211
concurrency control 2, 3
concurrency control principle 212
concurrency set 143
conflict 44
conflict equivalence 44

235